M000165776

COMPATIBLE CULTURAL DEMOCRACY

COMPATIBLE CULTURAL DEMOCRACY

THE KEY TO DEVELOPMENT IN AFRICA

DANIEL T. OSABU-KLE

broadview press

©2000 Daniel T. Osabu-Kle

All rights reserved. The use of any part of this publication reproduced, transmitted in any form or by any means, electronic, mechanical, photocopying, recording, or otherwise, or stored in a retrieval system, without prior written consent of the publisher – or in the case of photocopying, a licence from CANCOPY (Canadian Copyright Licensing Agency) One Yonge Street, Suite 1900, Toronto, Ontario, M5E 1E5 – is an infringement of the copyright law.

Canadian Cataloguing in Publication Data

Osabu-Kle, Daniel Tetteh, 1942-
    Compatible cultural democracy: the key to development in Africa

Includes bibliographical references.
ISBN 1-55111-289-2

1. Africa, Sub-Saharan—Politics and government—1960- . 2. Indigenous peoples—Africa, Sub-Saharan—Politics and government. 3. Africa, Sub-Saharan—Colonial influence. 4. Democracy—Africa, Sub-Saharan. I. Title.

DT353.082 2000   320.967   C00-930114-3

Broadview Press Ltd., is an independent, international publishing house, incorporated in 1985.

North America:
P.O. Box 1243, Peterborough, Ontario, Canada K9J 7H5
3576 California Road, Orchard Park, NY 14127
TEL: (705) 743-8990; FAX: (705) 743-8353;
E-MAIL: customerservice@broadviewpress.com

United Kingdom:
Turpin Distribution Services Ltd.,
Blackhorse Rd., Letchworth, Hertfordshire SG6 1HN
TEL: (1462) 672555; FAX (1462) 480947; E-MAIL: turpin@rsc.org

Australia:
St. Clair Press, P.O. Box 287, Rozelle, NSW 2039
TEL: (02) 818-1942; FAX: (02) 418-1923

www.broadviewpress.com

Broadview Press gratefully acknowledges the financial support of the Ministry of Canadian Heritage through the Book Publishing Industry Development Program.

Design and composition by George Kirkpatrick

PRINTED IN CANADA

CONTENTS

PREFACE

Africa has never danced well to the tune of alien political music. Is it not therefore most likely that Africans will dance more comfortably to the tune of a modified form of indigenous political music? This is the theme addressed in *Compatible Cultural Democracy: The Key to Development in Africa.*

Under colonialism Africa danced to the drums of colonial dictatorship. As a precondition for the granting of independence, those African countries that attained independence by peaceful means or by violent confrontation were manipulated or compelled in various ways to emulate Western-style political practice. The decision in country after country to emulate Western forms of democracy was not, however, an indication that indigenous democratic cultures, which were at their heart consensual, were in any way inferior. Rather, for the most part the African elite who assumed the levers of political power during the transition to independence calculated that their own interests—which were fused with the interests of international capital—would be best served by fashioning harmonious relationships and joint experiments with the same imperialism they had previously condemned. There were some committed and benign African nationalists, but they failed to appreciate the severe limitations of the Western world's so-called liberal democracy. The result was to be disastrous for African political stability, economic growth, and general well-being. Africa remains in a persistent state of crisis.

Compatible Cultural Democracy argues that only a democracy compatible with the African cultural environment is capable of achieving the political conditions for successful development in Africa. Successful development in Africa demands the existence in each country of an encompassing coalition capable of enjoying the support of all sections of society in such a manner as to be able to contain the stresses and strains emanating from both the local and international environments. A close look at the political histories of any number of African countries reveals that the required encompassing coalition cannot be forged through any wholesale transplantation of alien political organization or ideology, whether it is Western democracy, Western-inspired military rule, or Marxist-inspired socialism.

Africa's current political and social problems go back to the colonial treaties, and especially the Berlin Conference of 1884-85, where the

European colonizers conspired to share Africa among themselves—an unhappy beginning to modern times, followed by the imposition of indirect rule, an inappropriate colonial education system, and a colonial infrastructure that principally served the interests of the colonizer (chapter 2). The post-independence period of structural transformation brought with it the problems of integrating into the global economy, the necessity for achieving the appropriate political conditions for that kind of integration, and ensuing debates about democracy (chapter 3). A number of examples of African political systems—the Ovimbunda, Zulu, Ashanti, and Ga—though far apart, exhibit common characteristics, including consensualism and a balance between centralization and decentralization to check the abuse of power (chapter 4).

In looking at how the indigenous political culture can be modified and adapted to achieve the political prerequisites for successful development, we need to address issues such as nation-building, state-building, the empowerment of indigenous social movements and organizations, and the modification of the educational system and its orientation to serve nationalist interests. We also need to recognize the cultural dynamics that can lead to continuous but gradual modifications and improvements to cope with inevitable changes in the mode of production (chapter 5). It would seem best not to condemn Western democracy per se; but only, perhaps, to postpone its adoption in Africa. If as a result of economic and social development Africa becomes capitalist and its culture comes to approximate that of the West, Western-style democracy might become compatible and applicable at that point in time, but not now.

The case studies of Ghana, Nigeria, Kenya, Tanzania, Somalia, Senegal, Rwanda, and Congo (Kinshasa) all reveal the problems inherent in the introduction of the alien political practices of the West (chapters 6-13). All of these countries are typical and critical cases for the analysis of the variables responsible for the economic and political crises of Sub-Saharan Africa. Each suffered from the limitations of the colonial heritage. Each, in its different way, not only faced internal patterns of political instability in the attempts at structural transformation but also had to cope with external factors, such as the oil-pricing and monetary shocks of the 1970s and 1980s, unfavourable terms of trade, or (as in the case of Nigeria, which did have its own oil) a staggering foreign debt. These countries also faced internal variables such as drought, limited infrastructure, and a weak institutional framework. In each of these countries, again in their different ways, the ruling elites failed to create an encompassing and committed coalition capable of pursuing nationalist and coherent policies. Each has experienced the severe, chronic pains of an unfulfilled potential—in most cases, in the midst of vast natural endowment—stymied by these internal and external forces.

What these cases show most clearly is that Africans will only be able to solve their problems the African way. The cultural dimension of the development process should be recognized rather than be denied. The encompassing coalition required for successful development in Africa must be capable of enjoying the support of all sections of society, which would in turn enable it to cushion the stresses and strains emanating from both the internal and external environments. That kind of coalition will only be possible when it is organized in an African way to authoritatively allocate African values to Africans.

CHAPTER ONE

INTRODUCTION: VARIANTS OF DEMOCRATIC PRACTICE

*If we could first know where we are, and whither we are tending,
we could better judge what to do, and how to do it.*

Abraham Lincoln

The end of the Cold War has brought within its wake a new cry for democracy in Africa, and it is as if democracy is something unheard of there—as if it was unknown on the continent before European contact. But Africans are not inexperienced in the ways of democracy. They are not against democracy, because it is an integral and inseparable part of their historical consensual culture. Africa's political problems are not about democracy per se, but about what brand of democracy is suitable for the people of this era. Is it the British type, the French type, the American type, the new Russian type, or an African type derived from indigenous culture? To answer this question we need to understand what democracy itself consists of—its purpose, its function, and how it is put into practice in different ways in different cultures by the peoples of this world.

Democracy is above all else a means by which the people as a whole can determine their own fates, determine the directions of their societies. If democracy is truly a government of the people and by the people, the shape and conditions of African democracy should be determined by Africans and not by outsiders. The attempt by outsiders, including the IMF and the World Bank, to impose their brands of democracy on Africans is unacceptable. It has failed to work in the past, and there is no guarantee that it will ever work in Africa. This is the crux of the African problem, and it is a problem of cultural compatibility.

The word democracy derives from two Greek words: *demos*, which means the common people, and *kratos*, meaning authority or rule. The idea of authority or rule can be associated with the functioning of the state or sovereignty. *Demos* can be associated with the functioning of what is called *civil society*: the social formation intermediate between the family and the state. Civil society is the area of social life that constitutes the realm of the private citizen or individual consent, including the ensemble of socio-economic relations and forces of production that contrasts with public life. The combination of the two words *kratos* and *demos*, therefore, suggests the rule, authority, or sovereignty of the common people or civil society. In the course of history, the sovereignty, rule, or authority of the people at large tended to be usurped by a few powerful people and symbolized through titles such as rulers, kings, monarchs, or emperors. Over a time struggles ensued between civil society and the rulers for the transfer of the usurped authority back to the people. Out of these struggles came the constitutional state, aimed at the establishment of a harmonious relationship between the state (the ruling body appointed with the consent of the people) and civil society or the common people (the ruled). As a means of maintaining this harmonious relationship, institutions evolved to prevent the misuse of power by ensuring compliance with the principles of representation, accountability, responsiveness, and balance of power between the state and civil society. Still, true democracy—as the rule or authority of the common people—does not exist anywhere in this world. Democratic practice as we know it takes up only some of the principles embodied by the concept.

The struggles to realize democratic principles of institutionalized rule required supporting mechanisms, and different societies developed different ways of attempting to put democracy into operation. It was possible for the rulers to belong to one society and the ruled to belong to a number of societies, including the society from which the rulers were selected. In this way, the state (the activities and force fields that competed to rule) and the nation (the feeling of belonging to the same society) did not necessarily coincide. In Europe, the idea of state and nation coinciding—so that the rulers and the ruled have the feeling of belonging to one entity—began with the Treaty of Westphalia, which, in 1648, ended the Thirty Years War in Europe. With the Treaty of Westphalia, empire-states such as the Austro-Hungarian Empire and the Ottoman or Turkish Empire broke up into smaller nation-states while the smaller principalities or princely states amalgamated into larger nation-states.[1] One such amalgamation was the German unification under Prince Otto von Bismarck in the nineteenth century.

The creation of the nation-state led to further changes in the attempted practice of democracy. Eventually, in the West, so-called democracy took the form of elections in which the elements of civil society, with a feeling of belonging, could exercise their sovereignty by voting for candidates representing political parties. Partisan politics thus became one—but only one—of the many processes for putting democracy into practice—though not a condition that in itself ensured democracy. In partisan democracy, during their term of office, it is entirely possible—and only too common—for the elected representatives to not honour their election promises and to enact laws or introduce policies that go against the expectations or wishes of the electorate. The replacement of one political party by another party in the government, or popular demonstrations and strikes against the policies or actions of a partisan government, signify the convictions of the electorate that their representatives are not following the popular will or even that they have become elected dictators. This dictatorship of the elected is encouraged by the number of years in office before the next election, and the required allegiance or loyalty of the representatives to the party first before the electorate. The partisan democracy also demands the existence of certain preconditions and the satisfaction of some assumptions. For instance, it requires a freedom of association so that individuals can come together to form political parties and interest groups. It requires a freedom of expression so that people can exchange ideas and form opinions and enable politicians to campaign and express their ideas and convictions to the people. It also requires a civil society that has reached the stage of political development at which it is matured and informed enough to be not easily deceived by the vain promises of politicians, and disciplined enough not to resort to violence or any act that is not conducive to peace or harmony. It also assumes that all members of civil society have an equal right and opportunity to vote, an equal opportunity to join and gain access to political parties, interest groups, and other associations, and an equality before the laws enacted by those chosen to rule.

These preconditions and assumptions may not necessarily hold in all societies. Indeed, the preconditions and assumptions of partisan politics do not necessarily hold in all societies called democratic today. In societies that lack most of these conditions and assumptions, partisan politics as a democratic practice becomes a joke and a mockery of the tenets of democracy. Even societies considered to be democratic have emphasized different principles. Take, for instance, the view of Robert Dahl about the contrast between Madisonian ideas of democracy and the Jacobinic popular theory of democracy.[2] The Madisonian view of democracy focused on dividing and limiting the power of the state while simultaneously limiting the power of the transitory majority. The Jacobinic view of democracy focused on enforcing the will of the majority. Hence, in the same Western society the very practice of a partisan democracy might prove to be different, and it could, of course, alter over time. Furthermore, in partisan democratic practice, the notion of equality might be given different interpretations, resulting in a situation in which some are more equal than others. For example, democratic states always place a limitation on voting age, and although laws enacted by elected representatives apply to all residents in the country, a state usually invokes the notion of sovereignty to discriminate between a foreigner who is disqualified from voting and a citizen who can vote.

Despite these difficulties, however, partisan elections provide a means by which the people can participate in the affairs concerning them and exercise part of their sovereign right. On the one hand, elections provide a means by which the rulers are made accountable to the ruled and, on the other, they are a means by which the rulers legitimize their rule both internally and internationally. As a tool of accountability, the partisan election serves as one of the non-violent rituals for replacing incompetent political representatives or rulers. However, partisan elections do not necessarily ensure representation. For example, if all women candidates fail to win in their constituencies, Parliament will comprise only men, and women will not be represented. If all the candidates are relatively rich (and that is usually the case), the poor are not represented in Parliament. Societies are made up of teachers, doctors, nurses, engineers, and other professionals, but Parliaments tend not to fully reflect this microcosm. Promises may be forgotten soon after politicians have been elected, and political representatives may not necessarily seek the consent of their constituents before they take major decisions that have an impact on the lives of the electorate. Thus, election promises of more jobs may be replaced in reality with job cuts, and promises of tax cuts at election time may be replaced with tax increases. The dictatorship of elected representatives is the common tendency.

The propensity for governments and parliamentarians to be not responsive to the electorate led to the rise of interest groups to articulate and aggregate particular interests or values, and to draw attention to these issues in various ways, including peaceful demonstrations, strikes, and media coverage. Governments and parliaments continually come under pressure to satisfy the requests of interest groups. However, the existence of these interest groups—which implies the substitution of group rights for individual rights—works against a basic tenet of liberalism, which aims at the protection of the rights and liberty of the individual. Indeed, liberal democracy is supposed to be a delicate balance between the rights of the individual and the rights of the majority of the electorate, which is vested in the state in such a manner that the individual is protected from any arbitrary action on the part of the state. The pure form of liberal democracy, therefore, does not exist anywhere on this planet; rather, what exists is a polyarchal brand of democratic practice in which elites of organized groups hold sway.

The domination of the political process by organized groups and their leaders implies the existence of a dictatorship by the few combined with a dictatorship of organized groups in the partisan practice of democracy. The ballot-box political technology enables individuals to vote, but the levers of political power rest with organized groups and their leaders. Indeed, the political parties that compete are themselves huge organized groups with leaders. The political marketplace of the Western democracies is not perfect; it is the arena in which political oligopolies control the political game or political price and operate in a way that limits the choice of the electorate. The outcome of the political competition may be satisfying, but it is far from being the optimum.

Most importantly, though, partisan democratic practice is only one of many ways in which democracy can be put into practice. Various societies, including the ancient Greeks, have had different democratic experiences. Participation in the political process has been comparatively more open in some systems than others. In the case of ancient Greece, the participation process excluded slaves and those who were not Greeks.

In the course of history Africans, including the ancient Egyptians and the empires of Ghana, Mali, Songhai, and the Zulu, established their own systems of democracy in which participation was restricted in varying degrees. At the least, democratic discussions took place in the councils of the Pharaohs, the emperors, and kings or chiefs among the regional representatives that constituted the legislature. Many writers, including Ivor Wilks in his *Forests of Gold*, M. Fortes and E.E. Evans in their edited book *African Political Systems*, and Margaret Shinnie in her *Ancient African Kingdoms*, have variously described these African political systems and how they worked.

The accounts reveal commonalities, which far outweigh the differences expected in any comparative analysis of political systems. The African political culture was characterized by free discussions, consultations with respect, and consensual decision-making at all levels of government. The commonalities include the absence of political parties or partisan politics (which does not by itself mean that democratic practice did not exist) and the practice of approving the appointment of rulers through consensus. The consensus systems involved electoral colleges comprising elites who were themselves appointed with the consent of various sections of society to whom they were accountable. Thus, the democratic principles of government with the participation and consent of the people were fulfilled consensually at the various levels and sections of society. Moreover, in African traditional societies, the democratic principle of accountability to the electorate was applied more broadly than it is in Western democracy today. The ruler, for instance, was held accountable for the occurrence of unexpected events, including natural phenomena such as famine, outbreak of disease, earthquakes, or any other natural disasters. Such calamities would be taken to signify the unacceptability of a ruler, who might be deposed or even lose his or her life if they occurred. It was in this cultural context that Ghanaians, including the highly educated ones, blamed Colonel Ignatius Acheampong for the drought that occurred during his time in office (1972-78). The British-trained Colonel Acheampong, who was completely out of tune with the Ghanaian political culture, became offended and went to the radio and television to ask Ghanaians "Miye Nyame?" (meaning, "Am I God to make it rain?"). If the Colonel did not understand Ghanaian culture, Ghanaian culture equally did not understand him. Far from calming the temper of Ghanaians, that question made Acheampong more unpopular. It was no wonder, therefore, that he was later overthrown and executed by firing squad. African politics in its pure form is, therefore, not alien to the democratic principle of accountability, but rather a strong adherent of it.

Partisan politics was largely if not entirely non-existent in democratic practice in African political systems because of the underlying African cultural value of unity of purpose and action among brothers and sisters of the same nation and the perception of partisan politics as a weapon that the enemy might use in any strategy of divide and conquer. In Africa the nation as a whole was considered as comprising brothers and sisters, and this notion was repeated through the lower levels of town, village, clan, and sub-clans, and the common extended family system served to animate and maintain that notion. The consequence of this absence of partisan politics is that although constructive criticisms and free expression of views characterized the discussions in the ruling colleges before consensual decisions were taken, the Western concept of a politically recognized opposition did not exist in any African vocabulary. Furthermore, because representatives of the ruling councils at all levels were appointed on the basis of merit and moral character as observed from their childhoods on, they did not campaign to be elected; they were voluntarily elected by the consensus of the people of the areas they represented. The only known opposing force was, therefore, the enemy from outside. In African political culture and vocabulary, therefore, the concepts of opposition and enemy came to mean the same thing. This linguistic notion of enemy for the member of a different political party would be at the roots of the misfit and consequent unsuitability of the partisan political technology in the African environment.

How then, if African political systems were characterized by democratic practices with attendant strict accountability, did it come about that post-colonial African political systems became undemocratic, with little inclination to accountability? The answer to this question is located within the drift of the colonial legacy and the Cold War period. The countries in Africa today are essentially European creations, emanating in part from the Berlin Conference of the later nineteenth century. Colonial politics included divide and rule tactics that encouraged the development of pockets of nationalism—"tribalism," to the colonizers.

The consequence of this divide and rule tactic was that unlike Europe's Treaty of Westphalia and the subsequent transformation of city-states, principalities, and empire-states into nation-states, under colonial rule state and nation did not coincide to form nation-states in Africa. The transfer of the ideological symbols of nationalism from the ethnic, clan, and subnational levels of society to the state level to enable nation and state to be merged into nation-state never did take place in Africa, because the colonizers, with their vision of a new form of colonialism for the continued exploitation of the continent and its peoples (called neo-colonialism), were interested in keeping the African peoples weak enough to be dominated politically, ideologically, and economically. As part of this the colonizers also assumed that the transplantation of Western democratic institutions would help to contain communism. They assumed that the Africans, acting like robots, might dance faithfully to the tune of Western political music when given the appropriate commands. Moreover, colonial rule was not democratic. Although for the purposes of legitimization colonial power was sometimes channelled through the mechanism of indirect rule, it was principally a coercive and predatory dictatorship in which the colour bar figured prominently, and it had no accountability whatsoever to the African populations. The logic of colonial rule was to exploit the human and material resources of the African continent to the full. Thus, Emmit B. Evans Jr. and Dianne Long write: "The idea that international efforts could, or should, be undertaken to build the societies of the Other World is relatively recent. The Western colonial masters used the Americas, Africa, and Asia as sources of raw materials and cheap labour under the systems of mercantilism and capitalism that dominated world economies for 450 years prior to the end of World War II; they saw no reason to 'develop' these areas."[3]

Because of a general and pervasive alienation of Africans from the major decisions that would determine the shape of their lives, Africans employed within the colonial administration were not encouraged to be loyal or honest to the colonial authority. A colonial mentality that considered it heroic for an African to rob, cheat, or undermine the alien state developed. After decades of colonial rule, this brand of colonial mentality or mental colonialism became a permanent psychological set handed down from one generation to another.

The advent of nominal independence could not eradicate this mental slavery, because the introduction of alien partisan politics and the persistence of the neo-colonial administrative and economic structures encouraged the African populations to habitually perceive the independent state as alien. If the African state is described variously as dictatorial, of a personal rule character, repressive, or corrupt, it is because the African elites who assumed the reins of government learnt the lessons they were taught under colonialism far too well—and then passed these lessons along to later generations. And even today those who occupy the administrative apparatus as well as the general public have not yet rid themselves of the colonial mentality. Effective governance demands the eradication of this legacy and the encouragement of a new African who identifies with the state.

The attitudes and orientations of Africans towards political objects (African political culture) are not the same as the attitudes and orientations of Europeans towards political objects (European political culture). What Africans required were political systems with a balance between centralization and decentralization to enable effective participation in the political process at the local level in their own languages and cultures. What was imposed was a political opium in which the language of Parliament as well as the political practice was alien, parliamentary debates were published in a language that the majority of the population could not understand, and the only participation at the local level was a ballot box into which some piece of paper was dumped once every four years.

In the absence of cultural participation at the local level, the ballot box technology alone could not satiate the indigenous political thirst. This is not to suggest that the ballot box technology is inherently unacceptable to the African; it is to emphasize that it was presented on a European silver platter instead of being presented appropriately in an African dish. How, for instance, would the English or the French peoples feel if the language spoken in Parliament were Chinese, which most of the electorate would not understand, and if representatives were to be selected in the Chinese style and the parliamentary procedures were in accordance with Chinese culture? Would those conditions be acceptable? If not, why should Africans be expected to accept a similar situation? It is no wonder, given these conditions, that the African post-colonial state became relatively weak. On the one hand, the larger African population perceived the politicians as well as the occupants of the administrative apparatuses as artificial Europeans perpetuating European ideas and values and working for the same alien state, for nothing really changed. Indeed, the new rulers were regarded as coconuts— black outside but very white inside. On the other hand, because the politicians and the occupants of the administrative apparatus were embedded in the larger population, their inability to rid themselves of the colonial mentality acted as a political catalyst that perpetuated and accelerated the perception of the post-colonial state as still alien. It thus became heroic for the larger population to evade paying taxes or rendering any effective allegiance to the post-colonial state and simultaneously heroic for the politicians and administrators to habitually plunder or loot the coffers of the alien post-colonial state. Moreover, seeing a member of another political party as an "enemy" acted as a potent centrifugal force that created divisions among the larger population, the politicians, and the administrators. Consequently, the imposed partisan democratic process failed to work, and the former colonial masters wondered why. Meanwhile, with the Cold War in progress the West required African political systems strong enough to resist communism. The former colonial masters became increasingly concerned that because African communal culture had some rudiments of collectivization and the imposed democratic institutions were relatively weak, the potential existed for communist penetration.

Certain leaders of Africa, including Kwame Nkrumah of Ghana,

Sekou Touré of Guinea, Julius Nyerere of Tanzania, and, later, Siad Barré of Somalia and Haile Mariam Mengistu of Ethiopia, openly declared socialism as their political formula for development. Although these leaders, except Mengistu, declared that their brand of socialism was to be African in content (meaning, essentially, a modification of African communalism), the West was alarmed and disappointed. To the West, the propensity towards socialism implied that their efforts in grooming Africans to become Western Europeans had either failed or been rejected by African politicians to the extent that communism was winning the Cold War in the African theatre. Indeed, in that Cold War the West perceived any African who condemned imperialism or colonialism as being an ally of communism. The possibility that Africans might have their own ideology distinct from any of the ideologies originating from the West was completely overlooked or rejected.

In that Cold War context Western leaders turned increasingly from encouraging the achievement of "modernity" in both the political and economic spheres to a decided preference for African leaders capable of repressing the legitimate and democratic demands of African social formations. With the support of Western intellectuals, there was a complete shift of emphasis from democracy to order. Thus, Samuel P. Huntington, a member of the Social Science Research Council Committee on Comparative Politics (SSRCCC) in the United States, redefined political stability not as a factor of democracy but as merely the absence of open conflict, and political development as the mere development of institutions capable of dealing with the strains of social mobilization and political participation. He argued that the degree of government commitment and not its form was the key in determining whether or not a development policy might be implemented. In addition, the SSRCCC published a book, *Crises and Sequences in Political Development*, emphasizing order and the government capacity to respond to or suppress legitimate demands—the popular demands of the same civil society that confers authority on the rulers by consent or on whose behalf the elite supposedly rule. In most developing countries independence was granted on a liberal-democratic platter at a time when industrialization had not adequately taken root. Because of election promises to win votes, expectations ran high. The low development of the productive forces and the weakness of the economy meant that most of those expectations could not be met either locally or through imports. With high hopes suddenly dashed, political crises might ensue. To prevent political crises that might well precipitate a communist takeover, it was rationalized that a government capable of suppressing these legitimate demands was required. With this tendency in mind, political development was redefined in line with Huntington's thinking as the ability of a political system to cope with crises associated with legitimacy, identity, participation, and penetration and distribution. Governmental capacity was redefined away from democratic norms to mean the capacity of ruling elites favoured by the West to maintain order. Political crises were therefore interpreted as threats to the position of the ruling elites supported by the West, and the question of political necessity as the necessity of such elites to maintain order and contain communism.

In *Crises and Sequences in Political Development*, the Parsonian concept of order virtually became an end in itself. However, in a larger context and agenda, it was supposed that this maintenance of order was essential to the containment of communism. In its desperate search for allies against communism and strategic interests, the West compromised on issues of human rights and democracy and gave its support to military regimes and dictators, including Mobutu Sese Seko of Zaire, Jean Bokassa of the Central African Republic, and William Tubman of Liberia. Similarly, for the purpose of compelling developing countries to comply with debt obligations, the Western-dominated International Monetary Fund (IMF) and the International Bank for Reconstruction and Development (IBRD, or World Bank) imposed conditionalities and policies that required the political will and capacity of African leaders to repress the democratic demands of their people.

The cumulative effect was the shelving of any accountability to the people, the driving of the democratic forces and movements in Africa underground, and an African development that would follow trajectories that responded to the agendas of foreign interests. As Claude Ake plausibly explains, the development process saw a confusion of agendas in which the Western agenda predominated.[4] Africa became one of the battlegrounds on which the elephants of the East and West fought their ideologically stimulated Cold War as the innocent grass (the African populations) suffered. While the West preferred strong governments capable of containing communism, the communists of Eastern Europe and China preferred strong governments capable of establishing communism. Colonel Mengistu of Ethiopia, who erected a statue of Karl Marx in Addis Ababa, was a puppet of the USSR and not of the United States. The West, then, was not solely to blame for the ills of Africa during the Cold War. In the struggles between East and West on African soil, Africa became the land of coups—which were also alien to its culture.

As the Cold War progressed and African countries suffered, Western scholars diverted attention to trivial issues, including debates about the relative autonomy of the African post-colonial state, the embedded state, personal rule, the predatory state, and interference in the market-place by African states—as if a perfect market had ever existed anywhere in the world. Instead of investigating whether Africa had achieved the preconditions for successful development, the apostles of the market closed their minds to the oligopolistic pricing and protectionist character of the world market and compelled African countries through structural adjustment conditionalities to open their markets wide. All the while the West continued to dictate commodity prices and maintain strict projectionist barriers to Africa's products.

The same Western countries that recognize and accept the ability of the market to fail in allocating entitlements to individuals as a human right and have introduced welfare benefits in their social programs continue to act through the IMF and the World Bank to dictate to African countries to remove subsidies that are essentially welfare-oriented. Given the past five hundred years of slavery, then colonialism, and finally neo-colonialism, it is difficult if not impossible to deny that raw materials and human capital from Africa have been obtained cheaply to make the West rich and Africa poor. Uranium from Africa, for instance, provided the West with the nuclear arsenals to counter the threat of the communist bloc. With the end of the Cold War it was not Africa that made gains, but Russia, Eastern Europe, and China, the former enemies of the West, which began to receive special attention and billions of dollars in aid. Through its behaviour, the West has demonstrated beyond reasonable doubt that it prefers to aid and maintain close ties with its former enemies rather than pursue policies conducive to correcting the ills of Africa. In addition, while the former enemies of the West continue to practise their own brand of democracy and China remains communist, African countries are being compelled by the West with the assistance of the IMF and the World Bank to accept new manifestations of the same Western partisan politics that failed to work in the past and are suitable only to the capitalist mode of production.

Partisan politics did not come to the West overnight. They were preceded by centuries of gradual cultural transformation, and universal franchise was not granted until industries had been established to satisfy societal demands. In Africa, universal franchise was granted solely for making the African behave politically like the European, at a time when industrialization had not even been planned and when indigenous entrepreneurs who might direct any industrialization processes were non-existent. The lack of indigenous entrepreneurs was not the fault of Africa, given that the policies of colonial subjugation deliberately repressed their development. The development of indigenous entrepreneurs was perceived as a challenge to the logic of colonialism. Furthermore, the colonialists established a racial vertical mosaic with Europeans at the top, Asians in the middle, and Africans at the bottom. Thus, as exemplified by apartheid in South Africa, and the settler and Asian problems in East Africa, colonialism in Africa took an entirely different character from colonialism elsewhere. Indeed, investment in both infrastructure and the training of indigenous Africans was so minimal that Africa gained very little from its colonial history compared to Asia and Latin America. African culture did not, therefore, go through the gradual transformation into a capitalist makeup suitable for partisan politics, and the post-independence experience brought little or no further success along these lines, for even after the end of the Cold War Africa remained pre-capitalist. While culture may be dynamic, its change takes time.

What Africa needs, I believe, is a democratic practice that is compatible with indigenous culture and not the blind emulation of any foreign political culture. This compatible cultural democracy is the key to Africa's political, economic, and social development. A modernized form of Africa's own indigenous consensual and democratic culture would provide the necessary political conditions for successful economic growth. As Kwame Nkrumah, the first president of Ghana, once said, "Seek ye first the political kingdom and all other things shall be added on to it"—with the interpretation and understanding that the political kingdom is the attainment of the political conditions for successful development.

Successful economic development demands the existence of certain political conditions, and, essentially, by forsaking the indigenous political cultures and blindly emulating alien political cultures and ideologies, the "modernizing" elite of Sub-Saharan Africa found itself out of step with the general social environment of the region. This prevented the elite from achieving the appropriate political and social prerequisites for democratic and economic growth in Sub-Saharan Africa, resulting in a persistent deepening of the political and economic crises. In this context, political conditions are deemed appropriate if they enable the governing coalitions to integrate the social interests, cushion and control strife that might accompany development, and pursue and sustain coherent and nationalist development objectives while simultaneously enjoying the support of major sections of society. The appropriateness of political conditions depends upon the cultural environment.

Compatible Cultural Democracy as a Practice

Compatible cultural democracy takes into consideration both the history and culture of the environment. The rationale for its implementation in Africa is necessarily eclectic. No one Western theoretical approach can explain African political systems adequately, whereas an eclectic combination of these theories might approach the African reality more closely. In addition the eclectic approach affords the advocates of the holus-bolus transplantation of Western partisan politics in Africa an opportunity to understand and evaluate the rationale of compatible cultural democracy in Africa in their own political languages and discourse.

Compatible cultural democracy recognizes a wisdom advanced by contingency theory, to the effect that there is no single best organization for the solution of human problems. Outcomes depend not only upon the agent, but also upon the fit between that agent, the environment, and the applied technology. Postmodernists have argued along similar lines that no one ideal organization exists, and no standard or teleological modernity should be emulated by all nations, taking into account that the industrialized nations of today are not without their severe problems. The approach envelops Geoffrey Vicker's theory of decision-making, according to which decision-making depends upon the appreciative system of the decision-maker. The appreciative system itself comprises value judgement and reality judgement as its weft and warp and in such a manner that in any particular decision-making process, a section of it is evoked. Because the value and reality judgements of people of different cultures differ, their appreciations and decisions about objects, processes, and practices, including the political aspects, may differ. What is acceptable in one culture might be completely unacceptable in another. Thus, the outright transplantation of political practices from one culture to another may lead to disastrous consequences.

Compatible cultural democracy also takes into consideration insights provided by Marxist political scientists, who argue that social, cultural, and political phenomena are determined by the mode of production of material things. Although this insight assigns primacy to the economy rather than ideas in explaining historical processes, and French Marxist philosopher Louis Althusser proposed that the superstructural elements of ideology and politics are conditions for the existence of the economy, compatible cultural democracy accepts the central argument that each mode of production requires suitable political, social, and cultural arrangements. African countries that are still pre-industrial and culturally communal with strong extended family relations, then, cannot be expected to have the same political arrangements and practices as an industrial society. What they need are political arrangements and practices compatible with their respective cultural environments.

The notion of compatible cultural democracy in Africa might also be seen in the context of U.S. psychologist Abraham Maslow's hierarchy of needs. While an advanced industrialized and powerful country such as the United States may be aiming at the satisfaction of the self-fulfilment needs of continued self-development and the greatest achievements among nations, including feats of space exploration, young and weak countries such as Ghana, Zimbabwe, or Kenya may be at the stage of satisfying the physiological needs of providing bread to their hungry millions, striving to satisfy the safety needs of protection against danger, threat, and deprivation, and sweating to promote the social needs of nation-building, including the injection of the sense of belonging and the acceptance of one tribe by the other.

In addition, if the definition of politics by David Easton and Fred Riggs as the authoritative allocation of values is accepted, then African politics should be the authoritative allocation of African values and not the authoritative allocation of alien or foreign values. What compatible cultural democracy calls for in Africa is the authoritative allocation of African values to the African people by Africans within the context of African culture and African history, leading to the projection of the African personality and respect within the entire world community. Compatible cultural democracy when applied in the African context cannot be socialism, communism, capitalism, liberalism, or any other foreign "ism," but a reflection of Africanism—the ideological, economic, and political practice of Africans, on African soil, in accordance with African culture, and by Africans emancipated from colonial mentality and cleansed of foreign excrescence.

The concept of compatible cultural democracy, however, is of very general application in both the developing and developed worlds. Compatible cultural democracy emphasizes that although democracy may not perish from the Earth, at the same time, and in conformity with contingency theory, there is no best organization or political technology to which all nations of the world might aspire. Because politics is for the satisfaction of human needs, and because the needs as well as the attitudes and orientations of people to political objects, processes, and practices do differ, it is logical to find differences in the implementation of democratic theory. Thus the Americans practise a democracy that is compatible with the attitudes, experiences, and orientations of the American people; the British practise a type of democracy that they consider to be compatible with the attitudes and orientations of the British. The same might be said of the French, the Germans, and of the small European states. What might be suitable to the Americans might not be necessarily suitable for the French.

The lesson to be learnt from all these differences is that what matters is the compatibility of the particular type of application of democratic theory to the orientations and attitudes of the people towards political objects or compatible cultural democracy. An incompatible cultural democracy might lead to dangerous consequences. Indeed, the presidential, parliamentary, federal, and consociational democratic systems are all different and harmonious applications of compatible cultural democracy intended for the intelligent solution of human problems and the satisfaction of human needs within different cultures. Given that all these Western countries practise compatible cultural democracy, is it not reasonable and appropriate for African countries to practise a type of compatible cultural democracy that is suitable for their environment? Might incompatible cultural democracy or incompatible ideologies not be at the root of the political turmoil and economic chaos in post-colonial Africa? In general the consequences of incompatible cultural democracy and incompatible political ideologies in Africa have been political instability and economic chaos. The wholesale transplantation of foreign ideologies and political practice in the form of multiparty electoral systems or one-party systems under the banner of socialism has undermined the attainment of the political preconditions for successful economic development. Also, the blind acceptance and adoption by the military elite of Africa of the ideology of military rule propounded by some Western scholars in the 1960s aggravated matters. If Africans ignore the cultural and historical dimensions in their ongoing democratic fervour and blindly emulate foreign democratic practices, there is a potential danger that the mistakes of the past might be repeated, with disastrous consequences.

The Elite Framework

The classical political theorists Vilfredo Pareto, Gaetano Mosca, and Robert Michels explained in various ways that societies are ruled by organized minorities, called elites, who play the part of key actors in shaping the structures and character of their societies. In recent times, others, such as C. W. Mills and John Porter, have argued along similar lines. Their accounts show that partisan politics does not necessarily lead to democracy (the rule of the common people) but to the rule of the few, which implies that a form of democracy set in place through partisan politics is illusory.

Pareto argued that because of the unequal distribution of biological *residues*—universal elements that reflect basic human sentiments—human beings are physically, morally, and intellectually different to the extent that it is possible to divide society into two broad categories: the elite, who excel in whatever they do; and the masses, who are only average in performance. There are also divisions within and among the elite. An elite class, the governing elite, plays a significant role in political life and in government. The rest, the non-governing elite, play no significant role in politics or government. The typology of government depends upon the manner in which the elites in power choose to govern, but two basic types of government exist. One type relies mainly on physical force and religion or similar ideology. The other type relies mainly on intelligence and cunning practices. In practice these basic types may be mixed. However, elites in power are not self-perpetuating. Within the governing elite there may be elites who prefer the status quo and counter-elites who seek a drastic change to the status quo. The most serious mistake that a ruling elite can make is to fail to provide for "circulation," in which those with superior residues move up in the ranks and those with inferior residues move out—a process that renovates the governing class in number and in quality. Revolutions occur when the circulation of elites slows down or when the upper strata of the governing elite accumulate decadent elements who no longer possess the appropriate biological residues for the maintenance of power, while the counter-elites are enriched by those with the appropriate residues moving into their ranks. While Pareto's theory of a minority class of elites ruling a mass majority and the notion and implication of the circulation of elites might be convincing, the biological explanation he gives for the emergence of the two classes suggests that contrary to historical experience leaders are born and may not be trained to be so.

Mosca explained the emergence of an elite in society differently. In his book *The Ruling Class* (1896), Mosca agrees in principle with Pareto that two classes of people appear in society—a class that rules and a class that is ruled. However, according to Mosca the two classes emerge out of the struggle for pre-eminence concerning wealth, status, authority, and control over the means of directing human activities or wills, in which the winners become the ruling class and the losers become the ruled. He argues that, contrary to basic democratic theory that would have it that majorities rule minorities, in practice minorities rule majorities in all societies. Because the ruling classes are minorities, they have the ability to organize themselves while the ruled masses remain unorganized. This state of affairs makes the domination of an organized minority over an unorganized majority inevitable in human societies. But the ruling classes do not govern simply by brute force. They legitimize their rule by political formulas that are accepted by the ruled. When the ruling classes are successful in imposing their political formulas, when they manage society and render appreciable service to it and are open to talented people from the ruled, a continuous rejuvenation of the ruling class takes place, resulting in gradual change and progress. Otherwise, revolutions are likely. In this way, Mosca agrees with Pareto on the importance of the circulation of elites. Hence, the character and structure of the ruling class determine the political regime and the rate of change and progress. But there may be contentions, competition, and struggles among the ruling classes, resulting in the replacement of one ruling class by the other. When a ruling class is deposed, another minority ruling class takes its place. Indeed, history is characterized by struggles between ruling classes and their contenders.

Mosca argues that in an elected representative government, the candidates with any chance of succeeding are those who are supported by organized minorities. Because organized minorities impose their will on the disorganized majority, the notions of the sovereignty of the people, government by the consent of the governed, and majority rule sanctioned by democratic theory are all illusions. In addition, the ability of elected representatives to govern well may be distorted by their own egotism, especially by their interest in seeking re-election and supporting the interests of their party. Elected representatives may be tempted to concentrate power in their own hands, resulting in tyranny. But the elected representative system has certain advantages. Political forces that might be inert in the absolute state, when monarchs were considered as the representatives of God on Earth, with absolute power, become organized and exert influence on the government. The elected assemblies serve as a check on the power of those who govern, especially the bureaucracy—a process in which the power of representatives limits the power of appointed officials, leading to a power balance that retrains the arbitrariness of the rulers. The system permits government actions to be subjected to public discussion through individual, press, and parliamentary liberties, and the ruling classes are compelled to take into account mass sentiments on issues and on any public discontent. Furthermore, the disadvantages of the elected representative system may be trifles when compared to the harm that can be done under a one-principle political organization, such as in a one-party collectivized state. In a one-party organization, diverse social forces may find it difficult to participate in the political process to counterbalance each other, resulting in despotism. Contrary to the expectations of the proponents of the one-principle political organization, the bureaucracy might never wither away but increase in size, authority, and power. Mosca concludes that the regime that may promote liberty best is a mixed one in which different forces curb each other's power.

In effect, Mosca argues that the importance of an elected representative system of government resides in the prior existence of counterbalancing political forces arising from individuals, organized groups, and institutions and made possible by the political elite's grant of individual and press liberties, and the subjection of government acts to public discussion. The historical experience of Africa seems to substantiate most of Mosca's analysis and predictions. In a typical indigenous African political culture, Mosca's counterbalancing political forces were provided by a representation from diverse clans and interest groups at the ruling college of elites, a consensual principle, a decentralized structure, and a requirement for consultation and feedback from the lower levels.

Another classical account pertinent to the African experience comes from Robert Michels. In his book *Political Parties: A Sociological Study of the Oligarchical Tendencies of Modern Democracy* (1911), Michels argues that the nature of human individuals, of the political struggle, and, especially, of organization lead democracy in the direction of oligarchy. Focusing his analysis on organization, he argues that human instinct views power as something to be acquired and then passed on to successive generations, and in the process aristocracies develop. However, in democracies the very requirements of organization lead to the growth of oligarchy. Any group, association, or class wanting to have a meaningful impact on the political process needs to be organized. Each organization, even if it begins by being democratic, becomes divided into a minority of directors or leaders and a majority of directed or led. Initially the leaders are merely the executive organs of the collective, but in time the collective loses its control over the leaders, who gradually become independent of the collective and, instead, gain control over it.

The size of the modern political party, which makes it impossible for all members to participate in decision-making, reinforces the oligarchical tendency. The complexity and speciality of functions, and the organizational requirements, incomprehensible to the rank and file, call for a delegation of authority. Oligarchy is also perpetuated by the need for quick decisions; the need for expertise; the requirement for information and control of information; the acquisition of leadership skills by the leaders, which makes them indispensable; the need for continuity, which makes the members prefer to maintain the same people in office; the apathy of the members and their willingness, gratefulness, and happiness to be left alone as others run the show; and the reluctance of the leaders to relinquish their acquired power. Thus the needs and behaviour of both the leaders and members lead to oligarchy. Governments, as complex organizations, are oligarchic. Because of the nature of the organization, even if the leaders are replaced the new ones will be oligarchic. This general tendency of democratic organizations to develop and perpetuate oligarchy is what Michels calls the "iron law of oligarchy."

A number of case studies have confirmed elite theory and the notion of oligarchy in the complex organizations of government. Case studies are theory-testing tools, and crucial cases may be used to falsify theory. Some case studies, including studies carried out by C.W. Mills and John Porter in the United States and Canada respectively, seem to confirm that the few govern the majority. The studies by Mills and Porter looked, after all, at environments in which democracy, the rule of the majority, would appear most likely to hold sway. But because these crucial cases could not falsify the rule by the few, but confirmed it, elite theory may be accepted as a valid general theory applicable to societies, including Sub-Saharan Africa.

In *The Power Elite* Mills argues that, as a result of social and economic development, a power elite of three different elements—the military, the political, and the economic—has assumed control in the United States. His focus of analysis of the power elite is social position rather than personal or individual characteristics. Because the elite is not just an economic class that rules politically, he considers the term elite to be more appropriate. The liberal notion of political representatives controlling the state does not recognize the important interplay between the corporate power-holders, the military, and the state.

He argues that the power elite are not representative men. Their high position is not premised on any measure of moral virtue, and their success is not related to merit. The development of the power elite is accompanied by the simultaneous growth of a mass society, which is fragmented, passive, and powerless. Consequently, the power elite is not held in responsible check by the plurality of associations—a factor that militates against the ideals of democracy, open politics, and intelligent citizens debating political alternatives. What essentially exists is the domination and manipulation of mass society by the power elite and the acceptance of the situation by the mass majority. Mills's analysis confirms the notions of Pareto, Mosca, and Michel that Western democracies are not truly the rule by common people, but illusions in which the few rule the many. In addition, Mills implies that the actual holders of political power might be playing the game from behind the scenes. They need not be those with merit, of proven morals—the elected representatives or the appointed civilian officials.

In *The Vertical Mosaic*, Porter focuses on certain institutions of society and the backgrounds, education, social status, ethnic origins, religions, and political affiliations of leading elites in the economic, labour, political, bureaucratic, and economic fields. He argues that institutions are organized hierarchically and that individuals as well as groups who occupy the top positions are the elites, who may compete or co-operate depending upon circumstances. They may compete to share in societal decision-making or co-operate as a matter of concern for society. Moreover, the existence of various elite groups can lead to conflict and competition, resulting in a balance of political forces in which no single group of elites becomes dominant. In Canada, because of the existence of elite groups, the notion of a liberal citizen participating in democratic governance is unsatisfactory as a model for the analysis of both economic and political decision-making. In contrast to Pareto's notion of circulation of elites, Porter places an emphasis on the necessity for open recruitment from all classes into elite groups, which would ensure stability. His analysis essentially recognizes and confirms Western democracy as an illusion.

Elite analysis, then, holds that the characteristics and modes of elite domination determine the institutional structures of society. Leadership matters. In the structure-agency debate, elite analysis argues on the side of agency, holding that the forces that are most important in understanding any given society are not the social structures, arrangements, or processes, but the elites. Structures can be constraining, but they are not enslaving or impossible to change. However, the mode of domination chosen by the elite varies according to the mix of other factors, as evidenced by differences between the United States and Canada. In the United States, according to Mills, the interplay between corporate power-holders, the military, and the state maintains the balance of power. In Canada, according to Porter, conflict and competition between various elite groups maintains the balance of power. Indeed, because of historical and other factors, the mode of domination chosen by the elites of the electoral representative systems of the Western democratic societies varies from country to country. What matters, then, is the compatibility of the particular type of application of democratic theory to the orientations and attitudes of the people towards political objects—or what I call compatible cultural democracy. Still, we cannot rule out the possibility of similarities in the mode of elite domination between nations far apart geographically.

A mode of elite domination that comes close to the indigenous and consensual system of rule by the consensus of an encompassing coalition is *consociational democracy* as described by Arend Lijphart.[5] He uses the term to describe the stability of democracies such as Switzerland, Austria, the Netherlands, and Belgium, which, because of subcultural cleavages, could also tend towards immobilism and instability. Through consociational democracy, elites of the major subcultures are able to create and maintain stable systems. The essential characteristic of consociational democracy is co-operation at the elite level with the objective of counteracting the tendency towards disintegration. But consociational democracy has certain prerequisites and requires favourable conditions. The prerequisites include the ability to recognize the dangers inherent in the fragmented system; the commitment of elites to system maintenance; ability to transcend subcultural cleavage at the elite level; and the ability to forge appropriate solutions for the demands of the subcultures. When these prerequisites exist, the conditions favourable to consociational democracy include distinct lines of cleavage between the subcultures; a multiple balance of power between the subcultures; popular attitudes that favour government by grand coalition; perception of external threats; moderate and constructive nationalism; and a relatively low total demand on the system.

Another mode of elite domination that can be submerged in consociational democracy and is related to a typical African consensual system is societal corporatism, in which elites with different ideological orientations and political subcultures maintain a coalitionally based executive authority as an essentially political necessity for economic development.[6] An essential feature of societal corporatism—and one particularly applicable to Africa—is the co-operation of the political elites, the economic elites, and labour leaders in decision-making.

Elite analysis does reveal that the Western modes of political practice emulated by the elite of Africa are, after all, not truly democratic. Rather, they are illusions of democracy in which an organized minority rules a majority of people. Furthermore, blind emulation of this mode of domination can lead to disastrous consequences without a proper fit between the political agents and the prevailing political, social, and economic environments. Although the indigenous political systems of Africa did have their differences, their democratic practices had essential commonalities. Patterns of decision-making emphasized a consultation based upon the consensus of elites who represented the various sections of society. The various indigenous nations had no political parties at all—which means that even a one-party state is a contravention of the indigenous democratic practice. The election or appointment of an elite in the indigenous system depended largely on merit, although paternal or maternal considerations also played a role at times in the election of eligible candidates.

Today, African politicians and administrators have been trained mostly in the West or locally in accordance with the high standards of Western professional and academic institutions. These high standards have been substantiated by their commendable performances in international arenas such as the agencies of the Commonwealth, the World Bank, the IMF, and the United Nations. Compatriots and contemporaries with the same background in training, operating in the African environment with great human and material resources at their disposal, have not been able to achieve anything like political and economic success. Africa remains in persistent crisis. In the decades following the Second World War, neither the civilian nor the military governments modified and adapted the indigenous consensual cultures to suit the requirements of modern government, and no states were able to achieve the necessary prerequisites for successful development. The misfit between the African elite, the environment, and the transplantation of Western democracy, military rule, and socialism on the African soil has led to political chaos and economic ruin.

CHAPTER TWO

THE GREAT TRANSPLANTATION

*The number of persons engaged in the slave trade and the amount
of capital embarked in it exceeded our powers of calculation. The
city of New York has been of late (1862) the principal port of the
world for this infamous commerce; although the cities of Portland
and Boston are only second to her in that distribution.*
Dr. W. E. B. Du Bois, Pan-Africanist,
quoting a report of 1862 in a study of the American Slave Trade

The coming of alien ideologies and practices to Africa began to some
extent during the era of captive slavery, from the fifteenth to the nineteenth century, but it intensified during the era of colonial enslavement.
Slavery was abolished in most of Europe during the later eighteenth and
early nineteenth centuries—though abolition in oversees territories
came somewhat later—but the end of captive slavery did not bring an
end to all forms of enslavement of black Africans. The further development of capitalism required raw materials and markets. Africa's natural
resources, relative proximity to Europe, and ready access by sea—at
least at the perimeter—rendered it a preferred source of the raw materials required by capitalist Europe. Africa was also an easy target for
European goods, which could be exchanged for Africa's resources. The
logic of capitalism required secure markets if steady profits were to be
repatriated to the metropoles for reinvestment in the capital accumulation processes, and the exploitation of Africa's natural resources
required indigenous labour. But with the end of the slave trade Europe
had to find another rationalization for exploiting the labour and natural
resources of Africa to its capitalist advantage. Certain developments in
Europe and the Americas would provide the answer.

In the eighteenth and nineteenth centuries France lost most of its former colonies in the Americas to its Anglo-Saxon rivals. By 1871 France
had been humiliated in its conflicts with Germany. After the Franco-
Prussian War, the prestige of France in European circles waned. To

restore matters to the proper balance France decided to acquire colonies in North and West Africa, where it calculated that its military superiority compared to those of African social formations would provide an excellent advantage. As a result, the conditions for Africa's future development were undermined, and the freedom that Africans might have enjoyed after the end of captive slavery were to be disturbed, first by France and later by other European countries. The Ghanaian historian Adu Boahene explains the forces that led to what is known as the "scramble for Africa":

> The most important of these political factors was an exaggerated spirit of nationalism in Europe following the unification of both Germany and Italy and especially after Germany's defeat of France in 1871. With the emergence of a strong national consciousness, nations began to think not only of their power and progress but also of their prestige, greatness, and security. Unfortunately, in Europe of the last decades of the nineteenth century, the number of overseas colonies a nation possessed became a measure or a symbol of its prestige and greatness just as dispatching a satellite into earth orbit is today ... and France [went into Africa] to prove that she was still a great power despite her humiliating defeat by Germany in 1871.[1]

In 1879, armed with this prestige-seeking mentality, and having previously set down a foothold in North Africa and Senegal, the French embarked upon an exploration project aimed at establishing a trans-Saharan railway. The desire to establish this railway was not, of course, a response to any request by the African societies of those areas, but sprang from France's unilateral and conspiratorial decision to further its interests whether the African societies liked it or not. From the dominant European point of view, democratic principles did not apply to Africans. In addition, France assigned to its Major Gustave Borgnis-Desbordes the responsibility of expanding French holdings inland from Senegal.

The Colonial Treaties

In 1879 the French, acting in alliance with Belgium, also dispatched the explorers Henry Morton Stanley and Pierre Savorgnan de Brazza to enter into treaties with African kingdoms in the general areas of the

Congo River on their behalf. The circumstances and scenarios that led to the signings of these treaties are key. To the treaty tables the African rulers brought a minimal understanding, if any, of the language in which the treaties were written, still-vivid memories of the devastations of the European slave trade, and the knowledge that the Europeans themselves had been conflicted on the issue of the slave trade and on whether it should be stopped. The apparent confrontation among Europeans over the stoppage of the slave trade convinced African rulers that at least some Europeans were genuinely interested in protecting Africans against the onslaught of other Europeans. African leaders also undoubtedly recognized the European advantage in weaponry, which meant that the outsiders could—and would—always use force to achieve their goals in their dealings with Africans. They recognized that it was futile and unwise for an African ruler to reject the offers of Europeans, especially when those offers came at a time when those Europeans carried guns. They would not have known that European promises—expressed in words that implied friendship on equal terms with Europeans, including protection from the aggression of other Europeans—were empty promises.

For their part, the Europeans brought to the treaty table documents prepared in their own languages, and the subtle intention of subjugating Africans by deceiving their rulers into signing papers those African leaders did not have the capacity to read and understand. They brought weapons—and especially the Maxim machine gun—to compel any reluctant Africans to sign the treaties, and they brought the conviction that the signing of those treaties meant the acceptance of the imposition of European authority and all its attendant practices and goals—among which was the exploitation of the rich natural resources of Africa and African populations to the benefit of imperialist Europe. At that time it was a point of pride and honour to be called an imperialist, because the term implied affluence and commanded considerable respect; and the treaties were not treaties of peace but European documents of conspiracy that African rulers, without the requisite understanding, were either compelled to sign or deceived into signing.[2] The signing of these treaties marked the beginning of the formal transplantation of alien ideologies and political practices in Africa.

Meanwhile, the signing of these treaties in the Congo basin meant that France and Belgium were expanding their influence to regions that Portugal and Britain previously regarded as their treasured areas of influence. When, in 1883, France added Porto Novo and Little Popo to its list of annexations, the effect was to draw Britain and Germany into the competition to annex areas of Africa by whatever means deemed fit—through treaties of deception or by conquest. In the capitalist arena of this colonial logic, Africa was to serve as market for manufactured goods as well as the source of cheap raw materials and cheap labour. However, the keen competition to annex posed the danger of drawing the European competitors into war amongst themselves. It was to avert armed confrontation among the competing European nations that a conspiratorial conference in Berlin under the chairmanship of Otto von Bismarck (the German chancellor at the time) from November 15, 1884 to January 31, 1885 was attended by the major powers of the time, with the notable exceptions of Switzerland and the United States.

The Conference of Berlin: Conspiracy and the White Man's Burden

The famous Conference of Berlin was essentially the Conspiracy of Berlin. No African ruler was invited by the Europeans to participate in the discussions that concerned Africa, although, of course, no meaningful conspiracy would let the targeted victim participate in the planning. At Berlin the strategies for the colonization of Africa were formally drawn up, approved, and ratified by all of the participants. Africa was to be partitioned politically, economically, and ideologically. The political partition would place identified and demarcated areas of Africa under the colonial control of specified European countries. The economic partition would enable the Western countries to share the economic goods and resources of Africa according to how much each of those countries or its citizens invested in the exploitation process. The ideological partition would allow the Christian church to work at "taming" Africans to accept European rule as ordained by God. In recognition of this ideological logic, James Coleman noted that Christian missionaries were "the front troops of the Government to soften the hearts of the people and while the people look at the Cross white men gather the riches of the land."[3] Indeed, Coleman's view of the Church's role is confirmed by the resistance of some bishops and religious leaders to the abolition of slavery and colonialism. Bishop Maury of France, supposedly a holy messenger of God, argued strongly in a 1791 presentation to the French National Assembly: "If you were to lose each year more than 200 million livres that you now get from your colonies: if you had not the exclusive trade with your colonies to feed your manufactures, to maintain your navy, to keep your agriculture going, to repay your imports, to provide your luxury need, advantageously balance your trade with Europe and Asia, then I say it clearly, the kingdom would be irretrievably lost." A century and a half later, in 1936, pan-Africanist George Padmore would emphasize, "The Blackman certainly has to pay dear for carrying the whiteman's burden." The transplantation of European culture and ideology to Africa would be exclusively for the benefit and development of Europe.

The exclusion of African rulers from the Berlin Conference itself implied that, to the Europeans of that time, Africans had no right to make their own history. African history was, rather, to be fashioned by the West—by its transplantation of alien values and practices, and by its exploitation of the human and material resources of the continent. Although a few crumbs resulting from that effort might fall to African countries, the political, economic, cultural, ideological, and administrative structures established in the colonial era were oriented principally not to the service or benefit of Africans but to the service and benefit of the West. For the Europeans this purpose came under the cover of their deeply felt sense of superiority, and the resultant sense that they were carrying out a civilizing mission in Africa. This was the famous "white man's burden." In a clever twist of the facts, they defined the white man's burden as a humanitarian mission. That colonial-era claim of humanitarianism, though, has to be placed in the harsh light of the previous era of the European slave trade. During the era of captive slavery (roughly, from the fifteenth to the nineteenth century), the imperialist powers of the time (Spain, Portugal, and Britain) traded alcohol, firearms, and textiles for captured slaves in Africa and shipped them to North and South America, where they became the mainstay of an agricultural factory economy. Under colonialism, whole nations, including their kings, queens, emperors, and other rulers, were captured and enslaved in their own land. The individual members of whole African societies witnessed a kind of joint humiliation: their own, along with that of their noble rulers, at the same time, and in the same place.

British colonial enslavement demoted African kings to the status of chiefs, emperors to the status of paramount chiefs, and compelled these virtual captives to serve the interests of imperialism through a system of indirect rule. The logic of colonialism required that African societies remained weak enough to be thoroughly dominated. That logic would fall apart if different ethnic groups within the colonized area became united. As a result the colonialists applied a divide and rule strategy to set the various kingdoms of Africa against one another, and through this process tribalism, which was born during the era of captive slavery, was revived. Significantly, these words—"tribalism" and "tribe"—are not African words. If tribes or tribalism had existed in Africa, there would have been African words for the phenomenon. It was precisely because no African words existed for what was essentially a kind of discriminatory distinction that the colonists adapted the words *tribe* and *tribalism* to describe the human formations they were creating. The terms carried the connotation of backwardness, which suited the rationalization of centuries of captive slavery. Even today huge empires and kingdoms of Africa continue to be referred to as tribes and not, more properly, as nations. In reality African kingdoms were nations of people who spoke different languages, or sometimes dialects of the same language. Europeans also spoke different languages, had different cultures, and went to war with one another just as African countries did; but they did not use the word tribe to describe themselves: no references were made to the French, German, Dutch, and English tribes of Europe. The idea of tribalism represented the transplantation of a European myth into Africa.

Given that the European slave trade in Africans used the same divide and rule strategy to obtain captives, not much difference existed between colonialism and slavery in that regard, except that they were different stages of the same enslavement for the same purpose—the exploitation of the African. What was called a civilizing mission essentially worked at setting one African kingdom against another, at robbing African social formations of their mineral resources or siphoning off their created wealth. Writing in the 1950s, Walter Wallbank described one example of this kind of mission in what was then the Belgian Congo:

In 1953 the Belgian Congo exported over $400,000,000 worth of goods, and its gross national product was more than a billion dollars. It produces half of the world's uranium and 70% of its industrial diamonds. Other minerals produced in substantial amounts are copper, cobalt, zinc, manganese, gold and tungsten. In addition it produces yearly $40,000,000 of cotton, $32,000,000 of coffee, and $28,000,000 of palm oil.

A feature of this incredible industrialization has been the growing economic ties between the United States and the Congo. We now take 13% of its output, not including our purchases of uranium for our defense industry which is classified as secret. In turn,

24% of all the colony's imports come from the United States. We now realize the immense importance of having access to the natural resources of the Congo. During the last war, when the Japanese overran South Asia and shut off the supplies of rubber and tin, it was this area that furnished much-needed supplies of these and other commodities.[4]

In the case of Ghana, after a century of mining tons of gold, diamonds, manganese, and bauxite worth billions of pounds and dollars, followed by the extraction of billions of dollars through cash crops and forest products, including cocoa and timber, the government of Ghana received a meagre amount of about $200 million as payment in support of its new life at independence. As part of the civilizing mission, African lands were appropriated by white settlers in East Africa and South Africa—to the extent that both Kenya and South Africa were declared white man's country. Apartheid was the ultimate extent of this civilizing mission.

Africans have, not surprisingly, generally rejected this concept of the civilizing mission of colonialism because they hold the view that before the coming of Europeans they were indeed already civilized and had their own governments, which were fully compatible with their own cultures. Many Africans hold the view that the colonization of Africa was a product of the intersection of three fundamentals—European greed, technological advantage, and brutality—all of which had nothing to do with advancing civilization. The excesses of the European slave-raids in Africa and the European slave-trade in Africans, followed by the excesses of colonial rule, including the brutal use of force against unarmed civilians and the institution of forced labour, did not particularly support the notion that the Europeans were somehow more civilized than the Africans.

In many ways the white man's burden of a civilizing mission in Africa turned out to be, in reality, the white man's *leisure* for the establishment of political, administrative, ideological, economic, and cultural systems in Africa conducive to developing the West at the expense of Africa. In recognition of this colonial logic, the first president of the first country in Sub-Saharan Africa that became independent this century, Kwame Nkrumah, wrote in his famous book *Towards Colonial Freedom*:

The purpose of founding colonies was mainly to secure raw materials. To safeguard the measures for securing such raw materials the following policies were indirectly put into action: (1) to make the colonies non-manufacturing dependencies; (ii) to prevent the colonial subjects from acquiring the knowledge of modern means and techniques for developing their own industries; (iii) to make the colonial "subjects" simple producers of raw materials through cheap labour.[5]

In the physical partition of Africa, the colonial powers drew imaginary lines across the continent, serving their own interests and ignoring the interests of the peoples of Africa. These imaginary lines cut across indigenous national boundaries and divided families so much so that an African could wake up one morning to find one section of the same family under British rule, another under German rule, and yet another under Belgian or Portuguese rule. Indeed, the physical partition of Africa by itself represented a form of mass confusion based upon a European concept of property ownership in which European countries were to own territories carved arbitrarily by them in Africa in accordance with the strategies of the Berlin Conference.[6]

The Transplantation of Indirect Rule

In their drive to maximize their colonial gains, the British colonialists carefully studied the indigenous political systems of Africa and found them to be highly practical. One such study, by Sir Frederick Lugard, revealed a particular fascination with the Africans' inherent efficiency and saw how it could be put to use for the colonizers' benefit. In his book *The Dual Mandate in British Tropical Africa*, which appeared officially in 1922, Lord Lugard recommended a system of indirect rule as a means of governing Africa cheaply while at the same time making traditional African rulers feel so comfortably recognized by the King or Queen of England that they would not be tempted to rebel against the Crown.

To constitute this indirect rule Lord Lugard's recommendations implied the superimposition of a dictatorial system capable of imposing its will by the threat of force or the actual use of force (military strategy) on the indigenous systems. Essentially, after they had been conquered or subdued African rulers would become comfortable puppets of the British Crown. In the vertical integration of indirect rule indigenous rulers would be compelled and transformed into puppets who danced to the tune of alien political music, often with bayonets at their throats. This colonial dictatorship nicely left to one side the so-called

Western regime of discourse, with all its democratic principles and market theory of value.

In feudal Europe, after all, kings and queens had ruled indirectly through princes, barons, and knights. It was not therefore difficult for Lord Lugard to promote the possibility of indirect rule in Africa, especially given established indigenous systems and the prime objective of exploiting the colonies for the maximum possible gain. Strategically the system offered an impression of parallel legitimacy, but this apparent legitimacy was mythical at best, because the approach omitted any possible competition or contestation between the indigenous political system and the superimposed alien politics, which was an absolute dictatorship in which the governor was practically a demi-god whose word was power. Indeed, that the legitimacy was apparently *parallel* itself suggests a lack of any contestable intersection to justify competition or struggle between the two systems. The indirect-rule chiefs would at best be channels to facilitate the exploitation of the indigenous material and human resources. The indirect-rule system was calculated and designed to be an ally of the colonial logic of divide and rule, rather than its enemy, because it enabled Africa's various ethnic groups to view themselves as separate entities being ruled independently by a European power rather than Africans with a common destiny ruled by aliens from Europe. The purpose of this type of government was to implement British colonial policies, which served British interests.[7] Other colonial powers emulated the system of indirect rule. The *Mwami* indirect rule in Rwanda under the Germans and later under the Belgians was a typical example.

Indirect rule by no means implied a divided sovereignty, which the repressive apparatus of the colonial state would not tolerate. Rather, an alien country usurped sovereignty for its sole interests and benefits. That was what colonialism was all about, and that explains why kings were demoted to chiefs and converted into puppets who served the interests of alien powers. To deny that sovereignty was completely usurped is to deny that colonialism ever took place. Indeed, African chiefs learnt from the repressiveness of the colonial subjugation of resistive rulers—including the experience of Prempeh I of Ashanti, Ghana, who was banished to the Seychelles during the early part of the twentieth century—that they should think twice before attempting any challenge to the sovereignty represented by the Governor.

Although the colonialists, including Lord Lugard, recognized the indigenous political system as being efficient, the superimposition of the alien dictatorial system and the operation of the colonial system meant that the indigenous political culture itself became distorted and lost its respect among its own people. The system of indirect rule was effectively transplanted only after the use of ruthless force, and after thousands of Africans committed to the defence of their homelands against the unprovoked aggressor had lost their lives. The very imposition of indirect rule was a reflection of military superiority resulting from the Industrial Revolution in Europe—with the Maxim machine gun as its prime symbol—and reminiscent of the centuries of bloody brutality that preceded it.

Indeed, indirect rule tended to be intensely painful for the chiefs, because they witnessed decade after decade of plunder and oppression but were so powerless (and the oppressor so ruthless) that they usually dared not complain about it.

How Indirect Rule Undermined the Indigenous System

Indirect rule meant that the metropole determined the major policies and decisions that governed the lives of the colonized people, but the implementation of some of these decisions had to be channelled through the indirect rule of chiefs under the coercive thumb of the superimposed dictatorships headed by governors. Because the operations of colonial rule were geared to the prosperity of the metropole, land was acquired through the indirect-rule chiefs at prices dictated not by market forces, but by the colonial government. The implementation of colonial policies by the indirect-rule chiefs, acting essentially as unwilling puppets with no choice, was backed by the coercive apparatus of the state. Indigenous institutions and customary laws were redefined to serve colonial interests. For example, the superimposed system alone had the sole right of recognizing chiefs, so that the chiefs effectively became officers of the colonial administration and no longer responsible first to their own peoples, who had originally selected and made them chiefs. If for any reason the colonial state withdrew its recognition of a ruler, that person ceased to be a chief. Before European contact, rulers had been installed for life, and although African societies did make provisions for deposing rulers, it was not a common practice to do so because democratic councils kept the activities of rulers in check. Under European influence and rule, new procedures and conditions were created and so manipulated as to provide the necessary momentum for removing rulers to serve the interests of colonialism. These procedures for removing chiefs were revised continually, and the subjects of chiefs were manipulated to keep these head persons in check. The power, respect, and authority of the chiefs began to wane. Still, on the ideological level the colonial governments maintained that the indigenous system remained democratic, because, in theory, the power to elect and remove rulers still rested in the subjects.

The chiefs were in a precarious and embarrassing situation. Any time the colonial government acquired land, some communal land-ownership group suffered a loss, and the land-ownership groups would see the indirect-rule chiefs as puppets or colonial agents who were robbing them of their lands. Eventually the colonial system turned the people against their chiefs, to the extent that by the time of the independence struggles the chiefs had been identified as allies of the colonial system. The mistrust of chiefs explains why they were not the main architects of the independence struggle, for it made it difficult if not impossible for them to mobilize their own people against the colonizers. During the independence struggles the nationalist leaders did not trust the chiefs, and the subsequent constitutions refused to give them any meaningful political space. This same mistrust meant that in their attempts to govern and develop their countries even the benign nationalists were tempted to prefer the trappings of Western-style democracy to an adaptation of the indigenous system.

The nationalists did not adequately appreciate the chiefs' difficult situation and saw no reason why the same section of the community that had clearly identified with the oppressor in plundering the resources of their own country should be given any meaningful office. The temptation was to relegate chieftaincy and anything associated with it, including the indigenous democratic system, to the back seat. Instead of behaving like the Roman doorway god Janus, with one face pointing to the glorious past of the indigenous systems and the other looking into the desired future—and using those perspectives to define a type of democracy or system of governance compatible with the indigenous culture, the modernizing elite made the mistake of equating the distorted form of chieftaincy with the indigenous political system. As a result they discarded it from their agenda. In this respect the colonial education system influenced the behaviour of the African elite. The modernizing elite did not realize early enough that "in the Colonial society, education is such that it serves the colonialist.... In a regime of slavery, education was but one institution for forming slaves."[8] With colonialism as a form of enslavement, it is not surprising that the colonial apparatus should organize to transplant educational systems in the colonies to serve their own interests and for the purpose of forming colonial slaves. Furthermore, because that kind of enslavement takes place in the sphere of the mind, it is difficult for colonially formed slaves to appreciate that they are mental captives of the colonial education system, conditioned to think more like a European than an African. The products of that transplanted education prefer to wear European suits and ties in the hot African climate rather than African apparel; to wear blistering European shoes rather than airy African sandals; and they prefer the junk food of corned beef imported from Europe to the fresh meat of an African deer or gazelle.

The Transplanted Colonial Education System

Colonialism did not introduce education to Africa. Systems of education existed in Africa long before the arrival of Europeans, although they were not organized on European lines. The pre-colonial education systems of Africa were geared towards training Africans to provide service for themselves and to the African societies they lived in. The organization of education was integrated with productive activity; it was age-graded to ensure progressive development in successive stages of African value systems. The ancient empires and kingdoms of Africa, including the Ghana, Mali, Songhai, Ga, Ashanti, Zulu, and Ovimbundu, could not have survived for long without some system of education that handed over acquired knowledge from one generation to another to ensure continuity of government and the survival of society. As only one example, the ancient city of Timbuktu, situated close to the Niger River in what is now Mali, was a great centre of learning—an undeniable historical fact reflected in some classical songs of Europe.[9]

The colonialists did introduce a new type of education, though it was not geared principally to serve the interests of Africans. Its strategy was to train a few Africans to perform mediatory roles for the colonial administration and to staff the ideological apparatuses of the state, including the churches (which were to tame African societies by teaching that colonialism was ordained by God and that it was a sin to rise against the established colonial authority), the administrative machine, and the few schools. This type of training implied selecting some Africans over others and compelling them by their own needs of survival to participate in the colonial domination and exploitation of the African continent. This kind of education was not aimed at making

Africans proud of their societies. What is the pride in being educated to assist the colonialist in dominating the country of one's birth? The colonial education was for shaping the mind, volition, and personality of the recipients to conform to the colonial processes of subordination and exploitation, for that is what made it a colonial education system and differentiated it from the education system of the metropole, which was designed to train and free the minds of the recipients for greater achievements in their future careers.

The strategy of colonial higher education was to assimilate students into the value systems of the colonialists. That was achieved by the holus-bolus transplantation of an alien-valued educational system with all its trappings—capitalist-class and gender biases, a culture of competition—into pre-capitalist African societies based upon a culture of co-operation, compromise, and consensualism. The recipients of that education became misfits within their own societies. They were trained to look down upon African values, denounce African tastes, develop the tastes of the colonialists, emulate foreign lifestyles, and dress and behave like white people.

The educational syllabuses concentrated on European history, culture, and geography at the expense of African history, culture, and geography. Students recited passages from Shakespeare, which taught nothing about the African way of life. They learned very little about their own African proverbs and stories, which would have taught African virtues and culture. They became aliens clad in African skin.[10] It was no wonder, therefore, that the operation of the colonial system easily diverted the attention of the modernizing elite from the potentials of their own indigenous political cultures, which they knew very little about, to the blind emulation of the alien political cultures of the same imperialism they so condemned.

The colonial education system created further problems. Because, unlike the indigenous system, it was not integrated with productive activity and instead geared to assimilating Africans for mediatory roles in the imperial machinery, a colonial mentality developed to the effect that it was improper for an "educated" African to engage in the same productive activities being carried out by those who had not gone through the colonial education system, such as farmers. Educated Africans had to compete for the limited space within the colonial administration, the mines, and the military. Those who were not absorbed into the administrative system found comfort in petty trading and employment in foreign-owned private companies that paid very low

wages, and in so doing became compradors dependent on foreign mer-
chant capital for their very survival. When a farmer's son received a
colonial education, he became unwilling to be a farmer, for fear of being
ridiculed by his peers. As more Africans became educated in the European mode, the agricultural sector and especially the food-growing sector shrank continuously. While the cash-crop sector received incentives
because of the colonial interest in building revenues, the food-growing
sector became weaker and weaker.

Furthermore, unlike their experience in the pre-colonial education
system, African students now had to complete their education before
thinking about what they were to do with their lives. Unemployment,
non-existent in the indigenous system, became a reality of life. Indigenous education was so integrated with productive activity and graded
by age that youngsters were absorbed into the workforce long before
graduation. As Nkrumah recognized, the colonial education system was
to assist in perpetuating a situation in which the colonies were kept as
non-manufacturing dependencies. Its logic was intentionally not to
provide colonial peoples with knowledge or expertise that might afford
them the means, technology, or techniques for industrializing to compete with the metropole—because capitalists do not set out to create
other capitalists to compete with them, and colonialism did not mean
competition with colonized peoples. The areas of knowledge acquired
by Africans were only crumbs allowed to fall from the tables of the colonialists. The change in education style and the emphasis on assimilation were, therefore, solely to the benefit of the colonial system, which
required mediatory roles to be performed cheaply by Africans. The
infrastructure that these mediating elites of Africa helped to establish
reveals colonialism's exploitative stance.

The Nature of the Colonial Infrastructure

Except in those areas declared to be the domain of white settlers, such as
South Africa and Kenya, the colonial transportation infrastructure was
not only parsimonious, but also linked to the mining and cash-crop
areas and not much else. For example, in Ghana the railway system connected only the cocoa-growing areas and the mining areas to the sea-
ports. The food-growing areas of the North were not linked by rail. The
road system was limited and poorly maintained. In spite of Ghana's
many rivers, the British established no river transport and no hydroelectric plants. As a result the hinterlands experienced abundant food-

rotting, and the city-dwellers had food imported. The European companies that exported food to Africa, such as the United Africa Company, A.G. Leventis, and Companie Francaise de l'Afrique Occidental, gained benefits and made enormous profits—which were not invested in African development projects—including transportation in general—but repatriated to the metropoles.

The few schools and medical institutions of the colonial infrastructure were located in the large towns. Most rural Africans relied mainly on traditional methods of healing and had limited access to colonial education or medical treatment. The combination resulted in spatial inequalities between the urban and rural areas and among regions, because a colonial education provided access to work.

Colonial economic policies were aimed at creating a structure that drew labour from the food-growing areas into mining, cash-crop farming, or government service, including military service. African countries that were once self-sufficient in food production became transformed into food-importing and mono-crop economies that produced crops such as cocoa in Ghana, sisal in Tanzania, and coffee in Rwanda, not for the good of the population but to serve the interests of their masters. The colonial economic logic everywhere in Africa was to encourage Africans to grow cash crops cheaply on their communally owned lands for the European market. Where persuasion failed, Africans were subjected to compulsory labour either directly by force of arms or brutality or indirectly through taxation.[11]

The colonial banking system aided the process of subjugation of Africans. In West Africa the colonizers did not encourage the original banking system, called *susu*. (In East Africa a similar system was called *upato* or *kutunzana*.)[12] Instead, they suppressed it by requiring official licences, ostensibly to protect Africans from being taken advantage of by other smarter fellow-Africans. *Susu* posed a challenge to the foreign banks and to the process of maintaining the colonial requirement for a reserve army of African labour. If the African could get easy access to credit, there would be little incentive to work for the colonial system. Thus the established banks, which were all owned by the colonialists, denied Africans access to credit, although they were willing to lend to Asians living in Africa. In this way Asians became the interface between Africans and the European colonizers. As a result Africans, particularly in East Africa, came to see Asians—who had themselves come to Africa from colonized countries—not as colonial brothers but as economic vampires and agents of imperialism. Again, the profits that the colonial banks derived from African countries were not invested locally but repatriated.

The compounding of the transplantation process was the inheritance not only of weak mono-crop economies with a lack of competent entrepreneurs capable of meeting the demands of successful economic development, but also of societies divided along ethnic lines. The post-colonial African state would have to shoulder these problems as well as face a harsh international environment characterized by protectionism and ideological rivalry.

CHAPTER THREE

THE POST-INDEPENDENCE PROBLEM

The essence of neocolonialism is that the state which is subject to it is, in theory, independent and has all the outward trappings of international sovereignty. In reality, its economic system and thus its political policy is directed from outside.

Kwame Nkrumah,
First President, Republic of Ghana

Of course there must be differences between developing countries ... [but] to maintain that no common ground exists is to make any discussion outside or across frontiers of a single country meaningless.

Julian West,
Oxford University

Neo-colonialism did not occur by chance but by design, and African countries can extricate themselves from this grand plan only by attaining the political prerequisites for successful development. What will undoubtedly be needed if these objectives are to be realized is collective action, co-operation, and commitment to the nationalist cause by effective coalitions of African elites in each country, because the interests of imperialism are served whenever the differences between African countries are stressed and their commonality is downplayed. The strategy by which imperialism always wins is still the same: to divide and rule. That strategy worked well for imperialism during the eras of captive slavery and colonization, and it has continued to work marvellously during the long era of neo-colonialism. Thus, while representatives from imperialist countries are able to meet in Brussels, with no need for visas, to discuss a common policy and common currency in Europe, Africans—whom members of these same imperialist countries once considered to have the common denominator of characteristics that qualified them to be carried into slavery for over 350 years followed by

100 years of colonialism—are led to believe that they are somehow different. For example, although people from colonially created Ghana and Nigeria speak different dialects of the same West African language, and although once, before contact with Europeans, they roamed about freely in the general area of West Africa without any necessity for passports or visas, and have similar cultural practices, they are deceived by the historical forces of imperialism and colonialism to think of themselves as Ghanaians and Nigerians. Africans and people of African descent are manipulated by the centrifugal forces emanating from imperialism into the conviction that they require special papers to travel to each other's country. It seems that they cannot freely visit their brothers and sisters who were forcibly abducted to the Americas and the Caribbean and that they do not require a common currency because their difficulties in converting their currencies to the dollar, mark, or pound are mere illusions of the mind. The supposed freedom of African countries seems highly suspect, and it would appear that the yokes and shackles of imperialism have not been entirely cast off, or even loosened.

Freedom and the African Nation

The artificial boundaries drawn by the colonialists and imperialists over one hundred years ago remain in place and after decades of independence African countries still cannot even speak with one voice. The artificial boundaries themselves stand as evidence that the colonial monster is still around with its claws as sharp as ever, for before European contact Africans knew no such territorial restrictions. On one independence day after another, political appointments in the former colonies merely shifted from representatives with white skin to those of black skin, as though the colour of the skin mattered more than the exploitative colonial structures in which Africans found themselves. But a true decolonization of Africa means the breaking down of the exploitative structures of colonialism and their replacement with nationalist goals oriented to the service of the African populations. The nominal independence of African countries was only the first step towards decolonization.

The power to grant independence remained with the colonizers. Consequently, independence had to be granted on terms acceptable and palatable to the colonizer, who ensured that independence was not granted until conditions that would perpetuate the colonial relationship were soundly in place. For this reason, independence was not granted until after the formation of political parties that would divide the African populations on partisan lines and render them weak enough to be dominated as before. In cases in which the colonizers had no intention of granting independence, for example, it was unlawful for Africans to form political parties, because they would only disturb the colonial peace.

Despite their deep knowledge of Africa's original consensual democratic systems, none of the European colonizers took steps to educate the modernizing elites (those who were to lead and guide the development process) about the indigenous political systems, or even to encourage them along those lines. The colonizers could have educated the African elite to be proud of their own indigenous forms of democracy, but they did not. The colonizers' behaviour was, at least to themselves, rational given that they wanted African countries weak enough for the establishment of a new type of colonialism in disguise. Indeed, long before the grant of independence, the clever colonizers had contrived a neo-colonialist relationship with the African similar to the approach successfully established elsewhere in Asian and Latin American countries. Their embedded assumptions of their own racial superiority and the superiority of their own European political, economic, and ideological systems prevented them from doing otherwise.

Apart from the assimilation of Africans trained in the ways of European cultures in the metropoles—London, Paris, and elsewhere—the media of radio and newspapers of the time exposed the African elite in the colonies to information about current political campaigns in Europe—so much so that African elites in the British colonies identified themselves as Tories and Whigs and enthusiastically embraced the political systems of Europe. They saw the prime ministers and presidents of Europe as men who commanded a power that was notably different from the exercise of power in the consensual tradition of Africa. They were encouraged too by the prevailing notion in both Marxist and modernization circles at the time that the developed country served as the future image of the developing nation. In the West, partisan politics was considered the political tool of modernity.

The inexperienced political leaders of Africa were not able to discern the advent of neo-colonialism, at least in the early years. They were inexperienced, and given the operation of the dictatorial colonial system that effectively excluded them from major decision-making, it could not have been otherwise. The inexperience blurred their political visions and horizons, leading to miscalculations and misinterpretation. For example, in 1960, shortly after British Prime Minister Harold Macmillan, recognizing the growing impact of African nationalism, made his famous remark about a "wind of change" blowing through the African continent, Kwame Nkrumah, Ghana's first prime minister, reiterated that it was not a wind of change but a hurricane blowing away the shackles of imperialism. After four decades of independence, Macmillan has been proved right—and it is because he knew what he was talking about. The colonizers preferred a wind and not a hurricane. The shackles of imperialism were to remain in place. Nkrumah, for his part, miscalculated by harbouring the conviction that imperialism had genuinely volunteered to go into permanent retirement, whereas in reality it was only on the verge of changing its strategy, leaving its purpose— exploitation of the material and human resources of Africa—intact. The post-independence problem remains principally a matter of delivering what strategies are available to African countries to overcome in the long term, or alleviate in the short term, the pangs of neo-colonialism.

Analysts of the African crisis have advanced various explanations for the continent's failure to achieve political stability and economic success. Some have pointed to the problems of the agriculture-industry link, which suggest elite incompetence, self-interest, and an urban bias. Others have blamed the crisis on external variables such as unfavourable terms of trade, oil-pricing and monetary shocks, and protectionism in the international marketplace. But these explanations, though providing some insight, would appear to be either secondary to or reflections of a deeper politico-cultural problem: a misfit between the African political elite and the emulated alien political cultures. The resulting political tensions and discontinuities in government have prevented the political elite from defining and sustaining policies in the long-term interests of African nations. In other words, African nations for the most part have not attained the political prerequisites for successful development, whether by associative or dissociative means. This failure to attain the political prerequisites has undermined the structural transformation processes.

The Attempt at Structural Transformation

The struggle for independence was stimulated to a large extent by nationalist aspirations aimed at emancipating African peoples from misery, neglect, and abuse. Before and after the attainment of independence, therefore, the political elite in the developing countries, in general, focused on the need to restructure the economies of their respective countries in order to realize certain development objectives. Indeed, the nationalist spirit that animated the struggle for independence was due partly to the desire of the modernizing elites to restructure their economies. Because the economies of most developing countries were largely based on agriculture, that sector had an important part to play in structural transformation. Diversification of the agricultural sector, it seemed, could provide a sound basis for restructuring. At the aggregated level, agriculture might provide a flow of resources, such as labour and capital, to the rest of the economy. At a more disaggregated level, agriculture might contribute to the realization of development objectives, such as "economic growth; equitable distribution of wealth and poverty alleviation; improvement in the balance of payments; reduced dependence on the rest of the world; and greater price stability."[1] Agriculture might also contribute to the realization of other socio-economic objectives.

The mining and manufacturing industries, it seemed, might also benefit from the flow of resources from agriculture. With careful and dedicated planning, those sectors might also help to provide inputs vital to the development and strengthening of the agricultural base and other sectors. Indeed, African countries had a need for harmonious and supportive intrasectoral as well as intersectoral relations. If those relations were jeopardized through some means, the sectors might become severely damaged, culminating in a dangerous and unwarranted vicious cycle of economic and political crisis. The factors that might contribute to jeopardize these relationships might be external or internal.

Tension between National and Global Concerns

The structural transformation process takes place in a world environment that has an ongoing tension between the aspirations of national political economies and the global political economy. A national political economy is concerned with how a particular nation, given the current state of the world and its own developed national relations, can improve or at least maintain its economic conditions. These goals are essentially the concerns of the political economy. The concept of political economy recognizes that within any nation-state, in practice, economics and politics are not separable, for, by and large, politics is concerned with who gets what, when, and how; and economics is concerned with the production, distribution, and use of wealth. Thus, both disciplines are interested in what is produced and in the allocation of those goods. Thus, economics has to be viewed in its political context, and politics has to be viewed in its economic context.

Global economic concerns relate to a consideration of how the entire human race may attain prosperity and emancipation from misery. In contrast to the political economy of a nation, these global economic concerns may be said to relate to an international political economy. As Emmit B. Evans Jr. and Dianne Long explain, global economic concerns are relatively recent matters, because in the 450 years that preceded World War II, the Western powers were interested only in exploiting the resources of the countries in the rest of the world, including their peoples' labour, and saw no reason to help those countries achieve any "growth."[2] These global economic concerns make more sense if they are based upon the assumption of a perpetual state of peace and harmonious relations among the nations of the world, and, especially, the existence of a fair and unimpeded exchange of goods among nations. But the real world is not an arena of harmonious relations among nations. The global economy is propelled by Thrasymachian[3] greed to the extent that while the Western nations are the price-dictators of both the goods they export and import, the Third World and particularly African nations are the price-takers of both their exports and imports. In addition, the world market is characterized by protectionism, dumping, and fears of "beggar-thy-neighbour"—policies according to which a country intentionally produces and sells goods below cost to gain an advantage over another country's industry. The assumption of a fair and unimpeded exchange of goods is a myth at best. Some tension always exists between the global economic interest and the national political economy, with various claims and strategies advanced in respect of that tension.

Global economic concerns find expression through Adam Smith-inspired economics based upon efficiency arising from the division of labour. Because that economics assumes, again, a perpetual peaceful world of unimpeded and fair exchange, it does not recognize the inequalities that arise from this exchange on a world scale. Also, it implies a mono-economics[4] claim that the laws of economics are so universal that they operate in the same manner and with the same effect everywhere, and that in their endowments of productive assets the advanced industrialized countries differ only quantitatively, but not qualitatively or structurally, from the developed countries. This school of thought does not pay attention to the differing hierarchy of needs of countries at various stages of development, the cultural context of the acquisition of productive assets, and the possibility of structural consequences arising from economic relations. Another implication is the mutual benefit claim based upon the Ricardian notion of comparative advantage: that economic relations between the industrialized and the developing countries can yield benefits for both and make the parties concerned better off than they might otherwise be.[5] This notion of mutual benefit allows for a possible reversal of comparative advantage between trading partners in the long run, indicating, again, the underlying assumption that no qualitative or structural consequences attend to production and economic relations. These claims overlook the basic patterns of world trade relations, in which most countries in the South, and particularly African countries, are price-takers for both their imports and exports, while the advanced capitalist countries are the price-dictators. They do not take into account the undeniable fact that world market prices are determined not by any efficient operation of market forces but by oligopolistic pricing mechanisms that always yield distorted prices and never what could be said to be just prices. Furthermore, because development experience has been characterized by structural consequences and inequalities in economic relations, leading to unfavourable terms of trade for some and favourable terms of trade for others and an ever-widening gap between rich and poor, the claims fail to explain adequately the tension between the interests of political economy and global economy. The free-market ideology they propound has been the cause rather than the cure for the ailing economies of the South, and especially Africa.

The European experience in economic growth, for example, indicated that it was dangerous for weak economies such as Portugal and Spain to meet an industrially superior country such as Britain on the grounds of laissez-faire and free trade. Because of international competence differentials in the nineteenth and early twentieth centuries, as Dieter Senghaas explains in *The European Experience*, the more industrialized and powerful European nations undermined the weaker economies of Europe in their attempts to build up equally powerful economies. The weaker countries became transformed into tributary and highly dependent economies.[6] The European experience also showed that late industrializers had to initiate deliberate state intervention and adopt the judicious use of external tariffs.

Because the production of manufactured goods offered increasing returns to scale—a benefit that was very difficult to attain in the production of primary goods—the division of labour became hierarchical both in the structure of production and in the benefits reaped. The consequence was the ever-widening gap between the rich and poor nations.

Proposed Integrative Strategies

Given the possibility of unequal benefits in economic relations and the attendant danger of relegation to the periphery of development, the problem reduces to how developing countries, and particularly African countries, can integrate themselves into the world economy in order to maximize and sustain their gains and achieve development objectives.

Among the proposals put forward for tackling this problem is the associative posture of outward-oriented or export-led development strategy cherished by the World Bank.[7] The virtues ascribed to this strategy include the possibility of increased efficiency in the allocation of resources, competitiveness in the production of goods to the benefit of the consumer, and flexibility not only to adapt to the opportunities offered but also to learn from the experience of the constraints imposed by the world economy. As a means of adapting to changing opportunities offered by the world environment, in which some might be losers and others winners, economist John Maynard Keynes proposed a method of adjustment. In his vision for a new postwar international economic order, Keynes proposed a regime of penalty for both surplus and deficit countries. Countries would be penalized for accumulating a deficit or a surplus of more than 25 per cent of their quota in the International Monetary Fund.[8] Both Keynes and the Smithians assumed that the industrialized countries would discipline themselves willingly by adjusting to the changing international division of labour and refraining from protectionism, including support for their declining industries. Keynes, in particular, assumed that to avoid any world war arising from economic disorder the developed countries would willingly and faithfully respect his proposed regime of penalty. The objective was to integrate the developing countries on the basis of dynamic comparative advantage. However, the character of international trade does not show that the industrialized counties have been able to discipline themselves on the issue of protectionism, to have any respect for the Keynesian regime of penalty, or that they ever intended to do so willingly. Their behaviour has so far been in accordance with both aspects of the Thrasymachian logic: "It is the natural right of the strong to take more than their equal share of what the world has to offer" and in the arena of justice, "might makes right."[9]

Developing countries have long recognized that international trade is far from being equally or mutually beneficial for the developing and developed countries. The international market mechanisms proved unfavourable to developing countries, and in time developing countries became convinced that the industrialized countries were bent on refusing to respect Keynes's regime of penalty in the adjustment process, while they, as losers, were compelled by the IMF and World Bank to undertake one-sided, painful, and often inhuman structural adjustments. Armed with these convictions, developing countries proposed the program of the New International Economic Order (NIEO),[10] which called for the integration of the developing countries in accordance with a plan in which the allocation of resources was to be guided by redistributive principles rather than oligopolistic market mechanisms coupled to protectionism. This approach was, essentially, a modification of the associative posture on terms favourable to developing countries. Thus it called for commodity agreements with a common fund to stabilize or increase export earnings from raw materials; preferential and non-reciprocal measures for access to the markets of the industrialized countries; a greater share in world industrial production; easier access to credit and selective debt relief; codes of conduct for technology transfer and the behaviour of transnational corporations; greater influence over the decision-making of the IMF and World Bank; and a greater say over the UN's social and economic systems by the UN's General Assembly, in which the developing countries are in the majority. These proposals, made in the 1970s, fell more or less on deaf ears.

A further proposal for rectifying the problems of the global economy is that of dissociation or delinking,[11] which, unlike the approach of the NIEO, does not seek integration by developing countries into the international economy on any easy terms. To achieve development objectives, this proposal considered it necessary to pursue dissociative and self-reliant polices. Theoretically, this stance amounted to the negation of dependency and liberalization. The values of liberal capitalism, which focus on the individual as the primary unit of analysis, would be replaced by the community as the primary unit serving the purpose of the whole collectivity. The approach sees production as being aimed at use value and the satisfaction of basic consumption needs. The economy would be needs-driven rather than market- or profit-driven. Cooperation between like units rather than competition would be encouraged. The approach prefers an endogenous means of attaining desired objectives of the community or collectivity over imported technology or techniques that are more often than not inappropriate. The guiding principle is to use local factors to produce the requirements of local consumption as identified by the community or the collectivity as a whole.

However, the strategy is prone to misinterpretation by the West. The aspirations of collective self-reliance are compatible with socialism, which also embraces and encourages community achievements as opposed to the achievements of the individual. From this springs the danger of labelling any self-reliant strategy as ideologically socialist-inspired.

Although some countries, such as the former Soviet Union, Cuba, and post-revolutionary China, adopted a more radical dissociation stance, pure dissociation has been rare. For example, as Senghaas explains, prior to the split in relations between the Soviet Union and China, the latter received substantial assistance from the former. Cuba also received substantial aid from the Soviets. What exists in practice is selective dissociation, in which particular areas are selected for dissociation and preference is given to co-operation with those in the same economic or ideological position.

The program of collective self-reliance of the Group of 77, adopted at Arusha in 1981, is a form of selective dissociation.[12] Thus, its objectives included trade preferences among developing countries; co-operation among "parastatals" of developing countries; greater use of Third World payments and credit arrangements; industrial co-operation through the establishment of multinational enterprises by developing countries; and exchange of technical skills between developing countries aimed at building more appropriate and endogenous capacities. Selective dissociation, however, tends to meet the same fate as cartels. In such co-operation between developing countries in general, and African countries in particular, therefore, each country may try to maximize its gains, and there is a great temptation for the members of the trade alliance to cheat by not respecting certain aspects of the agreement. This danger is enhanced by the tendency of African countries to be producers of the same commodities. Hence, the arrangement may not be free from distortions and inequalities in the reaping of the benefits.

What matters in the African context is, therefore, that states should be capable of maximizing the gains from inter-African co-operation, be committed to this co-operation, and realize that Africans everywhere have been relegated to the bottom of an international vertical mosaic emanating from the Thrasymachian and racist forces of the past five hundred years of human history.

The Necessity for Appropriate Political Preconditions

Both associative and dissociative postures to development require a state capable of maximizing gains from external co-operation. In the associative posture and, particularly, in the export-led strategy, the opportunities opened in the international economy may produce inequalities and dislocating consequences. Therefore, success may depend upon the prior existence of a state capable of exploiting the opportunities as well as absorbing or bringing the adverse political effects under control. Moreover, because of tariffs, quotas, and various protectionist measures, free trade between countries does not take place under conditions of laissez-faire. Some additional problems may be encountered on the home front.

Left on its own, private enterprise may be tempted to pursue its narrow self-interests, which may be unrelated to the national aspirations of dynamic comparative advantage. Because of external economies, private enterprises may be unwilling to invest in certain areas. The achievement of development objectives will require some amount of government planning and intervention. Indeed, the difference between the export-led strategy and the inward-looking or self-reliant alternatives lies not in government intervention but in the ends of the intervention, the areas targeted, and the instruments applied. Thus, the development experiences of the Newly Industrialized Countries (NICs) of Asia (Singapore, South Korea, Taiwan), which adopted the export-led strategy, show that their governments followed market signals to identify their initial comparative advantage in the international division of labour. But they did not stick to this initial field of activity. They used government interventionist techniques as instruments to diversify and maintain their comparative advantage. In the process, they devised domestic means of controlling the adverse consequences of the associative posture.

Their experiences confirm that the mutual-benefit claim may be applicable only under the conditions of judicious governmental intervention, and the success of the export-led strategy would therefore require the prior existence of appropriate political conditions—which means that governing coalitions would be able to integrate the interests of society, cushion and control strife accompanying development, and define, pursue, and maintain coherent and nationalist development objectives. The appropriateness of political conditions also depends upon the cultural environment. For example, a society with a history of authoritarian relations would be more prepared to accept authoritarian instruments or measures of control than a society with a history of democratic relations. What may be described as a suitable prescription in one culture may be a misfit in another.

The success of the dissociative posture also requires the prior existence of appropriate political conditions. Groups that benefited from the previous associative posture may resist dissociation if their interests are jeopardized. Because such groups might have acquired the experience necessary for development, making their participation in the process indispensable, the problem becomes more complex. Moreover, the extensive and intensive planning requirements of this strategy may impose a heavy administrative burden. The problem is complicated further by the tendency in developing countries to look down upon indigenous products and processes and to stick to the foreign tastes acquired during the colonial period, or the period of association.

The success or failure of both the associative and dissociative postures may be determined, in the final analysis, by internal factors, but the influence of the international situation on the domestic factors will also play a role. Chief among these internal factors may be the ability and capacity of governing coalitions to define and maintain coherent policies and to control the adverse effects of development within their cultural environment. Historically these preconditions have not existed in most developing countries, and particularly not in Africa.

Reasons for the Absence of the Necessary Preconditions

Most developing countries were former colonies of the West, and they inherited alien and relatively weak political and administrative systems and institutions that fell short of the required political conditions. These political and administrative institutions were either imposed before independence by the former colonial masters to foster their own interests or were emulated blindly and ideologically by local elites after independence. Recognizing the weakness of their political and administrative institutions, but not the cultural incompatibilities, many developing countries undertook the task of training their own cadres and were assisted in this effort by the developed world, which had its own agendas. The training institutions were often in the industrialized West, and even when local institutions were used, their syllabuses were for all intents and purposes the blueprints of the syllabuses of the institutions of the Western world. Little consideration was given to the cultural appropriateness of the type of training.

Because development was conceived of as being equal to modernization, which was in turn equated with industrialization, it was thought that the acquisition of the knowledge, attitudes, and orientations of the industrialized West meant the acquisition of the necessary political and administrative prerequisites to development that might make the newly trained or modernizing elites competent enough to plan and implement development projects to attain the desired development objectives. Western approaches and methods were considered appropriate for the non-Western environments, and the indigenous cultural dimension (the orientations and attitudes of people arising from the history and experiences of the distant past) was of less, or no, importance. The political system approved by the colonialists before independence was the Western representative pattern of democracy. To complete the process of Westernization, the administrative system recommended to support both political and economic development also followed the Western pattern. Thus, the success of projects was supposed to require the creation of central planning agencies, improvement of central administrative systems, budgeting, financial control, personnel management, and organization and methods that pertained to the West.[13]

The Western administrative "ideal" for developing countries tended to be based on the Weberian assumptions of a legal, rational bureaucracy, classical scientific management, and the "Planning, Organizing, Directing, Staffing, Co-ordinating, Reporting, and Budgeting (PODSCORB)" principles that moulded the thinking of intellectuals in the late 1930s and 1940s. Students were often exposed to theories and concepts that were not, in the 1950s and 1960s, even applicable to developed Western societies. No Western societies followed the Weberian model, even though developing countries were expected to adhere strictly to that organizational form. Although technical experts such as engineers and agronomists had to carry out the real administration of development in various sectors, the training of local personnel in these fields was either ignored or minimal. In most cases, foreign experts assumed technical responsibilities, and most often these outsiders were unfamiliar with indigenous administrative systems and cultures. Although some of them were undoubtedly well-meaning, they tended to provide inappropriate advice, complicating the development process and giving rise to what is popularly called the false paradigm model of dependent development.[14] The momentum of the false paradigm model of dependent development was only compounded when developing country scholars were trained in accordance with the syllabuses of the advanced industrialized countries or in the advanced industrialized countries themselves, so that they became fully out of step with their own local cultures and situations. The attendant complications and confusions were enormous.

Also, by the time of independence the growth of indigenous private capital had been stifled by decades of colonialist discouragement, which meant that Africans had to obtain capital for investment from government funds, foreign aid or loans, or multinational corporations, which had their own agendas. These sources of finance implied the extensive use of the already culturally incompatible and, hence, incompetent government bureaucracy for development. This Western-oriented and incompetent bureaucracy was expected to control the financially powerful and politically influential multinationals, which were profit-driven rather than development-oriented. There was a clash of agenda, for while Third World countries saw development as a nationalist objective, the multinationals were interested in the exploitation of the material and human resources of developing countries at a minimum cost to themselves, and without regard to the problems of underdevelopment.

Other internal and external constraints posed severe problems for the emulated alien institutions. The internal constraints included the underlying infrastructure inherited after years of parsimonious colonialist policies; the underlying natural resource endowment; and the weather conditions, particularly the rainfall patterns so vital to the agricultural base. External constraints included the external terms of trade; foreign indebtedness; foreign aid with strings attached; unexpected crises such as the oil-price and monetary shocks of the 1970s and 1980s; and protectionism in the international marketplace. The external environment was also complicated by competition among developing countries that produced similar products, competition between developing and advanced industrialized countries in some products, competition between the advanced industrialized countries themselves, and competition between East and West in the prevailing Cold War logic. Another problem was the cross-default clauses of the foreign banks, an approach adopted as a protection against the potential default of Third World countries in meeting debt obligations. In accordance with this cross-default clause, any Third World country that defaulted in payment to any Western bank was automatically disqualified for loans from all the banks of the West. Despite the individualism inherent in Western democracy, this cross-default clause—which essentially meant that if one sinned against any individual, one sinned against all the brothers and sisters of that victim—was strictly upheld, confirming again that on the international scene the reigning principle was the doctrine of Thrasymachus.

The Western countries also administered a variable interest rate regime, which implied that if due to mismanagement in the advanced industrialized countries interest rates went up over there, the debt obligation of Third World countries that played no part in the mismanagement would also rise automatically. This second Thrasymachian notion of "might is right" continues to be the rule of the international banking system, and it continues to enable the West to milk the South. For every unit of interest rate, an estimated U.S.$12 billion are siphoned off from the poor developing countries to the affluent advanced capitalist countries, so that when the interest rate is 10 per cent, the advanced industrialized countries collectively enjoy a bonanza of $120 billion. This provides the advanced capitalist countries with an incentive to manipulate interest rates to invigorate their economies at the expense of developing countries. As Susan George explains in her article "How the Poor Develop the Rich," between 1982 and 1990 the advanced industrialized countries enjoyed a bonanza of $418 billion from the developing countries in interest payments alone.[15]

The Internalist and Externalist Explanations

Despite the complex nature of development, and the necessity of recognizing and encouraging culturally compatible political conditions, certain internalist and externalist views have been advanced as the sole explanations for the economic crises in Sub-Saharan Africa. Such views neglect more fundamental politico-cultural problems, and in so doing they scratch only the surface and fail to penetrate to the roots. Still, the explanations can serve as pointers to the nature of the root causes and provide useful insights as to how these root causes can express themselves under various conditions.

A number of externalist explanations—blaming the economic crises mainly on external variables—focus on the structuralist interpretations of development first advanced through the theses of the Economic Commission for Latin America and later by some Marxist structuralists, such as Samir Amin in his book *Imperialism and Unequal Development* (1977) and Andre Gunder Frank in his essay "The Development of Underdevelopment" (1966).[16] Externalist explanations attribute the crises principally to the international economic system and its many attributes: unfavourable terms of trade for Africa; low demand elasticities for Africa's products, accentuated by substitute products, including synthetics; economic recession and high interest rates in the developed countries; and unexpected events in the external environment, such as oil-price increases and monetary shocks. The overvaluation of the U.S. dollar is another factor in this stream, because both debts and external trade are denominated in U.S dollars. Inappropriate donor policies also come into play.

While these factors are undeniable, they obscure a more fundamental factor, of which they might be only reflections. The interpretations ignore the interplay of forces within Third World countries themselves—that local agents acting upon false paradigms models can be effectively checked within the underdeveloped countries themselves. The fundamental question is: can developing countries not do anything at all about the horrible situation in which they find themselves? Do politics matter at all? If structures are constraining, does it necessarily mean that they are determining? Certainly, the international situation is such that the advanced capitalist countries continue to enjoy their bonanzas, but perhaps developing countries are capable of reversing the situation, or at least of walking out of it. The elites of developing countries tend to be pleased with the externalist explanations, because they absolve them from blame. But apart from creating an illusion that the developing countries are not capable of overcoming their present predicament, blaming the crises solely on external factors obscures the necessity of achieving culturally compatible political preconditions for their emancipation and thus working towards a change of the international system and to successful development.

Internalist explanations, for their part, attribute the crises to the irresponsible action of local elites without adequately taking into account the politico-cultural context. The arguments advanced recognize the role of local agents and hence of politics but place too much emphasis on the negative aspects of this role. They blame local actors for problems associated with the agriculture-industry link—problems that, in turn, are supposed to have been responsible for the crises. The World Bank, the IMF, and some non-Marxist political economists, such as Robert Bates in *Markets and States in Tropical Africa* (1981) and Assefa Bequele in his essay "Stagnation and Inequality in Ghana" (1983), take this approach. Their arguments tend to please the West's right-wing political actors and financial institutions—both of them interested in propagating an angelic and immaculate image of the West in its relations with the developing world. Apart from the naked expression of hypocrisy, such a position is dangerous because it obscures not only the more fundamental and important politico-cultural factors undermining the attainment of the necessary political prerequisites for successful economic development, but also the hostility of the international environment towards developing countries and the inequalities and distortions in the international marketplace, which are not conducive to economic growth in the developing world.

Internalist explanations focus on the agriculture-industry link and identify several problems. They cite, for instance, the inadequate forward and backward linkages between agriculture and industry, which have contributed to an import-reproduction system with little transfer of technology and little use of local inputs—as opposed to an import-substitution system with a substantial transfer of technology and use of local inputs.[17] The resulting import-dependent industrialization cannot be supported by export earnings, and both the agricultural base and the industrial sector are weakened continuously, resulting in economic crises.

A second problem identified by the internalist approach is the expansion of industry in the context of misguided import substitution and capital-intensive policies. These import-substitution strategies include tariff protection for the industrial sector, which serves to turn the internal terms of trade against agriculture and means that enormous resources are extracted from the agricultural sector. African countries need to go more slowly on the industrial front and to use labour-intensive technologies in both the agricultural and industrial sectors. They can ensure industrial growth through sustained increases in agricultural output and productivity in combination with strategies that distribute income in a manner that increases the consumption of both agricultural and industrial goods locally and encourages investment. Advocates of this line of thought include John Mellor and B. Johnston in "The World Food Equation."[18] The approach does not adequately explore the blind emulation of Western culture and the interpretation of development as industrialization, which underlies the preference for quick industrial development.

The role of markets, institutions, or political structures that might achieve a successful co-ordination between the agricultural and industrial or non-agricultural development patterns is a third identified problem. This approach sees a lack of agricultural and economic success as the reflection of specific political and institutional structures that influence policies and are related to urban bias. The internalist approach, though, does not take into serious consideration the question of how these structures came to be and their cultural incompatibility. The *World Development Report* of 1986, Robert Bates, and Assefa Bequele express such views.

One suggested solution is for the peasants to wield political power, but such a solution has its own problems. Peasants are not a homogeneous group, other sectors must also be taken into account, and there is no guarantee that peasants will use their power wisely in the long run. Another solution is an encompassing coalition capable of formulating, sustaining, and implementing coherent policies, but the practical formation of that coalition remains a problem, as evidenced by both the political instability and the failures of the socialist experiments on the continent. This solution does not adequately explore the root causes of political instability and the failures of the socialist experiments, and the analysts do not draw upon lessons from the historical past and culture to arrive at methods of creating an effective coalition—as though powerful coalitions had never existed in Africa. They tend to ignore the glorious historical pasts of the Ghana, Mali, Songhai, Ashanti, and Zulu empires and other indigenous political systems.

A fourth internal issue springs from the emphasis on non-food production, which reduces the size of the food surplus provided by those who remain in production. Although trade is supposed to minimize this problem, the acute shortage of foreign exchange exacerbates matters. In his *Political and Economic Origins of African Hunger* (1966), Michael F. Loftchie supported this view. This approach does not pay adequate attention to the small size of the industrial sector in African countries and, again, the inappropriate capital-intensive industrialization strategies that employ a very small proportion of the labour force, as well as the land-tenure system that militates against agricultural production.

A fifth problem rests in the undermining of the agricultural base through the failure on the part of governing elites to introduce land reforms necessary to support effective production. In *Beyond Ujumaa in Tanzania* (1980), Goran Hyden goes so far as to suggest that the crises might be attributed to a failure to forcibly bring the peasants into the market through a drastic land reform that would deprive the peasants of land and enable capitalism to take roots. He argues that because peasants were permitted to own their means of production, they developed a consciousness that the state needed them but they did not need the state, and they became resistant to mobilization by both the capitalist and socialist systems. Again, this approach does not adequately explore the culturally compatible political preconditions for carrying out land reforms. Hyden failed to appreciate that what he called the "economy of affection" is principally what makes an African an African. African culture considers it demeaning for a person to think of himself or herself as an individual at the expense of the welfare of the extended family as a whole. Africans can never be Europeans, but given the chance and freedom from neo-colonial chains, they are capable of developing to the same level as Europeans within the context of their own cultures.

A sixth problem is that agriculture has been stifled through the manipulation of price signals by political and other vested interests. Prices on the world market are supposed to be the correct price, the one that should prevail. But world market prices are oligopolistically determined and can never be the "right" prices. Achieving the right price for any commodity assumes perfect competition between infinite competitors in a utopian arena with no intervention by any state measures, including taxation. Although the conditions for the right prices have never existed, the right prices are imagined to have some real existence despite oligopoly. Based upon this flimsy imagination, Africanist writers have assumed that the extraction of surplus from agriculture has been excessive, and African elites have unwisely invested that surplus in industry, to build political support. Or local officials have misappropriated it. Thus, local elites are accused of the deliberate suppression of agricultural prices to maintain a low-cost food supply for urban dwellers. This approach fails to consider fully the compensating and balancing mechanism of the African culture of the extended family in the distribution of food between the urban and rural dwellers. It ignores the reality that the majority of the population is rural and that, hence, any significant instrument of political support has to be targeted to the rural rather than the urban. It also accuses the elites of being deliberately responsible for currency overvaluation, which imposes hidden taxation on export goods, and for the widespread use of parastatal corporations, which are corrupt and inefficient. But it does not sufficiently explore the root causes of these elite behaviours. Advocates of this line of argument include the World Bank, the IMF, D. Lal in his book *The Poverty of Development Economics* (1985), and Bates.

The most dominant perception of the internalists is that the agriculture-industry link has become a destructive factor as a result of the counterproductive expansion of the industrial sector achieved through the manipulation of price signals by political and other vested interests. This view presupposes the existence of culturally compatible political preconditions for growth and integration into the world market, but concludes that the elites are not benign and have mismanaged the process. This incorrect presupposition dangerously obscures the more fundamental fact: that local elites have never been able to create effective and encompassing coalitions compatible with Africa's cultural values and capable not only of defining and sustaining coherent nationalist policies but also of channelling the gains from trade towards the building of a dynamic comparative advantage.

Despite their flaws, these internalist and externalist explanations provide insight into the root causes of Africa's agricultural and economic crises. The externalist position's extreme structuralist view leaves the impression that local actors cannot do anything at all about the situation. But history has shown that local actors can influence the course of change—as evidenced by the success of the struggles for political independence. The external and internal factors do influence the role of local actors and impose constraints, and the internal and global economic concerns do create ongoing tension; but successful development is possible if internal political coalitions are able to generate forces strong enough to contain and control external pressures. The central problem is therefore the inability of the African elite to set in place the culturally compatible political conditions necessary for successful development. It is in the context of establishing the necessary political conditions that with the demise of the Cold War democracy has become a subject of considerable debate.

The Democracy Debate

Despite the experience of the Newly Industrialized Countries of Asia, including Thailand, Taiwan, South Korea, and Singapore—with their consistent pattern of efficient dictatorships and strict control operating within an economic environment in which the geopolitical interests of the United States figure prominently—the only road to successful development is not authoritarianism. The European experience shows that successful development is possible under conducive democratic practice. Still, much depends upon the nature of the "democracy." Despite being the largest democracy in the world, India has made significant progress in modern times and might have made even more significant strides had its brand of democracy been tailored to its culture. The preconditions for successful democracy advocated by some scholars (a history of proto-democratic institutions, comparative capitalism and a small public sector, industrialization, high literacy levels, the emergence of a relatively strong middle class or bourgeoisie) have never existed in India, where liberal democracy has persisted for more than forty years.

Tekeste Negash, for example, expresses doubts about the effectiveness of the Western form of democracy in Africa and highlights the contradictions between Western democracy and African cultures.[19] Negash compares European political systems with the indigenous political systems of the Fon in Benin (where lineage is matrilineal), the Abyssinian in Ethiopia (where Judaism and Christianity date back to the biblical King Solomon), the Yoruba in Nigeria (where the king is one among equals and chosen by rotation from one of five royal houses), and the clan or stateless systems of Africa, using this comparison to explain why the blind imitation of Western political systems ultimately fails. African political culture, even the clan societies, is essentially democratic, he argues, though this indigenous politics has been little appreciated over the past hundred years. Under the prevailing conditions of the twentieth century, the most probable political culture of Africa would appear to be authoritarianism or ethnic nationalism. He sees both internal and external factors, including the maintenance of colonial boundaries and conditionalities associated with IMF and World Bank loans, as being unconducive to the Western form of democracy and as providing fertile grounds for the continuation of authoritarianism.

Rural Africa—where the majority of Africa's population resides—is not yet ready for Western democracy because the common view there of how issues should be resolved is vastly different from the view in the urban centres. Evidence from the continent points to the tendency of African states that experiment with multiparty systems to fragment centrifugally along ethnic and religious lines. The cultural preconditions for the institutions of Western democracy (including bureaucracy, incorruptible civil service, a well-grounded private sector, and individualism) are non-existent. The most pertinent question is "Who is demanding democracy in Africa and why?" Negash explains that the impetus to democratize Africa came from the West—and only after capitalism and democracy gained the upper hand over communism and socialism in the early 1990s. The new experiment with Western democracy has so far failed to bear fruits consistent with nationalist aspirations. It has, for one thing, overshadowed the most important need: for an overall strategy to resolve Africa's food crisis.

Other scholars, including Claude Ake, argue that democracy is conducive to economic and social growth because it is the people themselves who should be the end of development, the agents of development, the definers of the type of development they want, the determiners of the key societal values, and the selectors of the modalities for realizing their aspirations. In this regard, democracy indeed might have been an effective tool for development in Africa, but despite the rhetoric, the North's attitude has always been that democracy is not for Africa. That attitude was an ingredient in rationalizing the colonization of the continent. Even though European countries granted independence to African countries, they remained more or less indifferent to issues of democracy—almost expecting, it seemed, the whole experiment of self-determination to fail. The primary preoccupation of the North was the question of how to influence African governments, no matter the makeup, to protect Western interests. Furthermore, in the great quest for allies in the Cold War, Western powers tended to ignore questions of democracy or human rights in Africa. The spectacular role of the North in supplying arms to repressive governments that perpetuated underdevelopment in Africa—to the Mobutu regime in the Congo, for example—underscores the double standards at play.

Ake recommends certain characteristics for a democracy in Africa, including equal emphasis on both collective rights and individual rights.[20] He also recognizes that democracy is not new to Africa.[21] What is new is a type of democracy that does not fit the African environment and is not conducive to development. He argues that an African democracy must necessarily be unique, radically different from the liberal democracy of the West, and reflect the socio-cultural reality of Africa if it is to be effective.

While Ake and Negash agree in principle that the indigenous African political culture is democratic, V.G. Simiyu argues that historical democratic practice in African cultures is a myth.[22] Nearly all the indigenous political systems, he says, have hierarchical systems based upon age and family lineage. These systems are not conducive to political mobility and tend to support the aspirations of the more active, intelligent, and younger generations. The higher echelons of society control the land and cattle, which constitute economic power, and patronage mechanisms reduce access to people with less economic power. Instead of democratic traditions, African societies reflect centralized monarchies.

What Simiyu does not seem to recognize is that African democratic practice and European democratic practice are based upon entirely different cultural principles. While European democratic practice springs from a competitive culture, African democracy is based upon a culture of co-operation and compromise, in which competition is considered a destructive force that is advantageous to the enemy. Although communalism is frequently cited as an obstacle to democratization in Africa—which may be the case when political parties mirror communal divisions within society—when a political party or coalition draws support across communal lines it can become a channel for bargaining and reconciliation among groups. The coming together of various clans to constitute pre-colonial African states and representations in the ruling councils at various levels of the political system afforded this opportunity for bargaining and reconciliation.

Given Europe's competitive culture, the circulation of the elites themselves constitutes an important ingredient in a democratic system. In a consensual culture of co-operation and compromise, the circulation of the elites is not as important as the circulation of the input of all elites. Furthermore, chiefs or clan heads in Africa are not necessarily the oldest within the societies or clans; rather, they are those selected by consensus based upon merit. In Western democracies, despite the rhetoric of democracy, real political power rests directly or indirectly in the hands of those with economic power, undermining the practice of liberalism. Indeed, the political parties of the West are propped up by economic power, without which the expensive political campaigns and image-making might not be possible.

Thus in both Africa and Europe economic power may be translated into political power; but in African democracy this tendency is held in check by consensualism. Moreover, the apparent upward mobility within Western political parties or systems is not angelic; it depends largely upon *whom-you-know* or *who-sponsors-you*. In certain instances, as a result of *whom-you-know*, more qualified people with merit have been bypassed in the party hierarchy, and political representations and appointments have gone to the less qualified. The system of political oligopolies, in which the number of competing political parties is limited to two or three, does not provide adequate alternatives to political mobility.

Another view suggests that the merits ascribed to liberal democracy are themselves questionable, which establishes even more doubt about their possible realization in Africa. Still, this does not mean that something like the developmental dictatorship experience of the Asian NICs would better suit Africa. Richard Sandbrook, for example, defines liberal democracy as a political system characterized by a range of political and civil rights and regular free elections in which organized parties compete to form a government, with virtually all adult citizens exercising their right to vote. He argues that only four countries in Africa (Botswana, Mauritius, Gambia, and Senegal) come anywhere close to that definition and that it is more appropriate to refer to these four countries as practising semi-democracy or proto-democracy.

Sandbrook explains that the notion of liberal democracy materially benefiting the poor is only a myth. In practice, the power commanded by the dominant classes works to obstruct social and economic reform. Elected governments may become prisoners of privileged social groups. In the United States, for example, less than 1 per cent of the population owns almost 40 per cent of the nation's wealth. Liberal democracy does not necessarily prevent tyranny. As the Rwandan experience exemplifies, majoritarian rule can be translated into the tyranny of the majority. Sandbrook recognizes that although multiparty systems may be inappropriate for Africa, single-party regimes can slide into the kind of personalistic dictatorship demonstrated by Nyerere in Tanzania, or degenerate into the military autocracy that is so common on the continent.[23]

Dominant groups in society may accept the trappings of democracy in order to get international recognition, which can lead to the inflow of foreign aid and loans. They may also value democratic rules for their own interests and cherish liberty and open political competition for the same purpose. But when, for instance, the IMF and World Bank advocate economic liberalization accompanied by austerity measures, the most likely outcome is repression and not democratization.

Sandbrook also took up the issue of democracy in a comparative analysis of the experiences of Ghana, Mali, Niger, Zambia, Tanzania, and Madagascar.[24] He argued that despite hostile socio-economic, historical, and other conditions, democracy in Africa is not doomed or inconceivable. The problem rests in how to consolidate the existing democratic openings, which can be the product of four factors: strong domestic protest, splits among top government leaders, sympathetic impact of democratic experience elsewhere, and pressure from donor countries. Of these factors, strong domestic protest and pressure from donor countries seem to be predominant in instigating democratic transitions in the six countries considered. The consolidation of democracy itself might be achieved through free and fair elections and the institutionalization of two key intermediary organizations: political parties and independent organs of mass communications media.

Like other analysts, then, Sandbrook conceives of democracy in European terms and sets out to explore how this kind of politics might be consolidated not in Europe but in Africa. Still, he argues that democracy consists of more than the ballot-box technique of periodic elections. It includes accountability, transparency in decision-making, responsiveness, and legal processes that require the consolidation of a complex array of ancillary institutions. He concludes that the apparent transition to democracy in Africa does not necessarily herald the consolidation of a democratic regime, which requires a myriad of organizations and procedures that will in turn lead to transparency in decision-making and an effective responsiveness to governance.

Sandbrook's assertion that the consolidation of a Western model of democracy in Africa requires a myriad of organizations and procedures can be taken as a indication that Western democracy is not suitable for the pre-capitalist conditions of Africa. The establishment of those organizations in suitable numbers and quality will not happen overnight, and that project might prove to be too expensive for such fragile economies. The centrifugal forces arising from economic inequalities and the attempt to establish political parties could well shatter the political system itself. Only an encompassing coalition established in accordance with Africa's own consensual democratic culture and capable of containing the stresses and strains from both the internal and external environments would be capable of defining, implementing, and sustaining coherent and effective nationalist development policies.

CHAPTER FOUR

TYPICAL AFRICAN POLITICAL SYSTEMS

Before even the British came into contact with our people, we were a developed people, having our own institutions, having our own ideas of government.
   J.E. Casely Hay-Ford, 1922, Gold Coast (Ghana) nationalist

African political systems in pre-colonial times were essentially democratic, with all the trappings of government with the consent of the governed and a balance between centralized power and decentralized power to prevent the misuse of authority by any one person. They were systems with checks, balances, and accountability. And while these indigenous systems might not have been perfect, and they did to some extent exhibit exclusion, it can be equally said that no political system in the world is perfect and no political system is all-inclusive.

African political systems fall into two main types. One type of political system, exemplified by the Logoli, the Talensi, and the Nuer, did not have centralized authority, administrative machinery, centralized judicial systems, or sharp divisions in rank or status.[1] The second type—and the most common—had central authority, administrative machinery, and judicial institutions. Its systems comprised hierarchical and concentric levels with regions near the centre and zones, districts, towns, villages, and huts, in that order, towards the outermost periphery, with a declining degree of authority. The Zulu, the Bemba, the Bankole, the Yoruba, the Igbo, and the Kwa-speaking peoples of West Africa, including the Akan, the Ga, the Ijaw, and the Ewe, all had this type of political system. It would seem likely that the first type of system could evolve into the second; and here, with our emphasis on Africa's need for organized and effective government, we focus on the second type.

African political systems with centralized authority and separated by hundreds of miles displayed a number of common characteristics. Most of them represented a union of heterogeneous groups or clans, each with its own identity and history. The peoples may have found it necessary to establish centralized authority to ensure the cohesion of the various clans necessary for the realization of common interests. The head of state in these societies was a territorial ruler, but often power devolved to chiefs who acted as the administrative and judicial heads of some specified territorial divisions. These chiefs were vested with the power of economic and legal control over their divisions. The stability of the political system was ensured by a balance of forces. The political forces that ensured the supremacy of the head of state were balanced by opposing forces that tended to limit his or her power. Chiefs, queens, queen-mothers, courts, and democratic councils with a commitment to the norms of tradition and vested with power to depose the head of state when necessary contributed their quota to checking the abuse of power. In addition, the devolution of power to regional, zone, and district chiefs coupled with transport and communication problems and the requirements of an effective rule had the secondary effect of counterbalancing the power of centralized authority.

The local chiefs represented the interest of the central authority as well as the interests of their people. In relations between their respective regions and the central authority, the chiefs represented the interests of their people, but in relation to the interests of the nation as a whole, they represented the interests of the central authority. Balancing these two competing interests required a high degree of wisdom on the part of a chief. The structure of the political organization ensured that at any level of government a chief and his council ruled with the consent of those below and above him, and the head of state and his council ruled with the consent of the people as a whole.

The responsibilities of an African ruler went beyond normal secular functions. He or she was the embodiment of societal values and common interests, including mystical beliefs that constituted the ideological superstructure of the societies governed. The attachment to these mystical values expressed through symbols provided the society with the required cohesion. The symbols included myths, taboos, sacred places, and sacred persons. The shared values so provided the political system with legitimacy that the overthrow of an incompetent head of state did not mean a rejection of the political system with its norms, traditions, and customs. They also served as protection against the abuse of political power, as standards by which political performance might be judged, and as a means of compelling those in authority to perform their duties as required. These supernatural aspects of African rule—conditions that so puzzled the Western mind—constituted an essential cohesive force that kept destructive centrifugal forces and abuse of power in check.

Numerous African societies practise variations of this type of hierarchical and concentric political system, and the selected few examples taken up here—the Ovimbunda, Zulu, Ashanti, and Ga—highlight the commonalities of their political systems.

The Ovimbunda Political System

The Ovimbunda people make up about one-third of Angola's population.[2] In pre-colonial times the peoples of Angola were divided into kingdoms that comprised various concentric levels of political responsibility and administration. Each kingdom had its own ruling body, with the king as the head of state. During the colonial era the Portuguese administration redesignated these kings as paramount chiefs and the kingdoms as chiefdoms. One of these kingdoms, the Ovimbunda kingdom, was located on the west coast of Angola and organized in a pattern similar to the other kingdoms of Angola, including the Bakongo, Chokwe, Nganguela, Nyaneka-Humbe, Herero, and Ambo.

The king of the Ovimbunda, the Osoma or Sova, was selected from among the male lineage of the royal blood, but simply belonging to the royal lineage did not automatically confer upon a person the right to kingship. A king had to be elected by merit by an electoral college of elites who acted as the king's councillors. These councillors were representatives from the various regions of the kingdom. They had the power to dethrone a king who had become unpopular with the people or who, in the eyes of the council, had become incompetent. A king's duties included responsibilities in the political, economic, military, and cultural spheres. He was the supreme commander of the Ovimbunda army, which also performed police duties. He had the power to declare war and to make peace. He presided over judicial appeals referred to the council from the lower courts of the kingdom. The decisions of his supreme court were final. He was responsible for foreign relations, including trade agreements with neighbouring kingdoms. His traditional responsibilities included ritual ceremonies to ensure rain supply and prevent natural calamities. Some of his responsibilities were delegated to the lower levels of government.

The second level of government was the *atumbu* (plural) or *etumbu* (singular). The heads of the *atumbu* played the role of sub-kings, regional kings, or sub-chiefs. Members of the royal family as well as court officials who did not belong to the royal family might be elected or appointed head of an *atumbu*. They performed similar duties and responsibilities as the king, but at a lower level. They swore oaths of allegiance to the king, were responsible to the king, presided over the regional courts, and performed rituals to make rain and to prevent natural disasters. They were expected to promote and control internal trade.

A third level of government was the town or village ruler, called the *sekulu yimbo*. This ruler represented the town or village at the regional or *etumbu* council. In addition to his political, economic, administrative, and judicial duties, he was also the village priest. Disputes in the local community were referred to him for judgment, which he pronounced with the help of his local representative council. He was responsible for agriculture as well as the health of his people. He was expected to perform rituals at the local level to induce rain and prevent natural disasters.

These levels of government were linked by a system of information flow. Decisions taken at the higher levels were passed down to the lower levels for their implementation, comments, and advice. Feedback also went from the lower levels to the higher levels. The two-way information flow enabled participants to gauge the temperature of the political waters to prevent surprises. The military organization, which also performed police duties, followed the same pattern as the political division of the Ovimbunda, with a central control that ensured co-ordination in the defence of the nation. The political arrangements enabled the Ovimbunda to nurture their society politically, socially, and economically—at least until the raids and wars to produce captives for Portuguese slave trading, and then the colonial conquest and colonial rule that followed, destroyed their political system and disrupted their society.

The Zulu Political System

The Zulu nation, as reorganized by the great ruler Shaka (c.1788-1828), consisted of hundreds of clans organized into chiefdoms united by their common allegiance to the Zulu king.[3] The chiefdoms that made up the Zulu nation—which is still today South Africa's largest ethnic group—spoke dialects of the same language and shared a common culture. The Zulu chiefdoms were, in turn, divided into sections. The political organization was a delegated authority over decreasing community sizes. At the very bottom of this organization were the kinship groups and their leaders who arbitrated in disputes within their own groups. Decisions at the lower levels might be appealed to the higher levels, moving up to the court of the Zulu king, where decisions taken were final.

The Zulu king was a political authority as well as the highest judicial authority, and he ruled with the help of councillors called *indunas*. Most of these *indunas* were chiefs who ruled areas of their own. Some *indunas* were commoners promoted by merit. The most important *induna* was the head of the army, who was also a chief or a prince, followed in importance by the *induna* responsible for the affairs of the state, who was appointed by merit and never a member of the Zulu royal family. The king was expected by tradition to follow the advice of the council of *indunas*, and if he did not follow that advice the council could penalize him by taking one of his cattle.[4] This tradition derived from the belief that the welfare of the Zulu nation depended upon wise *indunas* and their ability to criticize the king. A free expression of views was encouraged by the arrangement that, in council, the king should put the matter before the council and be the last to speak so that no *induna* was intimidated. The king was expected to adopt the view of the majority of the *indunas*, but the majority view had to be approved by consensus. Thus the Zulu king was not an autocratic ruler, but a king who respected what we would now call traditional democratic values. Succession did not go automatically to the most senior son of the king. It went to the son of whichever wife the king declared as his chief wife.[5]

Despite the hereditary nature of succession, upward mobility did exist in the political system. The kings on occasion rewarded their personal body servants, brave warriors, and *indunas* for exemplary performance by making them heads of districts or senior administrative officials. Zulus who distinguished themselves could become *indunas* in the councils of the chiefs or the king. A notable characteristic of Zulu political organization was the creation of new groups as people moved about already settled land and occupied uninhabited territories. Leaders emerged within these groups who, with time, achieved enough prominence to become chiefs. The constant creation of new leaders coupled with the promotion of brave warriors and men of merit led to a high degree of social mobility. Any man irrespective of his rank by birth could rise to a high political office by merit. The system of upward mobility was encouraged by the intimacy between the Zulu chiefs and their people and the non-existence of class snobbery among the Zulu. The intimacy was such that the chiefs might attend the weddings and funeral rites of their subjects. The chiefs were essentially the representatives of the king at the regional or district level, but they were not only political heads. Chiefs and their *indunas* shared common social and economic activities and were expected to promote the trade, welfare, and prosperity of their subjects.

The authority of the king was delegated to and exercised through the chiefs, who in turn ruled through the sub-chiefs and *indunas* of smaller districts. Indeed, the Zulu nation might be considered as a federation of autonomous clans or regions, whose identities were symbolized by their chiefs but who were all united together under one king. The political arrangement was such that in quarrels with the king, a large number of the group might support their own chief and some might have divided loyalties. But in quarrels among chiefs, support for the local chief was unflinching. Although the chiefs of the various Zulu groupings had administrative and judicial powers delegated to them, they had no taxation power of their own, though they periodically sent large herds of cattle as gifts to the king. These chiefs also had their own councils of *indunas* and tried cases that were referred to them from the lower districts under their jurisdiction. However, their decisions might be appealed to the council of the king. Like the king, the chiefs were bound by tradition to abide by the advice of their councils of *indunas*.

The delegation of authority contributed to the balance of political forces and acted as a check on the abuse of power. The king had to treat his brothers as well as the chiefs well to avoid any rebellion against him. Tension between the king and his own brothers and the provision for an incompetent or unpopular king to be deposed and be replaced by another member of the royal family served as the first check on the king's rule. The free discussion at the council and the king's obligation to take the advice of the council of *indunas*, and the participation of chiefs as members of the council of *indunas* of the kings, served as a second check. A third check was provided by the strong attachment of the Zulus to their local chiefs, which the king could not overlook in any action against a chief. The chiefs had similar checks on their power. In addition, misrule by chiefs could be reported to the king or drive subjects to other chiefs through migration. Because the respect and power of a chief depended to a large extent upon the number of his subjects, the chiefs and their councils of *indunas* were careful not to allow their style of rule to drive away their subjects to the jurisdiction of other chiefs. In spite of the delegation of authority from the king and the autonomy of the chiefs, the Zulu military structure enabled the king to keep the chiefs in check and the Zulu nation united.

For military purposes the Zulu nation was divided into regiments along lines similar to the political division. The regiments belonged to the king alone and lived in barracks around the capital where the king lived. The chiefs sent their subjects to serve in the regiments, which were cared for mainly from the king's cattle and grain, although the men might receive supplements of food from home. The concentration of the regiments in the king's area ensured the continuous and common standard of training and co-ordination of their activities under the watchful eyes of the ruler. Still, all the men of the regiments remained attached to some chief other than the king, and the king had no personal followers among the regiments. This served as another check, for although the king could send forces to discipline a particular chief, he had to be careful that his arbitrary use of power did not lead to divisions within the regiments.

In addition to his political duties and the power to declare war, the king was also a spiritual ruler responsible for the health and prosperity of his people. All Zulu doctors were expected to teach the king the workings of their herbal formulas, and the king was regarded not only as a great doctor who could heal his councillors but also a spiritual leader who could make rain. Shaka is reported to have gone to the extent of expelling all rainmakers from his kingdom, claiming that as the Zulu king he alone had the power to control the forces of the sky and of the heavens.[6]

The Ashanti Political Organization

The succession to political rule in the Ovimbunda and Zulu political systems was essentially patrilineal. In the Ashanti political system succession was matrilineal. In the Ashanti region of what is now Ghana the king was succeeded by one of his sisters' sons, the one who, in the view of the royal council, was the most competent among the nephews. The matrilineal succession is said to derive from an ancient story, which was recorded by R.S. Rattray in his book *Ashanti Proverbs*.[7] According to the story, Abu, a linguist of the Adansi (one of the Akan ethnic groups to which Ashanti also belongs), was fined heavily for incurring the displeasure of the king of Adansi. Abu's children refused to help him pay the fine and deserted to their mother's relatives. But the children of Abu's sister helped their uncle to pay the fine. Later Abu became rich, and when he died he left all his belongings to his sister's children. Other people emulated Abu's example and it soon became the tradition of the

Akans. This emulation of Abu's example is called *Abu-sua* (copying Abu).[8]

The Akan matrilineal clans of Ghana and neighbouring regions in West Africa comprise the Oyoko, the Bretuo, the Asona, the Asenie, and the Aduana. These clans came together to build towns and villages at various places and established several independent states that spoke dialects of the same Akan language. However, these Akan states fought against one another. First the Adansis emerged as the dominant group. They were eventually defeated by the Denkyiras, who exacted enormous tribute from the other Akan ethnic groups and, in the process, incurred the displeasure of the other Akan societies. In 1701, five Akan states—Dwaben, Nsuta, Mampong, Bekwae, and Kokofu—joined another state, Kumasi, to fight against the Dankyiras under the leadership of Osei Tutu, who was the ruler of Kumasi and allied to Kumawu state. The states that came together for the purpose of war called themselves *osa nti fo* (because-of-war people) or, for short, Asantifo (Ashantis).[9] Because these states came together under the leadership of Osei Tutu for the purpose of war—the ruler was proclaimed Asantehene (king of the Ashantis) only after the war—the people of Dwaben believed that they had the right to withdraw from the union at any time. When Dwaben attempted this secession in 1732, the rest of the Ashantis united under the leadership of Osei Tutu to crush the rebellion. After the defeat of Dwaben, the Ashanti grew to be the most powerful nation in the region.

The Ashanti political organization is a typical example of how symbols of the ideological superstructure served to unite African social formations under one leadership. The two most important ideological symbols of the Ashanti are the golden stool and *apafram*. Rattray provides an account of the Ashanti belief concerning how the Golden Stool came to be:

> [Okomfo Anokye announced in Dwaben] that he had a special mission from Onyame, the god of the Sky, to make the Ashanti into a great powerful nation. Osei Tutu was informed and a great gathering was held in Coomassie [Kumasi].... Anotchi [Anokye], in the presence of a huge multitude, with the help of his supernatural power, is stated to have brought down from the sky, in a black crowd, and amid rumblings, and in air thick with white dust, a wooden stool with three supports and partly covered gold.
>
> This stool did not fall to the earth but alighted slowly upon Osei Tutu's knees.... Anotchi told Osei Tutu and all the people that

the stool contained the sumsum (soul or spirit) of the Ashanti nation, and that their power, their health, their bravery, and their welfare were in this stool.[10]

The Asantehene, the occupant of this stool, automatically became the human symbol of the soul-power, health, bravery, welfare, and unity of the entire Ashanti nation. This ideological symbol served to unite the Ashantis together under their king, even under very difficult circumstances. The other ideological symbol, the *apafram*, was a charm contained in the spiralled horns of an antelope. Osei Tutu was said to have obtained the horns from the district of Akim.

Once a year the Ashanti nation celebrates a feast for *apafram*, representing the bonds between the Asantehene and those who swear the oath of allegiance to him. The dignitaries of the Ashanti nation arrived in Kumasi, the Ashanti capital, on a Saturday to swear oaths of allegiance to the Asantehene, and on Sunday the skulls of slain enemies of the Asantehene and *apafram* were brought to the palace of the Asantehene. With the skulls arranged before the *apafram* charm, the Asantehene, dressed in a traditional dress of bark cloth, smeared the *apafram* charm with traditional red dye, offered it some yam, and poured a libation to it, reciting words to the effect that *apafram* should help him to kill any chief who compromised his oath or refused to serve him (the Asantehene), and they would include the skull of that chief among the assembly of skulls that were before *apafram*.[11] The celebration of *apafram* was arranged to coincide with the annual *odwira* (purification) festival.

The *apafram* symbol served two purposes. It brought the Ashanti chiefs together once a year to renew their allegiance to the Asantehene. It also reminded the Ashanti chiefs that the rebellious ones among them might be executed and their skulls displayed annually and forever before *apafram*. The psychological effect was to remind the chiefs of the need for loyalty and unflinching support, and that their contribution to the unity of the Ashanti nation could not be compromised under any circumstances.

The Asantehene delegated authority to the chiefs and sub-chiefs of the Ashanti nation. He had the power to make chiefs or depose chiefs, and the making of new chiefs ensured upward mobility by merit. However, the Asantehene also ruled through a council whose advice he was expected to respect. To encourage free discussions at the council, the Asantehene normally introduced a topic through an eloquent linguist without giving any indication of his views. He was the last to express his opinion, which normally reflected the position of the majority, but the final decision had to be approved by consensus. The same process of decision-making was repeated at the regional town and village levels.

The Asantehene as well as the chiefs could only rule with the consent of the people as expressed through the council, and any Asantehene or chief who proved incompetent could be deposed. For example, in 1874, when the Asantehene Kofi Karikari did not comply with the wishes of the council, he was deposed and replaced by his junior brother, Mensa Bonsu. In 1883 Mensa Bonsu was himself deposed by the citizenry of Kumasi, who stormed the palace in reaction to his incompetence. Because of the matrilineal nature of succession, the queen mother had either to approve of the electoral nomination of an Asantehene by the council or nominate a candidate for the approval of the council. She also had the power to initiate the dethronement of an incompetent Asantehene. The respected position of queen mother of Ashanti was a political appointment. She was seen not as the mother or wife of an Asantehene, but the mother of the whole Ashanti nation.

The Asantehene was the final judicial authority, with appeals from the lower levels referred to him and his council. He was also the supreme commander of the Ashanti army, which performed police duties as well, and he was responsible for the appointment of the senior military commander. He accompanied the army to war. Designated sub-chiefs and divisional chiefs identified by their titles commanded regiments that fought as the vanguard, the rear, the left, the right, and the centre, all according to the positions of their respective chiefs.

The Ga Political Organization

In every village or town in the Ga state of Ghana, various clans live together in peace. These clans may be differentiated from one another by name, by the names of the members, and by their particular religious allegiances and rites. The clan structure and practices suggest that the towns and villages were founded by previously independent groups who at some point in history decided it was safer and more convenient to live together. Every clan was assigned a role to play in the life of the community.

Each clan is subdivided into families, and the families are further subdivided into houses—with the word "house" referring to people of the same ancestral origin. Members of clans, families, and houses are patrilineal blood relatives, with the relationship the closest at the house level.

Each house is headed by an elder who, under normal conditions, is the oldest but still most able man. The oldest woman heads the women in the house, and she is respected by all as the mother of the house. Her position is no less important than the male head of the house, except that the male leader presides over all meetings of the house. The same structure is repeated at the family level. Because of the role and responsibilities of the clan at the level of the town or village as a whole, the selection of the head of the clan is more complicated and involves the participation of other clans and groups.

The selection of the clan head is based more on merit than on age. The heads of the various houses and families of a clan meet to prepare a list of candidates arranged in order of preference by consensus. The list of candidates is then presented before an electoral college consisting of the heads of the various clans, professional groups, the chief priest, and captains of war—"*asafoiatsemei* and *asafoianyemei.*"[12] This same college of elites governs the town or village. The chief priest, or *wulomo*, of the town or village is, also, the speaker of the college responsible for order as discussions proceed. Each clan is represented at the electoral college by four people: the head or acting clan head, the "mother" of the clan, an *asafoiatse* (a male war captain), and an *asafoianye* (a female war captain). An acting clan head represents a clan whose head is to be selected.

The college selects the clan head by consensus from the list of candidates. In the past both the nomination of the candidates and the selection of the clan head were secret to avoid competition and petty jealousies, both of which tendencies were considered dangerous. Hence, no candidate was ever aware of his nomination. After selection, at a predetermined date, the candidate was presented ceremonially to the people of the town or village, and he swore an oath of allegiance to the ruling college and to the ruler or chief. In addition he swore an oath of unflinching service to the people, stating that he would uphold this service even at the peril of his life. The ceremony was crowned with the chief priest or "*wulomo*" invoking the blessings of the gods and of God upon the selected clan head, in particular, and upon all the people.

The selected candidate was obligated to take office; refusal was a taboo and a disgrace that invoked automatic banishment from the town or village. There was a provision for the clan to prefer charges before the college against a leader who did not live up to expectation and depose him if he was found guilty, subject to an appeal to a higher college.

However, before colonialism, the deposing of a clan head was either rare or unknown. Also, clan leaders might be replaced on grounds of insanity or be represented in an acting capacity by a selected member of the clan in case of some illness other than insanity.

The heads of the various professional groups, such as the heads of farming or fishing, are selected in a similar fashion. They are appointed for life. There is a provision that they may be deposed if they do not live up to expectations, or they can be represented in an acting capacity on health grounds. Again, before colonial rule the deposing of professional heads was very rare. A person is not allowed to be simultaneously a clan head and a professional head. Indeed, no person is permitted to hold more than one appointment or office.

The nomination of the candidates for selection to the office of a chief is the responsibility of the clan from which the chief is selected. However, the same electoral college meets to select a chief. The chief swears an oath of allegiance not only to the people of the town or village, but also to the council of chiefs at the next higher level. In the past, appointment to the office of a chief was for life. Although there was a provision that a chief might be deposed if he did not live up to expectations, before colonial rule the deposing of chiefs was either unknown or very rare. At the state level, chiefs of the various towns, the chiefs of the captains of war, the various queens, and the chiefs of the main professions form an encompassing college of elites, the Ga council, which rules by consensus.

All principal chiefs of the Ga traditional areas swore oaths of allegiance to the Ga manche, the Ga council, and to the Ga state council. The Ga manche, in turn, swore an oath of allegiance to all the principal chiefs, to the Ga council, and to the Ga state council.[13] The Ga manche was the president of both the Ga council (Sanhedrin of the Gas, which includes divisional chiefs) and the Ga state council (the council of the principal chiefs of the Ga state). In the distant past, the Ga manche, the head of the Ga state, was selected from the Asre traditional area as the *primus inter pares* among the principal chiefs from the various towns who together form the Ga state council. Due to some historical occurrence related to marriage, the selection of the Ga manche shifted from the Asre clan to the Abola clan. The Nai Wulomo, the highest priest of the Ga state, was the speaker of both the Ga council and the Ga state council. As a first among equals the Ga manche was not an absolute ruler, but a rubber stamp of decisions taken by the Ga council and the Ga state council. Those decisions, after the swearing of an oath before the Nai Wulomo, became law or obligatory.

The system recognized the importance of stability, experience, and continuity of government. At all levels of the college, a member of that body might be represented by a person appointed in an acting capacity if the member became sick or too old to function effectively. Continuity of government was ensured by the appointment for life of the members and the provision for representation in an acting capacity.

The system was also amenable to changing situations and conditions. At all levels, elites of the college might change the membership structure and the rules subject to approval at the next higher level. For example, the membership structure might change as villages developed into towns and as small interest groups developed into major ones. Eventually, when the growing size of the membership made consensus more difficult, alternatives were found (the *ajina* procedure), and the behaviour of the elites would determine the political structure, even though a given structure, when in force, could shape the behaviour of the elites to some extent.[14]

The system had no political parties, administration was decentralized to the family level, and decision-making at all levels was consensual. Its focus was on organization and co-operation rather than competition and conflict. Political competition was regarded as dangerous and a tool that the enemies of society might use to their advantage. Constructive agency was considered to be best achieved through consensus within a tolerant and collegial organization that permitted debate, criticism, and the free expression of views. The decentralized nature of administration ensured democratic participation in the decision-making process by elites at all levels. Proposals and decisions from the higher levels were passed down for discussion and feedback from the lower levels and vice versa before final discussion and decisions occurred at the higher levels (a democratic process popularly known as "*amaniebor*"). Because of the consensual principle, circulation of elite input (*amaniebor*) was considered more important than the principle of the circulation of elites. Final decisions at all levels were crowned and legitimized by oaths of unflinching support, and invocations of the blessings of the gods and of God by the *wulomei* or priests.

But decision-making by consensus might be difficult and prolonged. Moreover, emergency and crisis situations sometimes required quick decisions. The system recognized these problems, and a process of quick decision-making known as the "*ajina*" was built in to overcome them.

The *ajina* was an ad hoc committee appointed at the family, clan, or college level to deliberate over an issue on which a quick decision or expert advice was desired or when consensus-building at a meeting became difficult. The decision of the *ajina* or *ajinafoi* (the *ajina* members) was final and binding on all within the jurisdiction of the college. To facilitate quick decision-making, the members of the *ajina* were always of an odd number. Members of the *ajina* were selected from those present at the meeting except when expert advice was required. The process of *ajina* provided the state with relative autonomy at all levels. Because of its decentralized nature, the political organization did not require large and expensive bureaucracies, even at the state level.

The military-police organization was relatively inexpensive. The military and police duties were combined to avoid duplication of resources. There were no standing or regular armies that drew heavy salaries. Every able-bodied person was a member of the military organization, with the able-bodied women providing logistical support to the fighting men. On reaching adulthood, every male was trained to fight and was presented with his weapons of defence by his clan. Every female, on reaching adulthood, was trained to provide logistical support. Adult males and females were trained in the art of providing care to the wounded. Indeed, all able-bodied women were trained in the art of providing nursing care. Graduates from the institutions of herbal medicine, both men and women, provided the required medical care.

Each clan maintained an arsenal of weapons, and the men of a clan were commanded by the *asafoiatse* or the military captain of the clan. Designated clans fought on the rear, the vanguard, the flanks, and the centre. The battle faced by a town was co-ordinated by the chief captain of the town, the *Akoashongtse*, who took his orders from the chief of the town, and again designated towns fought in certain positions during war. The chief military captain of the Ga state co-ordinated the whole war effort, taking his orders from the Ga manche. Police duties followed the same pattern of administration. The military-police organizations were banned when Ghana was colonized, but the traditional administration continued to exist, and as a result the titles of the indigenous military-police organization also still exist today, though they are of no real significance.

The administration of justice was not expensive. Lawyers were not required, and the courts focused on truth based upon evidence rather than technicality. Courts existed at the family, clan, village, town, and state levels, with provisions for appeal to the higher levels. The highest court of appeal was the Ga state council. Justice was based not on the opinion or conviction of a single judge, but on the consensus of an appointed panel of people conversant with the traditions and the law. If someone considered a sentence to be too harsh, that person might plead for leniency on the spot, but could not do so more than three times for the same offence. The members of the panel of judges were not paid regular salaries, but received a token fraction of the fines imposed by the court. Thus the administration of justice did not pose any financial burden upon the state; it paid for itself and provided net revenue. Because the consensus of a panel administered justice, it was almost impossible for a person to bribe his way out of trouble. Moreover, because lawyers were not required to represent any person, and the experienced members of the panel posed relevant questions aimed at unearthing the facts of the case, the poorest person was ensured of justice. Like the military-police organization, the traditional administration of justice was replaced by the British system of justice when Ghana was colonized. The system did continue to exist in traditional administration, though playing the role only of arbitration and not serving as a legal entity.

Consensus also characterized the workings of the economic marketplace. The Gas recognized that competition could be destructive if not controlled. The consensus of the heads of the various houses forming a family allocated land, giving priority to members of the family or clan. To avoid competition the sellers of a commodity had a meeting to decide on its price range. Sellers could then compete within the price range based upon the quality of their products. If the price range was reported to be too high, the leaders of that interest group might be invited to the ruling council of the town or village for price negotiation by consensus. The people thus saw constructive intervention by the state at the goods marketplace as being both desirable and acceptable. Both the interests of the customers and sellers were fused, served, and protected through the consensual process. But with the advent of colonialism, traditional rule lost its power to intervene constructively in the marketplace.

They attended to problems in the labour market and at the workplace in the same consensual manner. Leaders of the professional groups met to decide by consensus on the price range of labour. If the price of labour was unacceptable to labour, the leaders of labour might meet with the leaders of the professions for negotiation by consensus. If either side was not prepared to compromise, they referred the matter to the ruling council, which arrived at the final decision either by the normal process of consensus or by the consensus of the *ajinafoi*. Decisions and disputes at the workplace followed similar patterns of administration to ensure the peace and satisfaction of all groups involved. Groups were held together by pragmatic bargains struck by their leaders at the college. In this way, the society encouraged workers to participate effectively and constructively at the workplace. These interventions in the economic marketplace by the political elite and the bargaining and compromises by the groups involved within a consensual atmosphere gave the indigenous political system its near-corporatist character.

The advantages of the indigenous political system were experienced by all the ethnic groups. But like all human organizations, the indigenous system had its imperfections. One notable disadvantage was that, for security reasons, hereditary or ancestral considerations played a heavy role in the nomination of candidates for selection by a college. Because of the appointment for life at the college and the emphasis on circulation of elite input through the democratic process of *amaniebor*, the rate of circulation of elites was relatively low.

Still, the advantages of the system far outweighed these disadvantages. Its decentralized nature and the associated procedure of feedback from the lower levels, the process of *ajina*, and decision-making by consensus all combined to provide a balance between decentralization and centralization. Because the various clan and major interest-group leaders were part of the college of elites, they were more apt to give their support to the decisions of the college and to convince their members that the decisions were in their best interest. The legitimization of decisions by the swearing of oaths motivated the elites to support the consensual decisions. The members, for their part, were confident that their representatives at the college would not compromise their interests. The confidence in the college was enhanced through the representation of every person in society by at least two people: a representative from the clan and a representative from the professional group.

Also, the representation of men and women of the various clans and leaders of interest groups at the college combined with the decentralized and consensual process to ensure the balance of political forces in which no particular clan or group was dominant enough to abuse power. Political compromises across clans, villages, and towns at all levels ensured political acquiescence and reinforced political control. The free discussions at all levels of the college encouraged the free expression of diverse views and the airing of grievances for redress, and contributed immensely to diffuse centrifugal tensions and preserve the unity not just of the villages and towns but also of society as a whole. It was this ability of the elites at the college level to maintain the unity of the various clans, villages, and towns, despite the diverse traditions and religious allegiances, that gave the indigenous political culture its consociational character. Moreover, the near-corporatist intervention at the market-place coupled with the process of *ajina* reduced unnecessary frictions and stalemates in the economic arena.

The election of elites at the clan, professional, or interest-group and college levels on the basis of selection by merit ensured that the most competent people in the society assumed office. Because of the non-existence of partisan politics, elites at all levels of the college were able to express their views freely and to seek the interests of their constituencies and the society as a whole rather than the interests of a political party. The possibility of being deposed for misconduct or failure to live up to expectations served to keep elites on their toes, making sure they would deliver their best efforts.

Moreover, decentralization made the workload at the state level relatively light for the capable and competent selected elites to handle. It insulated the leadership at the state level from most of the demands of society, so they could concentrate on the more important affairs of the state. At the same time, the decentralized structure ensured the penetration of society by the state and enhanced nation-building. The decentralized structure and the voluntary nature of the military-police organization enabled the state to discharge its duties with relatively small and inexpensive civil and military bureaucracies.

The involvement of all able-bodied men in military and police services had certain advantages. It contributed to make the crime rate almost negligible, because suspects might be watched and apprehended by anyone who happened to be around the scene. Because the nature of the military organization required a large force or superior technology to defeat it, enemies were dissuaded from attacking by counting the cost of an attack. Coups were non-existent as well. Continuity of government was ensured within a flexible political structure that might be altered gradually and judiciously to accommodate changing conditions or situations without compromising the principles of decision-making by consensus and of co-operation and compromise rather than competition and conflict.

The Common Habermasian Character

The indigenous systems of the Ovimbunda, Zulu, Ashanti, and Ga were all consensual, with a balance between centralization and decentralization to check abuses of power. These people did not leave decision-making in the hands of any one person. Under a strict system of accountability, their political appointees had to live up to expectations or they would be deposed before the completion of their terms of office. The benefits of this consensual character may be compared to a call made, in the twentieth century, by Jurgen Habermas for social and political institutions to permit open, unconstrained dialogue through consensus. Habermas's vision of a just society is a society in which social arrangements result from unconstrained consensus achieved in an open and well-informed dialogue.[15] To realize this noble situation, Habermas, in various books and articles, alluded to conditions of discourse ethics that establish an ideal speech situation. These conditions are: the parties involved should regard each other as equals by paying equal attention to the interests of all participants (which is difficult to realize under majoritarian democracy, in which the government and the opposition are never equals); there should be an absence of direct constraint or force or indirect pressure of any kind (which the party loyalty inherent in partisan politics makes difficult); rational argument should be the only form of persuasion (party loyalty undermines this condition); any assumption should be subject to inquiry; assumptions should be accepted only if all the parties agree (in partisan politics, it is honourable for the government and the opposition not to agree); and no authority should declare any issue settled forever (in partisan politics majority vote ends the matter without consensus). Given that Habermas's intervention was lamenting the absence of this ideal speech situation in the advanced Western societies, we could conclude that on these same terms the political systems of Africa were actually far more advanced than the European ones—and they were so hundreds, perhaps thousands of years before Habermas laid down his principles. The African systems had a great potential for social justice, they were democratic—and they were the very structures that colonialism either destroyed or, at the very least, polluted.

CHAPTER FIVE

TOWARDS THE MODIFICATION OF AFRICAN POLITICAL CULTURE

The British have gone further than any other African power in passing over the reins of government when it appeared that an influential, albeit small, minority of Westernized Africans was insistent on self-determination. There is no doubt that this is a gigantic gamble.

T. *Walter Wallbank,*
Contemporary Africa: Continent in Transition
(Princeton, N.J.: D. Van Nostrand, 1956)

If there is not to be disillusionment with the educated group as leaders, it must mean an end to condescension toward traditional African customs, and sincere and studied attempt to represent the interests of the majority, and not only the wage labourers and the elite.

Ralph Linton, ed.,
Most of the World
(New York: Columbia University Press, 1949)

Colonialism had several structural dimensions, including the political, the ideological, and the economic, all of which served the interests of the colonizers at the expense of the colonized. Decolonization means the complete eradication of the colonial structures and their replacement with the structures that primarily serve the interests of the new nations. The transformation processes of decolonization require not only united elite coalitions committed to the nationalist cause but also appropriate political conditions that enable the coalitions to cushion the inevitable stresses and strains of independence. But instead of adapting the deeply embedded indigenous political cultures to achieve the appropriate political conditions, the new nations adopted alien democratic practices and socialism, which served to undermine the attainment of the political prerequisites for genuine decolonization, divided the elites, stifled economic and social growth, and enabled the resulting neo-colonial structures to perpetuate the colonial mode of exploitation and repatriation of profits to the metropoles.

The Inappropriateness of an Alien Political Culture

Central to the inappropriateness of the party system of government is the notion of "enemy" for any person or group that does not belong to, or is opposed to, the ideas, aspirations, or policies of a particular party. Because in their traditional forms of government, the concept of an opposition member did not exist and the only opposition to the collegial decisions endorsed by the "king" of the nation could come only from external enemies, Africans have a fixed tendency to associate the concept of opposition with enemy. Local vernaculars sometimes even translate the word "opposition" to connote "enemy." For example, the Ga language (the language spoken in Accra, the capital city of Ghana) translates "opposition" as *mei-ni-ke-wo-yee* (those who do not like us) or *mei-ni-ke-wo-wuo-le* (those at war with us) or *wohenyeloi-le* (our enemies). The psychological impact of such interpretation or translations on political behaviour is not conducive to coalition-building. One effect of this notion of enemy for opposition or member of another party is the tendency to regard as a defeatist attitude, a sign of weakness, or treacherous behaviour any attempt to continue the policies, programs, or projects of a former government of another party, accept the constructive suggestions of the members of another party, or co-operate with the members of another party.

Another factor militating against the institution of partisan politics is the difference between the economic and political histories of Western Europe and Africa. In Western Europe, before the universal franchise was introduced as form of democratic process, industries had been firmly and successfully established and entrepreneurs capable of further industrial expansion were in place. In Africa, colonial policies prevented the development of indigenous entrepreneurs, and the universal franchise was introduced as a form of democratic process at a time when the plans for industrialization were yet to be drawn. The legitimate and democratic demands of the people for goods and services could, therefore, not be met. The potential for the development of economic crises that could culminate in political crises was therefore strong. The situation demanded the existence of an encompassing and committed coalition to cope with the stresses and strains along the development path, and this coalition would have to be different from the political coalitions of Europe. While partisan politics may have been suitable for the relatively luxurious life of Western Europe, what Africans required was a political system capable of the authoritative allocation of African values and needs. What the African elites did was to supply the luxurious values of the West to the few at the expense of the many, and what materialized in Africa was not the greatest happiness of the greatest number, but the greatest happiness of those privileged few who had assimilated European culture.

Modifying and Adapting the Indigenous Political Systems

The political systems of the Ovimbunda, Zulu, Ashanti, and Ga were only four among many others capable of being modified to enable the adoption and adaptation of capitalist development. Other African political systems and other African kingdoms were organized along similar patterns. With no political parties, administration was decentralized to the family level, and decision-making at all levels was consensual. The focus of these systems was on organization and co-operation rather than on competition.

The decentralized politics made the workload at the state level relatively light for the capable and competent elites at the centre to handle. It insulated the leadership at the state level from most of the normal demands of society and enabled them to concentrate on the more important affairs of the state. At the same time the decentralized structure, with its information flow between levels of government, ensured the penetration of society by the state and enhanced nation-building. Continuity of government was ensured within a flexible political structure that might be altered gradually, and judiciously, to accommodate changing conditions or situations without compromising the system's basic principles.

This consensual decision-making principle was pervasive on the continent. Its origin as a political culture may be found in a well-known African proverb that teaches that one person does not take a decision for a group without consultation with and the consent of that group. Compliance with this proverb existed in all spheres of life, including the economic, and played a significant role in the setting of acceptable prices for goods and services in the marketplace. For this reason the chiefs at all level were expected to promote and control trade. The consensual culture existed in the workplace, in communities, and in every organization in which discussions took place, in durbars under roofs or trees by elites representing various groups. Farming communities discussed how to pull together their labour power (whether co-operative or communal) and in what order before cultivation began.

Chieftaincy or kingship is only one of the many reflections of the African consensual culture. Indeed, before African social groups came together to constitute nations for the realization of their common and interests, free discussion among the groups took place and the decision to unite was taken consensually. This is not to deny that sometimes other groups were absorbed through conquest. But even after conquest, the conquered had the right to choose between becoming part of the nation or maintaining their original identity—though they would pay heavy tribute. If the conquered decided to become part of the nation, that decision was consensually accepted and the payment of tribute was no longer applicable.

Due to the historical experience of colonial rule, which thrived on the divide and rule principle, the consensual decision-making process became polluted to the extent that it is no longer reflected in present-day chieftaincy or kingship. Chieftaincy has instead become an arena of conflict among rival traditional elite groups. But the consensual culture still exists, and it could be modified and adapted to suit the requirements of modern government, taking into consideration the ethnic and clan diversity of most African countries, the principles upon which the indigenous political systems were founded, and the advantages inherent in their structure. The weighting of the nomination of candidates by hereditary and ancestral considerations might give way to a modified system that offers equal opportunity based on merit within and among ethnic groups or clans. In other words, the institution of chieftaincy, which does not offer equal opportunity, may have to be discarded, but the cultural values and symbols binding the people together could be preserved, modified, and expressed in nation-state terms.

Modifying Indigenous Democracy, Nation-Building, and State-Building

The African cultural process of nation-building and state-building should not be overlooked. In this context, nation-building refers to the injection of the sense of belonging, and state-building to the penetration, presence, and exercise of state power within national boundaries.

The historical experience of the Ovimbunda, Zulu, Ashanti, and Ga shows that nation-building and state-building in Africa involved first the transfer of political power with all its ideological symbols of unity and allegiance to the state followed by the delegation or devolution of power to the regions and from the regions to the districts. The resulting political system was essentially a balance between centralization and decentralization in which decentralized power served as a check on the abuse of power by the state and centralized power served to keep the nation united.

The transfer of the ideological symbols of unity to the state meant the dissolution of ethnic diversity so that the whole nation was reduced to only one ethnic group speaking the same language in different dialects. Unfortunately, during colonial rule and also at the time of independence, the symbols of unity and allegiance were not adequately transferred from the various ethnic groups or clans to the state. Elites with Western European values who were themselves alienated from the principles of their own political cultures assumed political power, occupied the state apparatuses, and began the authoritative allocation of Western values to Africans as if Africans were Europeans. The resulting situation represented a form of internal colonialism in which the majority of the population, people living and practising African culture, were colonized by the minority ruling elites, who were now practising the ways of European culture. While the majority of Africans struggled to meet their basic needs, these internal colonial masters became experts in rigging elections and entertaining themselves with imported drinks, imported turkey tails, and luxurious mansions with swimming pools, and by dancing on their toes with joy to the tunes of Western music.

The institution of partisan politics in Africa was a luxurious attempt at an authoritative allocation of Western European values to Africans by a culturally alienated African elite in African cultural environments that were entirely different from Western European culture. Partisan politics was particularly a luxurious attempt because the imposed or emulated European values were luxuries when compared to the basic needs of African populations. The politics demanded the formation of political parties and the building of political support, which required the expenditure of scarce resources. Resources were, therefore, diverted away from development projects. Furthermore, in an African political system, the nomination of a candidate was based upon relative merit, and the well-known candidates were groomed to rule from their childhoods. In the transplanted system of partisan politics, the African public perceived that any crooks who were rich enough could mount the political platform to campaign and appeal to the people to vote for them. The consequence was the election of corrupt and uncommitted elites who served their selfish interests by compromising the interests of the nation.

The first step in the process of modifying and modernizing the indigenous system to suit the requirements of modern government is a recognition of the type of democracy that Africa needs given the diverse ethnic composition of society (social pluralism), the high level of illiteracy, its relative poverty, low development of the productive forces (the instruments of production constitute a force, the organization of the direct producers constitutes another force, and the combination of the two constitutes the productive forces), and the communal character of rural society. These characteristics require a type of democracy that is pragmatic. They require a political arrangement with a balance between centralization and decentralization, a system that fosters the articulation and aggregation of interests, and in which people take part in the decisions affecting their lives and do not merely give electoral consent to elites who then renege on their pre-election promises. They also require a democracy with teeth that is capable of investing and organizing to deliver the basic needs of the people such as health, education, and productive job creation. They require a democracy that respects individual as well as collective rights and balances these two conflicting rights so that nobody is considered dispensable, and they must ensure that the collective interest is simultaneously not compromised. They require a democracy in which representation reflects the microcosmic structure of society by proportion.

What is necessary, then, is a form of consociational arrangement that is inclusive, responsive to the different aspirations within society, and decentralized enough to enable local participation in indigenous languages. The microcosmic structure of representation means an opportunity for the creation of a committed and encompassing coalition capable of defining, implementing, and sustaining coherent nationalist policies while simultaneously containing the stresses and strains from both the internal and external environments.

Within the scope of this modified system is the recognition that the assembling of diverse ethnic groups or clans to constitute a united nation is similar to the coming together of diverse clans to form towns or villages, the amalgamation of villages and towns to form traditional areas, and, at various points in a society's history, the joining together of traditional areas to form ethnic states. Indeed, based upon this same principle of African nation-building, the whole of the African continent might become united into one great supranation—like the United States, Canada, or China—that could hold its own against external political and economic forces, although it would, of course, be expedient to achieve internal unity first. At the nation-state level, representation at assemblies, colleges, or councils on the basis of the ethnic composition in any particular area would not pose insurmountable difficulties. Ethnic or clan sensitivities would seem to call for a nonpartisan but consociational political organization. Indeed, the indigenous principle of decentralized political organization that ensures a balance of political forces through consensus, and the penetration of society by the state resulting in nation-building, would appear to be indispensable to national development. What might be required and revised periodically are the records of the ethnic and interest group structures at the various levels of the political mapping of any country.

Politically, and taking into consideration the geographical origins of the ethnic groups, a country might be divided into regions, traditional areas, districts, towns, and villages with colleges or assemblies at all levels. The representation at any level of assembly would reflect both the ethnic population structure of that area and the professional or interest-group structure by proportion. Hence, a person might be represented at least by two people: one from the ethnic group or clan and the other from the professional or interest group. There would be no political parties until the dominant mode of production became capitalist enough to justify a gradual move to a political culture of partisan politics, although the ballot-box political technology could be used in the non-partisan selection of candidates. The appropriate representative would then be elected consensually from among the selected candidates on the basis of merit and moral conduct. Microcosmic representation would help to ensure the interpenetration of the economic and the political, and the simultaneous penetration of these within different strata and sections of society, and induce a sense of belonging by all members of society. The resulting social integration might also reduce rural-urban differentiation, spatial or regional inequalities, the gap between the privileged and underprivileged, and centrifugal tensions.

Adequate circulation of elites as well as circulation of elite input could be ensured by a provision that each tenure of office at the national assembly would not be more than four years. The president, appointed by the consensus of the members of the assembly and free to choose his or her cabinet to be approved by the assembly, would not serve more than two terms. Decisions at any level of assembly might be consensual to ensure a balance of political forces. Legitimization of decisions by oath—an essential part of the indigenous culture—would be preserved. Because of the ongoing secularization of society and the diversified religious allegiances of the various ethnic groups, the role played by priests in the legitimizing process would probably be dropped. At all levels, the speaker of the assembly and members of the executive might be appointed by the consensus of the members for a tenure not exceeding four years and for not more than two terms. At the national level the president and his executive selected by the consensus of the national assembly could be sworn in by the chief justice. However, in compliance with African culture, if the president and the cabinet were found to be incompetent or to be compromising the national interest in preference to their own, they would be deposed before the expiration of their terms of office through a vote of no confidence by a consensus of the members of the national assembly. The same provision might apply at all levels of government to keep elites at all levels on their toes—so they would deliver the political goods to the best of their abilities.

The political role of kings, queens, chiefs, and queen-mothers in African political systems suggests that no sexual discrimination whatsoever should be tolerated in the African political arena. Men and women should be equally eligible for election to political office and appointment to any public office. A clear separation of the political from religion to enable the laws of the state to be independent of religion would be required. It would be necessary to eradicate the misogynistic or patriarchal behaviour inherited from the Abrahamic religions of Christianity and Islam. It should not be forgotten that long before Islam and Christianity set foot in Africa, African culture carried a basic respect for the honourable role of women in politics. The male chauvinism inherited from European colonialism should be eradicated from the African political culture, which, in its original form, permitted women not only to be queens and queen-mothers but also military commanders, including Yaa Asentewaa of Ashanti and Dode Akai of the Ga state. The majority of African productive farmers are women, but misogynistic policies encourage agricultural extension officers to provide needed productivity information to men only, thus alienating a great number of producers and suffocating productivity. Women should participate in the political and economic decisions that affect their lives.

Reviving and Empowering Compatible Indigenous Structures

The African elite also failed to modernize and adapt the indigenous democratic structures that characterized African society and made it resilient to shocks and unfavourable conditions. Among these structures were various voluntary organizations and social networks originating from African communal practice, and the African principle of voluntarily helping a brother, sister, friend, relation, or a community member in need. Among these voluntary institutions were funding or rotating savings organizations, organizations for local policing, organizations for co-operative labour, self-help organizations, and spiritual organizations. Africans generally joined these voluntary organizations based on trust, integrity, and accountability to further their economic and social interests. The fundraising voluntary organization was essentially the traditional African banking system (the *susu* in West Africa and the Caribbean, to which African culture was transported, or *upato* or *kutunzana* in East Africa), which was highly decentralized to the grassroots level.[1] The fundraising, self-help, and policing organizations are particularly important to compatible cultural democracy in Africa. Other voluntary organizations should also be encouraged and empowered.

The fundraising voluntary organizations could be modernized into potential sources of funding for development, pension, and welfare purposes. Usually, members of a group contributed specified amounts per week, and at the end of the month the total collection went by rotation to one member to fund his or her project. No payment of interest to members was involved. The advantage was that the recipient got an interest-free loan from the rest of the members. African governments could assist by appointing bank officials to maintain lists of the contributors and to deposit their collective contributions per week into specified bank accounts, with rules guiding withdrawals and distribution of the funds. Members could be educated into accepting that some small percentage of the amount contributed per week be allocated to pension, insurance, and welfare schemes for their benefit. The flow of funds from these fundraising organizations, which could exist in all workplaces, communities, and villages, might render the high-interest government premium bonds unnecessary. Because the rotation takes time and no interest payments to the contributors are involved, the monthly interest payments accruing to the government could provide funds for development projects. Furthermore, by adopting proper timing, governments could borrow from these funds with minimal or no interest to invest in development projects.

The voluntary policing organizations could serve as a source of training for all able-bodied people and help an African government reduce its expenditure on the police. Usually local people know who the criminals in their own community are, but are discouraged from exposing them for the simple fear that the corrupt, Western-oriented, and salary-minded police are allied with the trouble-makers. The empowerment of the voluntary policing organization could discourage the regular police from co-operating with the criminals and contribute to a reduction of the level of crime.

The self-help voluntary organizations might enable the government to reduce its budget on development projects. Self-help voluntary organizations are known to have contributed funds and labour to construct roads and bridges, build and staff schools and health clinics, construct wells and earth dams to provide water and to breed fish, and care for the helpless. Both the government and population might therefore gain from their activities. Their proliferation must be encouraged because, in a situation of economic crisis, they could well be the indispensable allies of the government. Their humanitarian character and disposition to provide basic needs justify their empowerment through incentives such as the award of medals, prizes, and other national honours.

Modifying the Education System

The pre-colonial education systems of Africa were geared towards training Africans to provide service for themselves and to the African societies they live in. That system of education was so integrated with productive activity and culture that the recipients did not face problems of unemployment and cultural alienation. The colonial education system was geared primarily to satisfying colonial interests. The education system now has to be revamped and oriented so that it satisfies the material needs of the recipients and society as a whole. In conformity with the indigenous character, education has to be integrated with productivity, African culture, and African history. Injection of African values and African nationalism, which recognizes Africans as one people with one destiny, must be emphasized and, simultaneously, the syllabuses must be such as to prepare the recipients for the occupations of their choice.

The colonial education system denied access to the majority of the African populations. Recognizing that education enhances productivity in various ways, the majority of the population living in the rural areas and the suburbs of the cities must be the target of organized mass education programs that integrate education with productivity and culture. To reduce cost, these mass education programs could be organized on a voluntary basis and offered in the local languages first before the introduction of any other language.[2] Television and videocassettes could be assets in these programs. The mass education program could be one of the potent channels for an ideological re-education of African society to create the new African who can contribute effectively to the realization of nationalist objectives. It could enable effective communication between the state and the masses in local languages that recipients can read, understand, and use to explain matters to the less fortunate. The programs could well have snowballing effects. Those who receive the education would be encouraged to teach others, including their own extended family members. Thus the extended family system, which Goran Hyden identified as militating against the operation of the capitalist market by providing a means by which the peasantry escaped capture, could be a channel through which productivity could be enhanced.[3] Through mass education programs, Africans could gain a means of understanding the society they live in and of participating effectively in the affairs that concern them.

Recognition of Cultural Dynamics

The constitution of the political system should recognize that culture is dynamic, and it should be flexible enough to enable adaptation to cultural variation over time. For example, in response to cultural changes, as African society approaches the capitalist mode of production the consensual political culture might gradually assume the characteristics of the consociational systems of the small states of Western Europe in which partisan politics plays a part; but this should certainly not happen at the present stage of African culture, in which members of a political party are still considered enemies and centrifugal political forces can break the system apart. Furthermore, partisan consociational democracy requires the diversion of resources from development projects to the formation of political parties. When Africa becomes more industrialized, when its economy becomes stronger, and when its culture approaches that of the capitalist mode of production, the building of a partisan consociational democracy may become a practical project. Indeed, I do not condemn partisan politics in itself, but rather, I question and challenge its contemporary compatibility. The pre-capital-ist mode of production of African countries does not justify the practice of partisan politics, which divides the people instead of uniting them to achieve the political conditions for successful development.

The Modified System and Social Choice

Africa's survival in a world economic system characterized by protec-tionism and oligopolistic pricing—and in which the continent lags behind the rest of the world and has been reduced to a price-taker both in its imports and exports—demands the existence of a political system in which consistent and coherent decisions enable it to free itself from economic colonialism. It is a world in which apostles from the developed world with double standards and with the assistance of the IMF and the World Bank preach the free-market ideology outside their borders, but within their own borders preach protectionism. Given such a situation, Africa requires a political system in which decisions that have an impact on the well-being of the African populations are not left in the hands of a few elected dictators who might as well have rigged the elections to serve their own narrow interests, which are closely linked or fused with the interests of imperialism. Indeed, Africa's present situation demands a system that offers a potential for consistent social choice in which the preferences of individuals comprising society are reflected; and a system that not only promises the greatest happiness of the greatest number but also the greatest happiness of all individuals of society—a goal that is called the Pareto optimum, in which everyone is better off and none is worse off.

The partisan political system characterized by elected dictators is def-initely not that kind of political system. Economist and Nobel laureate Kenneth Arrow, who studied the problems of collective choice based on uncertainty and doubt, argued that the conditions required for such a system are not possible in any non-consensual democratic decision-making society of elected dictators.[4] According to Arrow, the required conditions are:

a. Social choices must be such that if A is preferred to B and B is pre-ferred to C, then C cannot be preferred to A.

In the Western partisan political system, the basic tenet of liberalism means that individual right is preferred to group right, which is in turn preferred to party right. In practice, party loyalty rules the day, and the political right of the individual is usurped by groups, so that both B and C are preferred to A. Thus the first condition is violated, making it impossible for social choice to reflect the preferences of the individuals comprising society.

b. Social choices must be such that an alternative that society might choose to take up should not be turned down just because particular individuals who are not liked are identified as liking it more.

In the partisan political system, a social choice that society might otherwise have chosen is likely to be shelved if the ruling party perceives it as likely to boost electoral support of the elites of another party or parties.

c. Social choices should not be dictated by anyone either inside or outside the society.

At the time of independence, it was the colonizers who, through manipulation of the political levers they controlled, chose partisan politics for their former colonies and placed political power in the hands of elected dictators. At present, the IMF, World Bank, and foreign political forces are forcing partisan politics down the throats of African societies as if it is the only way in which democracy can be put into practice. The elected leaders, who might as well have rigged the elections, are then in a position to dictate their policies—their likes and dislikes—to society.

d. The social preference between one alternative and the other should be based on the beliefs of people about those two alternatives and not on their opinion of other alternatives.

Competitive political propaganda engaged in by different political parties of varying ideological spectrum makes the realization of this alternative impossible. Society, constantly bombarded with varying and confusing ideological propaganda, is compelled to choose between two dominant parties while armed simultaneously with opinions about other alternative parties. Their volitions are shaped by these propaganda machines, which very often fail to honour their promises. In the process, one party is replaced by another party, leading to inconsistent social choice.

In the modified, non-partisan, and consensual democratic practice, with a balance between centralization and decentralization, African society would make decisions based on a consensus forged at all levels of government, in a Habermasian manner. Hence this practice carries a high potential for the realization of Arrow's four conditions. The social choice in that system is more likely to reflect social justice in which the preferences of individuals comprising society are more consistent and coherent.

The Characteristics of the Modified System

A modified indigenous political system would have a number of desirable characteristics:

1. A decentralized, consensual, and consociational system with the participation of interest groups, ethnic groups, clans, and professional associations directly in the decision-making process.

Thus the military, police, peasants, workers, entrepreneurs, and traditionalists would all be represented in government and participate actively in decisions that affect them and the nation as a whole. Because of incorporation of the *ajina* quick decision-making process of the Ga political system, the difficulty of prolonged discussions in consensualism would be eliminated to enable quick decision-making, especially under crisis and emergency situations. Indeed, the state would encourage openness and freedom of expression of views before reaching final decisions.

2. A democratic system that offers equal opportunity for men and women to participate at all levels in the political process.

3. A democratic system without political parties.

The absence of political parties would potentially mean the vanishing of the problems of instability associated with the party system, such as frequent changes of government, frequent cabinet reshuffles and changes in major ministries, threats of decrease in the electoral margin of government parties, that divert the attention of governments from more important issues, and fractionalization of the party system with its attendant weak minority governments. Party loyalty might be replaced by loyalty to the electorate and hence to the state.

4. A relatively stable state in which coups would not be justified and with a periodic circulation of elites in number and in quality.

5. A responsible state that is insulated adequately from society by the

decentralized process to concentrate on more important issues.

Such a state could develop the capacity of defining and sustaining nationalist-oriented policies in the long-term interests of the nation and enjoy the support of all sections of society through the decentralized process. At the same time, the decentralized process could enable the deep penetration of society by the political elite to explain the rationales of government policies.

6. Relatively small and inexpensive but efficient regular armed forces and police organizations, augmented in their effectiveness by compulsory training for all able-bodied people, and with an associated highly disciplined society with a low crime rate.

7. A relatively small and efficient central state bureaucracy made possible by the decentralized nature of the political structure and the responsibilities assumed by local authorities.

8. A largely privatized but mixed economy with a near-corporatist intervention in the market that reduces tension and promotes peace in the economic arena to encourage development initiatives.

9. A political system that recognizes that culture is not static but changes over time, and is sensitive to and adaptable to such cultural dynamics.

10. A state in which the participation of voluntary organizations is encouraged with the understanding that communal democracy expressed through voluntary organizations is an integral part of Africa's cultural democracy.

11. A state in which the elected representatives are kept on their toes to deliver the political goods to the best of their ability.

12. A political system whose constitution is altered gradually in response to cultural dynamics.

13. A political system in which social choice reflects the preferences of the individuals who comprise society.

14. A political system in which social choices are coherent and consistent.

Critics might argue that because consensus-building is difficult, consensual democracy works only in small communities and would not be suitable for today's large and complex nations. I would remind such critics that if consensus-building is possible in the United Nations, as exemplified by the consensus to drive Iraq out of Kuwait, it is also possible in nation-states whenever the issue at hand is perceived to be in the interests and to the benefit of society. It should not be forgotten that the Ghana, Mali, Songhai, Zulu, Ovimbunda, Ashanti, and Ga political organizations—with their forms of consensual democracy—were not small city-states. Furthermore, the *ajina* process can overcome the problems that critics associate with consensus-building.

Critics might also ask, "How can the Zulu spear, which symbolizes the subjugation of other ethnic groups, ever represent a national symbol of South Africa, or how can the Golden Stool of Ashanti, which stimulated the Ashanti to conquer other ethnic groups of Ghana, ever be transferred to the centre to become a national symbol?" But remember: the Union Jack was created by King James VI of Scotland when he became King of England in 1603. Because of the history of wars between England and Scotland and the resulting enmity between Scots and English, King James thought it wise to transfer the ideological symbols of those separate realms—the red cross of Saint George on a white background (the ideological symbol of England), the white cross of Saint Andrew in the shape of an "X" on a blue background (the ideological symbol of Scotland), and the red cross of Saint Patrick in the shape of an "X" on a white background—to the centre in London to constitute a single and united nation with a common aspiration. In 1803, when Northern Ireland became part of the Union, the ideological symbol of Northern Island was also transferred. Also, despite the U.S. Civil War, the U.S. flag has many stars, with each one representing the ideological symbol of a state that was transferred to the centre to constitute the United States of America. The various clans of Africa that came together in pre-colonial times to constitute distinct ethnic groups for the realization of common objectives also transferred the ideological symbols of unity from the clan level to the centre.

These questions themselves suggest that the transfer of the ideological symbols of unity to the centre has to be preceded by a process of ideological re-education in which the mistakes of the ancestors are brought to light with the view of inducing national reconciliation and ridding the mind of society of historical excrescence. For example, in the past the ancestors made the mistake of thinking that a different dialect meant a different people or an enemy society, and they fought among themselves on that basis. They failed to recognize that if a Zulu baby grows up in an Ashanti environment, she will almost certainly grow up to speak Ashanti and will consider herself an Ashanti. Language or dialect is therefore not a barrier. What matters is common destiny. When the Zulu spear is transferred to the centre, it is no longer a Zulu spear symbolizing the unity and conquering spirit of the Zulu, but the unity and spirit of all South Africans to conquer the evils of South African society. Every symbol and dialect of South Africa shall become the symbol and dialect of all South Africans irrespective of their colour or creed. Thus, the misconception of white-skinned South Africans that they are still Europeans just because of the colour of their skin would vanish. Similarly, the misconception of black South Africans that white South Africans are Europeans would vanish. Through the ideological re-education process, all South Africans would recognize that they are one people with one destiny and that language, the colour of the skin, and all other physical characteristics are nothing but illusions. When the Golden Stool is transferred to the centre, it is no longer an Ashanti stool symbolizing the unity and soul of the Ashanti, but the unity and soul of the whole of Ghana. The Ashanti slogan *Ashanti Kotoko*, symbolizing the conquering spirit of the Ashanti, could symbolize the determined spirit of all Ghanaians to conquer the evils of Ghanaian society. The Ga slogan *Ashiedu Keteke Odomni Amamfo* shall no longer symbolize the indomitable courage of the Gas to fight on despite overwhelming odds, but the indomitable courage of all Ghanaians to continue to fight on despite overwhelming odds from both the international and local environments. The *Togbe* or *Amega* slogans of the Ewe would no longer symbolize the respect that Ewes have for the rulers and for the elderly, but the respect that all Ghanaians have for the rulers and for the elderly. Indeed, if all these symbols are conveniently and appropriately invoked, the whole of the African continent would be united into a very great nation.

This idea of transferring ideological symbols is by no means unrealistic. It is a pragmatic view, because it is based on the understanding that what has been done before in Africa is capable of being repeated. The nations of ancient Africa, including the Zulu and the Ashanti, were built through clans or sub-ethnic groups transferring their ideological symbols to the centre. What they accomplished in the past is capable of being accomplished in the present through effective processes of ideological re-education. Undeniably, Britain is a nation in which the

ideological symbols of the English, Scots, Welsh, and Irish were transferred to the centre, and sub-ethnic groups gradually faded as the spirit
of British nationalism grew. Germany is a country in which various
Germanic tribes transferred the ideological symbols of unity to the
centre to create a united and stronger nation under Bismarck. Ruling out
the possibility of Africans transferring the ideological symbols of unity
to the centre is not only an insult to the African personality but also
relegates the African to the status of an inferior being who is not capable
of moving forward and achieving a better future.

The critic may also ask, "Should the transfer of the ideological symbols of unity be by a top-down or by a bottom-up process?" The historical experience of British, German, and Russian nation-state building
followed the top-down approach, involving the use of persuasion, force,
or conquest—which may well have been appropriate in certain, earlier
times. The use of force or conquest within the nation-states of Africa in
an exclusively top-down approach would certainly be inappropriate; but
the required balance between centralization and decentralization in the
modified system itself suggests that a balance between the top-down
and the bottom-up approaches would be appropriate. That is why an
ideological re-education of society is required to convert the present-day
African into a new African who places the unity and common destiny of
the nation as a whole above his or her narrow self-interests. The modified education system coupled with mass education programs are
among the effective channels for the ideological re-education of society.
The top-down element could be used to introduce the new education
policy to be implemented at all levels. The bottom-up approach could be
used to identify and channel problems to the top echelons for resolution,
and to mobilize the grassroots for the purpose. Pre-colonial African
education was not by compulsion or by force but by interest, persuasion,
and co-operation. Ideological re-education has to be carried out in the
same manner before it can be considered compatible with African
culture.

This ideological re-education would be followed by the simultaneous
involvement of the top and bottom strata of society in the transfer of
the ideological symbols to the centre and in the delegation of authority
from the centre to the regions and from the regions to the districts—all
to ensure that decentralized power checks the abuse of centralized
power. Force is not necessary, and especially not in this process of ideological re-education. Change instead requires commitment, persuasion,
and perseverance.

CHAPTER SIX

GHANA: TACTICAL ACTION, SOCIALISM, AND THE MILITARY

When Ghana became an independent nation in 1957—the first country in Sub-Saharan Africa to achieve that status in the twentieth century—it was a country created not in accordance with any principles of African nation-building, but a foreign creation resulting from the Berlin Conference of the late nineteenth century. It was through the imperialist design to divide up Africa and the economic logic of capitalism that what is now Ghana became The Gold Coast, a colony of Britain, under the force of British guns. Before European contact, the various ethnic societies of Ghana had constructed their own effective patterns of political, social, and economic life, and the indigenous systems would have continued to evolve if they had not been undermined by the retrogressive forces of slavery and colonialism.

British colonial rule was not at all aimed at uniting the various ethnic societies of Ghana to meet their own needs, or at bringing them together to constitute a strong nation capable of autocentric development. Rather, the strategy of colonial rule was to keep the clans and ethnic groups or nations divided and weak enough to be dominated and exploited. Ghana's struggles with nation-building and state-building have their roots, therefore, in the eras of slavery and colonialism. Still, during the colonial era Ghanaians proved themselves able to bury their ethnic differences and to unite to protect and defend their interests. In 1897, for example, the Aborigines Rights Protection Society (ARPS) successfully campaigned against a colonial lands bill that threatened aboriginal land tenure by proposing that all lands not in actual use be placed under the control of the British government. In September 1911 a bill enacted by the Legislative Council of the colonial government and intended to establish forest reserves was dropped, again after ARPS opposition was raised against it. And in 1937, after foreign cocoa-buying firms formed a trust to control the producer price of cocoa, Ghanaians effectively united in a boycott movement to oppose that outside control.[1] What the Ghanaian elite of that earlier era achieved, the Ghanaian elite of today are capable of surpassing.

At the time of its independence Ghana not only had great aspirations for a better future but was also a source of inspiration to other countries in the region and, indeed, in other parts of the so-called Third World. At that time it was, comparatively, a country with a full complement of educated elites. Its economy, although dependent largely on cocoa, had a potentially strong base. Its dependence on a monocrop economy justified the desire to restructure the economy through a diversification of the portfolio of production. Partly because of deteriorating terms of trade for agricultural products and partly because industrialization became synonymous with development, the country's leaders and advisors preferred a shift away from agriculture rather than a shift back to the multicrop economy of the pre-colonial past. The political climate within the country, however, was never stable enough to nurture and support coherent policies.

But Ghana has faced more than a pattern of political instability in its attempts at structural transformation. Other internal and external factors have also had an impact on its development. The new country encountered internal variables such as drought, a colonial heritage of limited infrastructure (the transportation network, for example), and a weak institutional framework, despite the thousands of tons of gold and the millions of tons of cocoa delivered to Britain. Also, like most non-oil producing countries, Ghana was badly hurt by the oil-pricing and monetary shocks of the 1970s and 1980s.

The Ghanaian Elite, Partisan Politics, and Development

By setting Ghana on the course of the party system of government, the Ghanaian political elite set the nation on a path of political enmity and disunity that would be characterized by discontinuity in government, a lack of co-operation, and violence. The political platforms and the national assembly became the arenas in which uncompromising enemies were always in combat-readiness. During the independence struggle, the political enmity between the United Gold Coast Convention (UGCC) and Kwame Nkrumah's political party, the Convention People's Party (CPP), compelled Nkrumah to adopt the recommendations of the Coussey Committee Report, which he had previously described as a Trojan Horse and rejected. It also compelled him to take up a policy of "tactical action," whereby the CPP would work through the established channels of the British colonial system to liberate The Gold Coast from colonial rule.[2]

The policy of tactical action meant that there would be no direct confrontation with the British administration and no radical changes to the economic and political structures established by the colonial government. In other words, Ghanaians were to abandon the process of decolonization during the process of independence, which would in turn be granted on British terms. From the point of declaration of tactical action onward, time itself became an ally of the forces of political and economic stagnation in Ghana. The country entered a vicious cycle of political and economic crisis characterized by discontinuity in government, economic decline, political discontentment, and general frustration. The political elite was not able to define and sustain any coherent and nationalist economic policies.

The policy of tactical action surprised and infuriated the more militant and nationalist-minded members of the CPP, particularly the trade union leaders, who had expected that Nkrumah would take a more radical approach to break the colonial chains of ideological, economic, and political dependence. They perceived—and later events confirmed their perception—that instead of creating the political conditions for successful development, which was buttressed by Nkrumah's famous dictum "Seek ye first the political kingdom and all other things will be added unto you," the CPP was compromising the country's economic future for worthless political gains. The spirit of nationalism that once animated the CPP began to wane. Bob Fitch and Mary Oppenheimer summarized the problem:

> The mother country still controlled the police and the army; the Colonial Governor retained his "reserve powers" ; British bureaucrats held most of the senior positions in the civil service; British stockholders owned the gold mines; over 90 per cent of the import-export trade was controlled by 13 foreign trading companies (the firms); the yearly budgets were prepared back in London by the Colonial Office.
>
> Yet the most obvious instrument of foreign economic control— the one which had the most long-lasting and destructive effects on the Ghanaian economy—was a government agency on which the CPP dutifully served. This was the Cocoa Marketing Board.[3]

The militant nationalists saw tactical action as a perpetuation of the colonial relationship and feared that Nkrumah's political course might lead to nominal independence without proper decolonization. They were bitter about the Cocoa Marketing Board (CMB), not so much because of how it acted to extract a surplus from cocoa production, but for the use to which the surplus was put. The CMB had been established by the British Labour government in 1948 as part of a strategy to ensure that the remaining colonies transferred their cash surpluses to London to support the ailing pound after the Second World War. Due partly to its heavy borrowing to finance the war and partly to import requirements for its postwar reconstruction, Britain was facing serious balance of payments problems, and marketing boards in the colonies would help supplement aid being received through the Marshall Plan.

The operation of the CMB was essentially part of Britain's attempt to control the marketplace to its advantage. At that time it looked as though the efficient free hand of the market—a concept that the IMF, World Bank, and monetarists preach to developing countries today—had either become sick or amputated. Also, the economists' mutual-benefit claim appeared to be dead and buried in a coffin. But in their presentation of the CMB to Ghanaians, the British strategists offered an entirely different picture. It was as if the primary purpose was to insulate the cocoa farmers against the vagaries of the international market and to aid Ghana's economic growth. Thus the domestic price of cocoa was set lower than the world price ostensibly for the purpose of creating a reserve fund, which could then be put to various important ends, such as providing a source for stabilizing the cocoa producers' income, combating inflation by draining the excess purchasing power, and providing savings that could be used for further economic ventures. For these purposes, the CMB was to accumulate the difference between the world price and the domestic price. But the CMB's accumulation process meant that the resources that should have gone to Ghanaian farmers were diverted into the hands of the government in power. In the colonial period this meant that money that might have gone into the development of private enterprise was diverted to the colonial government for investment in Britain.

The British were the winners and Ghanaians the losers. The accumulated surplus was not used fully for the proclaimed purposes, but rather mainly went to satisfy British economic interests. The British strategists stealthily compelled Ghana, through the CMB, to lend money to Britain at the very low interest rate of "0.5 percent before 1950; 2 to 4 percent after 1952."[4] The terms were determined by the borrower, Britain. Ironically, since the 1960s, when its economic crisis began, Ghana has by no means found it easy to borrow from Britain, and the interest rates on those funds that the country was able to borrow from Britain have not been determined by Ghana, the borrower, but by Britain, the lender.

Ghana required a strong, knowledgeable, and united coalition to challenge the clever British strategy of siphoning off its surplus funds, and the nation was indeed blessed with a competent and knowledgeable human capital of economists and other professionals and intellectuals. Unfortunately, partisan politics divided the elite. The more qualified among the Ghanaian elite (including lawyers, engineers, and economists) mostly if not all identified with the opposition. Nkrumah drew his support from the lower classes, and as a result the ministers of his first government of the pre-independence era were high school graduates at best. The notion of opposition as "enemy" discouraged any cooperation between the two sides. In addition, because Ghana sold large amounts of cocoa to the United States, the country was in turn able to supply substantial amounts of dollars needed for Britain's economic reconstruction. Ghana's contribution to providing Britain with the needed capital was, according to Fitch and Oppenheimer, "larger than that of any other country except Malaya," in appreciation of which the former colonial secretary, Arthur Creech Jones, remarked, "I think we should be conscious of the very substantial contribution which the Gold Coast has made to the Sterling Area."[5] Interestingly, again, Britain has never volunteered to be the largest supplier of dollars for Ghana's recovery from the economic crisis.

For its part, the CPP leadership had a selfish interest in the continuation of the siphoning of the surplus from Ghana. Because of the competition between the CPP and the UGCC for British favour, Nkrumah and the moderates within the CPP thought it wise to maintain the CMB approach even though it was detrimental to Ghana's economy. This disposition might not have been possible under the indigenous consensual system, but under partisan politics it was considered rational. Nkrumah and the moderates within his party had learned from the experience of the Coussey Committee, when the British authorities had openly showed a preference for the UGCC, that if they were not prepared to abide by the colonial rules of the game, the British, the real holders of the levers of political power, could lay down difficulties on the road to independence and might even use their levers of power in favour of the UGCC.

As the CMB continued to siphon off the cocoa surplus, Ghana was

Table 6.1: The Cocoa Marketing Board and Ghanaian Reserves in London (millions of pounds)

Year	Total CMB Proceeds	Paid to Cocoa Producers	Total Ghanaian Reserve
1948	41.5	15.4	n/a
1949	37.5	21.2	n/a
1950	45.1	21.2	113.3
1951	70.3	4.2	137.2
1952	51.6	31.4	145.1
1953	57.1	32.5	160.1
1954	74.7	28.0	197.4
1955	77.5	29.5	208.2
1956	52.3	35.0	189.8
1957	50.7	39.9	171.4

Source: Bob Fitch and Mary Oppenheimer, *Ghana: The End of an Illusion*, p. 45.

deprived of the opportunity of using that surplus to diversify its economy and thereby embark on the cherished road to economic independence. The CMB contributed to the building of reserves in London at a time when Ghana needed investment to restructure and diversify its economy and save itself from its monocrop economy, so vulnerable to fluctuations in the price of cocoa on the world market (Table 6.1). In addition, during the pre-independence CPP rule, Ghana was permitted to retain only a meagre percentage compared to the value of its exports to the dollar area (Table 6.2).

The siphoning of cocoa surplus to Britain did not just undermine the nationalist hope of building an infrastructure vital to Ghana's economic development. It also reinforced and continued the colonial pattern of preventing the development of an indigenous group of big-business entrepreneurs who might otherwise have engaged in an import-substitution industrialization leading to production for export—similar, perhaps, to the historical processes of development in South Korea. It prevented the CPP government from spearheading industrialization initiatives where necessary.

In effect, the CPP government compromised Ghana's economic future. Indeed, independence was not freely won. Through the policy of

Table 6.2: Ghanaian Dollar Allocations 1951-54

Year	Value of Ghanaian Exports to Dollar Area* (in pounds)	Per Cent Allocated to Ghana %
1951	30,047,000	17
1952	25,539,000	18
1953	25,407,000	21
1954	20,009,000	16

Source: Fitch and Oppenheimer, *Ghana*, p. 46.
*"Dollar Area" refers to geographical areas in which exports were paid in U.S. dollars and not in pounds sterling.

tactical action, the CPP government purchased independence from Britain by sacrificing the country's future at the very time when Ghana should have been laying the foundations for its own well-being.

How Partisan Politics Undermined Coalition-Building

The policy of tactical action not only sacrificed the economic future of Ghana, but also contributed to the intensification of partisan politics. The tactical action phase created problems for coalition-building within the CPP and blocked almost all chances for coalition-building by the political elite. It contributed immensely to depriving the Ghanaian political elite as a whole and the CPP, in particular, of the opportunity of establishing the political prerequisites for successful economic development. In addition, at election time the CPP was challenged by the National Liberation Movement (NLM) in Ashanti and the Togo Congress (TC) in Trans-Volta Togoland. Independent candidates represented ethnic and splinter groupings such as the Ga Shifimo Kpee of Accra. (Later the opposition parties merged to constitute the United Party.) Almost all these political parties engaged in vote-buying as well as in episodes of bloody violence in which many Ghanaians lost their lives. This behaviour itself was a signal that the model of partisan politics was neither well understood nor appropriate. While the opposition parties resorted to appeals to sentiments of local nationalism in their respective areas, the CPP exploited rivalries between chiefdoms and localities to its own advantage. For example, in exchange for votes from the Brongs and the Ahafos, the CPP promised the creation of a separate region to be carved out of the Ashanti region—a plan that would weaken the Ashanti nation. The CPP campaign for votes also sowed seeds of disunity or, like the British, adopted divide and rule tactics. A campaign agent working against the CPP recalled:

> We made it an issue that it was a fight between the Chianas and the Pagas. We will not like the Chianas to be paramount over us. We would have to walk to Chiana for court cases and pay our levies to them; we made it known that if we allow the Chianas to win, that means Chiana-pio would be paramount and would dictate to our chief in Paga.
>
> Owing to this news the whole of Paga went haywire. Enthusiastic representatives from all sections volunteered to help Paga win the election so that we might not become servants to the Chianas but masters of our own.[6]

Funds that might have gone into productive economic development instead went to unproductive vote-buying by both sides:

> We slept in the town for two days and at night called on the headman and explained what (the CPP candidate) was trying to do, tipped them heavily, gave out cola and drinks, i.e., spirits and clothes, etc. Before leaving ... we left two of our men and a native who helped us a great deal; we gave them about five pounds each for canvassing, i.e., buy cola and tipping them, etc. We spent heavily in this constituency. The other side also spent heavily. In one case, a headman who was supporting us turned out later to be our enemy. We understood the other side gave him about 40 pounds cash as he was a popular man in the area and having many subjects under his command.[7]

Given that neither the CPP nor the opposition was a strong mass-based coalition, each side went about trying to outbribe the other—and thereby denying any real democratic gains. The alien ballot-box partisan politics introduced, encouraged, and intensified political corruption. Certainly, that kind of democracy might best be described as a demonstration of craziness. When, for instance, oil is substituted for petrol or gas in a petrol engine the engine goes crazy and the performance drops sharply. When someone is injected with a drug he is allergic to, that person's health will go crazy. And in Ghana, when alien party politics were substituted for an indigenous political culture, the political machinery went crazy. When Ghana was injected with a dose of Western-style democracy, it experienced a politico-cultural allergy and its health went crazy in both the political and economic spheres.

A government that offers this demonstration of craziness is no democracy or even a polyarchy. Ghanaian society, in general, became confused and apathetic about the meaning of democracy. Despite heavy expenses on all sides, the country's elections were characterized by an apathy indicative of a public loss of confidence in the political elite. In one typical election just before independence, in July 1956, the CPP won 55 percent of the total votes cast, but that proportion represented only 32 per cent of the registered electorate and only 16.5 per cent of those eligible to register.[8] Separatist movements, such as the National Liberation Movement (NLM) in the Ashanti region and the Togo Congress (TC) in the Volta Region, as well as the associated high level of political violence, exposed the divisions in the Ghanaian political elite and the extent to which partisan politics was compromising the national interest.

The Preventive Detention Act and Transplantation of Alien Socialism

Spurred on by the violent trend in national politics, the CPP government introduced the Preventive Detention Act (PDA), which would essentially become an instrument for attacking, and putting away, the main enemy—the parliamentary opposition. The PDA enabled the government to detain for a period of five years any person considered a security threat. It was first applied to detain suspected criminals and hooligans—people popularly known as canoe boys—in Accra, and most peace-loving Ghanaians, including members of the opposition, were happy about that. Ironically, the canoe boys were staunch supporters of the CPP, but because they were not of good behaviour they embarrassed the party. Later the PDA was used to detain members of the opposition. For fear of the PDA many opposition members went into exile and many supporters of the United Party went underground. Some pretended to support the CPP while, in reality, they supported the opposition. As time went on the PDA was used to detain CPP members whose political views were opposed to those of Nkrumah.

After using the PDA to virtually eliminate the opposition, the CPP government embarked upon another dangerous course. It boldly and openly declared socialism (another alien ideology) and the one-party state to be the political means for the attainment of the national objective of self-sustained industrial growth by the year 1967. The problem with this was that socialism was even more alien to the indigenous political culture than was Western democracy. Hence, the crazed atmosphere of the Ghanaian environment became even worse than before. Because Ghana had not attained the capitalist stage of development, the country had no viable foundation for the establishment of socialism, and because the elites apparently did not understand the basic tenets of socialism, the attempts to introduce the ideology floundered. This was a "socialism-gone-crazy." Indeed, what was established out of the confusion was not socialism at all, but something else with a mixed economy content that was given a wrong name.

The declaration of socialism as the guide to Ghana's development confirmed earlier opposition fears that Nkrumah and his CPP were communists. It set up an ideological basis of conflict among the Ghanaian political elite that was fuelled by foreign interests opposed to the socialist ideology. It encouraged opposition members in exile and operating underground in the country to intensify their operations with the help of foreign sympathizers; and it thus made more difficult the task of organizing a united nationalist coalition. The British, allies of the CPP government during the tactical action period, felt betrayed and became open critics of the government's policies. With hindsight, the British concluded that Nkrumah had not been sincere in his pre-independence statement that he was not a communist and would never be one.

Moreover, the government declared itself socialist at a time when the CPP leadership had no clear understanding of socialism as an ideology. They considered socialism simply and mistakenly to be similar to the indigenous political culture, in which organized political opposition did not exist. The CPP forgot that the indigenous culture of rule by the consensus of encompassing coalitions had no parties at all. In that respect, the declaration of Ghana as a one-party state also did not conform to any indigenous political culture. Given the mistaken interpretation, socialism became a misnomer in Ghana. Furthermore, the confines of the one-party state made it relatively easy to identify "political enemies." In a one-party socialist state, the political community outside that party can readily identify the conspicuous members of the only party as the real enemy. The political community polarized dangerously into two camps.

The conceptualization of socialism by the Ghanaian political elite carried other difficulties. Whereas socialism or Marxism has a fundamental belief in the existence of classes and class struggles in every society, the CPP leadership denied that classes existed in Ghana. Indeed, Marxism holds that class struggle is the motor of history, so that without class struggle there is no history. Marxism does not deny that citizens exist. It emphasizes that, at any particular instance, there is a class structure of citizens and a struggle among the classes. For example, the transition from feudalism to capitalism did not occur by chance but represented a struggle between the landed aristocracy and the bourgeois class. In contemporary society, wage-bargaining, strikes, and absenteeism are reflections of class struggles occurring primarily at the economic level, while reforms of trade union law, maintenance of the welfare state, and the formulations of economic policies are reflections of struggles at the political level.

Despite these strong socialist views about human society, J.H. Mensah, a member of the CPP and chairman of the Economic Planning Commission, maintained, for example, that Ghana had no classes, but only citizens. He argued that in the absence of classes and hence of class conflict, Ghana had no need for a socialist party to mobilize the poor peasants and landless labourers in any process of transformation of the countryside. He stated: "We are using the chiefs and other leaders of village society in laudable programmes of community development. Our political theory should not be based on the assumption that the chiefly class is an antagonistic class."[9] Mensah was right to some extent in his argument. The extended family ties are so strong in Ghanaian society that class consciousness has been negligible. But if, as he said, Ghana had no need for a socialist party, then what need was there for socialism in the first place? And why was the CPP necessary as an agent of socialist development?

The CPP leadership argued that the reorganization of the means of production, which is a central issue in socialism, was not a central issue in the developing countries as a whole, for "by and large the means of production do not exist."[10] According to the CPP, the central problem to be addressed was, rather, the building up of the nation's stock of productive assets. Again, in the assumed absence of the means of production, was socialism necessary? But in any case, certainly the accumulation of productive assets is not purely a socialist project. After all, it occurred even under feudalism, as well as under the empires of Egypt and Rome. Not only that, but to some extent the accumulation of productive assets also took place in the pre-colonial African empires of Ghana, Mali, Songhai, and Zimbabwe. It also took place under capitalism. Considering that Marxism teaches that the socialist revolution is preceded in history by the capitalist stage of development, the accumulation of productive assets in itself is not socialism per se, and the initial stages of the accumulation process from which even primitive societies are not excluded may be far from the point of initiation of any socialist revolution.

The CPP also assumed that mere state ownership of some portion of the productive assets of a nation meant socialism, and that competition between the state and private capital might enhance efficiency of allocation. For example, citing the guide to the implementation of the Seven Year Development Plan (launched after the termination of the Five Year Development Plan), Mensah stated, "This should not be done by hindering the growth of the private sector. Private enterprise will not be killed; it will be surpassed."[11] The statement presupposed the possibility of a harmonious competition between the state sector and the private sector, and a state sector that was capable of surpassing the private sector in the accumulation of capital. The ruling elite paid little attention to the possibility of the private sector resorting to dirty tactics, such as destructive competition involving price wars, to drive the state sector out of the competition. Furthermore, the accumulation of a nation's stock of capital through the joint efforts of state enterprises and private capital is what a mixed economy is all about and, again, does not necessarily constitute socialism.

Indeed, if state ownership of production side by side with private capital alone did constitute socialism, then the small European states with considerable public ownership of industrial enterprises, and all other countries with mixed economies, including the United States and the United Kingdom, might have all qualified, at one time or another, to be called socialist countries. The CPP architects of socialism did not understand that a socialist mode of production and a capitalist mode of production do not function in the same way. Marxism holds that every mode of production comprises the forces of production and the relations of production. It is the different characteristics of the *forces* of production and the *relations* of production that differentiate one mode of production from the other. The instruments of production (tools, capital, land) constitute one force; the organization of direct producers constitutes another force; and the two together constitute the forces of production. A system of relationships exists between the direct producers, the non-producers, the instruments of the production process, and the product, and that system is what constitutes the relations of production. Although the instruments of production in the capitalist mode of production may be the same as those in the socialist mode of production, the relations of production and the organization of the direct producers may not be the same. In a capitalist mode of production, private capitalists own the instruments of production, and direct producers are alienated from the products of their labour. In a socialist economy the state owns the instruments of production, and direct producers are not alienated from the products of their labour because those products belong to the state and are socially owned. According to Marxism, in a capitalist mode of production the state sector primarily serves the interests of capital, but in a socialist economy the state sector serves the interests of the people as a whole. The CPP apostles of socialism did not understand the socialist conception of the role of the state under the two different modes of production and thus could not appreciate the difference between the mixed economy of the advanced capitalist states and the socialist economies.

The CPP demonstrated its misconception of socialism further by assuming that the monopoly and finance capitalists of the West were setting out as good Samaritans to create capitalists, and thus competition for themselves, in developing countries. But, even more disappointing, the CPP apostles of socialism closed their minds to the realities of the ongoing ideology-based Cold War between the East and West and trusted that the same foreign private capital that was so ideologically opposed to the socialist development path might be exceptionally willing to co-operate in the establishment of socialism in Ghana. Armed with this misconception, the CPP government assigned a major role to foreign private capital in its socialist Seven Year Development Plan. Because of its conceptualization of a combination of mixed economy and African communalism as socialism, the CPP did not perceive any fundamental contradictions in its development policy, and did not suspect foreign private capital of any conflict of interest, or of any hidden agenda to sabotage the development plan. Thus, the government expected that over 40 per cent of a proposed state expenditure of £1,000 million would come from foreign private sources—all for the realization of a socialist plan of development.[12]

What the CPP saw as socialism was, in reality, a type of mixed economy in which the state would compete with private capital in the capital accumulation process and the state would expand or provide the necessary infrastructure, such as transportation, to the benefit of both sectors. By calling this type of mixed economy socialism, the CPP created unnecessary enemies for itself. It provided the opportunity for the government's genuine nationalist efforts to be misinterpreted and opposed on ideological grounds. In the ensuing ideological conflict, both sides of the political elite—the government on the one hand and the opposition (which had merged into the United Party after independence) on the other—failed to realize that the central issue was the ultimate economic and social well-being and growth of Ghana, and that no Western theory of development, be it socialism or liberal democracy, was perfectly suitable to the newly independent country.

Military Rule as a Transplantation of Alien Ideology

Meanwhile, a number of Western intellectuals—Lucien Pye, Morris Janowitz, and S.E. Finer, for instance—were expounding the virtues of military rule as a means of achieving the prerequisites for implementing development.[13] In *The Man on Horseback* Finer went as far as describing how to organize a successful coup—how it might be planned, organized, and executed. Without much serious consideration to the new ideology of military rule, some of the military elite in Sub-Saharan Africa became converts to that way of thinking. In 1966, while Nkrumah was out of the country visiting China, he was deposed in a coup led by General Joseph Ankrah. Since then coups and counter-coups—and attempted coups—have been rampant.

This new military rule was as alien to the indigenous political culture as what had gone before. Indeed, the government of the National Liberation Council (NLC), which replaced the Nkrumah government, also failed to achieve the political prerequisites for successful economic development. How could it, given a military government that was a misfit in the environment, and confused to the extent of acting irrationally to the detriment of the nation? Serious divisions within the military, among the coup leaders, led to a pattern of martial-organizations-gone-crazy. Indeed, the Ghanaian elite was so divided, and the notion of enemy so strong, that the few projects started by the Nkrumah regime and vital to Ghana's economic development were abandoned.[14]

The Post-Colonial Experience

The first NLC military government was succeeded by others: the National Redemption Council (NRC), Supreme Military Council (SMC), Armed Forces Revolutionary Council (AFRC), Limann's regime, and the Provisional National Defence Council (PNDC). Not surprisingly, none of these attempts were able to establish the preconditions for successful economic development. Successively, they deepened the economic crisis.

The NLC regime proved to be inadequate. It exposed itself as a stooge of imperialism. Diplomatic relations with Britain—broken during the latter part of Nkrumah's rule in compliance with a recommendation of the Organization of African Unity (OAU)—were restored almost immediately and the link with the British Commonwealth was simultaneously affirmed. In so doing, the NLC demonstrated its preference for the colonial rule of the British to Ghanaian self-rule under Nkrumah and association with the British Commonwealth to the African nationalism and unity championed by Nkrumah. The name of Nkrumah became synonymous with the notion of "enemy," to the extent that any praise or achievement associated with his name or regime became an abomination.

The Ghanaian political elite as a whole failed to realize that the coup was itself alien to the Ghanaian political culture and could set a precedence for removing governments through the barrel of a gun. It failed to realize that military intervention reflects only a shift in the internal balance of political forces and that while it may determine temporarily who might rule, it cannot change the character of society or provide an effective substitute for a consensual culture.

Instead of concentrating on solving the economic problems of the country, the coup leaders were busy promoting their own interests, thereby casting doubts on the sincerity of the motivations that had precipitated the coup. As a consequence the military coalition began to disintegrate. A bloody abortive coup took place on April 17, 1967, and serious cracks within the regime's leadership led to the forced resignation of General Ankrah, the chairman of the NLC, on April 2, 1969. Compelled by the growing cracks within its ranks and the high incidence of worker and student protest, the NLC handed over power to a civilian government.

The following period of partisan and electoral politics divided the country dangerously on ethnic grounds. The Progress Party (PP), led by Kofi Abrefa Busia, won the elections of 1969, and its majority in Parliament became a licence to flout constitutional provisions. It formed a government with a cabinet that included no members of the Ewe ethnic group, because all the Ewe members of Parliament belonged to the National Alliance of Liberals (NAL), a party in opposition. The Ewes, alienated from power, longed for the day when the PP government of Kofi Abrefa Busia would fall.

Wanting to fulfil the promises that had contributed to its election success, the PP introduced an unwise general open licence for imports, which weakened Ghana's already precarious balance of payments position. As the economic situation worsened, Busia (who had promised more jobs for his supporters) began to blame the situation on the aliens in the country, and on November 18, 1969, using the Alien Compliance Order (ACO), the government ordered the expulsion of all aliens without resident permits. Most of the so-called aliens were not aliens at all in the legal sense. Most were fellow Africans born and bred in Ghana but who had retained their ethnic identities as a convenient means of association. Many were hardworking illiterates who had no idea about resident permits and had never been requested to obtain any even during colonial days.

What the Busia government did not take into account was that the supposed aliens formed a large part of the productive farming population of Ghana. They provided the required labour as well as managed the farms for the Ghanaian communal land-owners who were traditionally satisfied with reaping two-thirds of the farm produce. The actual experience and knowledge of the technology of farming were in their hands. Their departure, therefore, left a vacuum that was difficult to fill. The quantity as well as the quality of Ghana's cocoa production, which constituted the backbone of the economy, dropped and the ACO became a curse rather than a blessing to the nation's economy. With the economy growing worse, the Busia government diverted attention to another scapegoat, the civil service. In a dictatorial manner, elements of the civil service considered not in tune with the PP government were targeted for purging without due consideration to the provisions of the Constitution. In February 1970, 568 civil servants lost their jobs. When these dismissals were successfully challenged in court, the Busia government refused to respect the court's decision.

Meanwhile, the government continued to dispose of the state corporations and to flout another section of the Constitution that required members of Parliament to declare their assets. Suspicions about the intentions of the PP government ran high, and its popularity began to wane. It became obvious that the Busia government had failed to forge a strong and united coalition. In April 1971 the National Union of Ghana Students (NUGS), which had been supportive of the Busia government, distanced itself from the PP policies by openly demanding wholesale nationalization of businesses and amnesty for all political exiles. In July, without prior consultations, the government embarked upon implementing austerity measures recommended by the IMF in which essential public services and employee benefits were cut, taxes were raised, and the cedi was devalued by 43.9 per cent. To curb reaction to its unpopular policies, the government proceeded to dissolve the Trade Union Congress.

The military government of the National Redemption Council (NRC), which replaced the Busia regime after a coup in January 1972, started well with an appeal to Ghanaians for self-reliance and a stress on returning the economy to health. Its leader, General Kutu Acheampong, belonged to a group of CPP activists in the Ashanti region who were radically opposed to the NLM during the Nkrumah days and had never liked Busia. Acheampong's allies were a group of Ewe officers who supported NAL, did not like the CPP of the Nkrumah era, and resented the alienation of the Ewe from the Busia government.

The overthrow of the Busia regime introduced an arena of struggle between the Busia and the non-Busia forces in the political arena in which the non-Busia forces were themselves divided between those who wanted the erstwhile CPP government to be returned to power and those, mainly Ewes, who did not. Barely two days after the announcement of the coup, General Kwesi Afrifa, an ardent supporter of the Busia government, was arrested for plotting against the new government. A series of countercoup attempts followed, indicating the severity of the disunity within the political elite in general and the military elite in particular. Under the threat of coups the National Redemption Council government was compelled to act on the economic front to reduce tension as well as legitimize its position. Because the devaluation of the cedi was one of the reasons advanced to rationalize the coup against Busia, on February 4, 1972, the regime revalued the cedi by 42 per cent, but this did not stop the coup attempts. On July 16, 1972, the government announced the foiling of another coup by the Busia forces. On August 31, 1973 came a coup plot involving Kojo Botsio, a former minister in the Nkrumah government. In December another plot by CPP supporters was uncovered.

On the economic front the Acheampong government introduced an Operation Feed Yourself (OFY) policy, aimed at transforming Ghana into a country that was self-sufficient in food production and eliminating the high import bills on food. Food imports were immediately stopped, mechanized agriculture was encouraged, and the cedi was overvalued to encourage the heavy importation of agricultural machinery, equipment, and inputs. The NRC also made a hasty decision to repudiate foreign debts, leading to an irretrievable loss of confidence in Ghana by foreign governments and investors. Subsequent divisions within the military led to a palace coup on October 9, 1975, in which, although General Acheampong retained his position as the head of state, the name of the ruling body changed to Supreme Military Council (SMC) and the NRC was relegated to a lower status.

Concerned about the centrifugal political forces threatening to break up the nation, Acheampong embarked upon a Union Government (UG) idea—essentially a reincarnation of the consensual culture in which political parties did not exist. But by 1978, as historian Mike Mason sums it up, "Acheampong was himself thrown off, to be succeeded by another general, Frederick Akuffo, who lasted only a year before he, in turn, lost his grip on power. By this time the economy of Ghana was in a 'catastrophic' state."[15] Elections held in 1979 were won by Hilla Limann, but before the new SMC government could hand over power to Limann it was overthrown through a mutiny in the armed forces by junior officers led by Flight-Lieutenant Jerry Rawlings—with both General Acheampong and General Akuffo and several senior officers executed by firing squad. The junior officers formed an Armed Forces Revolutionary Council (AFRC), with Rawlings as the head of state, but serious divisions among their ranks compelled them to hand over power to Limann within a few months. Limann, though, had not completed even half his term before he was overthrown in 1981, in another military coup led by Rawlings.

The military government of the Provisional National Defence Council (PNDC), with Rawlings as chair, suspended the constitution, dissolved parliament, and banned political parties. It experienced many challenges to its authority. The middle class, including lawyers, professionals, and religious groups, denounced the Rawlings revolution. Several unsuccessful attempts were made to overthrow the government, to which the PNDC responded with ruthless force and the summary executions of suspects. One foreign writer commented on the situation at the time: "By the early 1980s, it was apparent that Ghana had forfeited its ability to maintain external or internal order and to hold sway over its population.... The Ghanaian state thus seemed to be on the brink of becoming less relevant."[16]

The Rawlings camp itself became divided. Certain elites whom Rawlings labelled as leftists at least partly to gain sympathy and financial and economic support from the Western world were arrested, sacked from the government, or harassed into exile. In November 1982, after another unsuccessful attempt to overthrow his government, the terrified Rawlings voluntarily sought refuge in the arms of the IMF and the World Bank. In 1983, under the veil of structural adjustment, the sovereignty of the country was surrendered practically to the IMF and World Bank and placed virtually under IMF dictatorship and direction.[17] Ghana embarked upon an economic recovery program (ERP) with no serious debt burden, but under the banner and tutelage of the IMF and World Bank it developed a serious debt, which between 1987 and 1993 grew about half a billion dollars per annum. In 1983 the national debt stood at about $1.7 billion and 45 per cent of GNP, and the debt-servicing ratio was about 10 per cent of export earnings. By 1993 the external debt was about 66 per cent of GNP, and the debt servicing ratio was about 23 per cent of export earnings despite grants, excessive borrowing to service the loan, and a generous write-off of some of the debt in return for the country's obedience to IMF and World Bank dictatorship.

In 1992 the PNDC held presidential elections for a transition to Western democracy. Most enlightened Ghanaians and the opposition parties objected to the proceedings, while Western observers claimed they were free and fair. One candidate, General Emmanuel K. Erskine, for example, was reported to have received no vote at all although he indicated that he had at least voted for himself and was very sure that his sons and daughters voted for him. When confronted with the evidence that his signature appeared on three different ballot papers, President Rawlings offered his apologies. Obviously, in the Ghanaian political arena, even after the Cold War, it was not who voted that mattered, but who controlled the ballot box and announced the results of the vote. Not surprisingly, the opposition parties boycotted the subsequent parliamentary elections. As a result only parties sponsored by the crafty Rawlings participated in the elections, and the resulting Parliament was virtually without an opposition. The government's accountability was compromised and corruption became endemic.

Rawlings, who had military officers and civilians executed or jailed for alleged corruption, was head of a government with a level of corruption unprecedented in Ghanaian history. Colonel Osei Owusu, the minister for the interior, and P.V. Obeng, the virtual prime minister, were found to be fabulously rich by international standards. The government found itself unable to account for an amount of U.S.$128 million, and when the finance minister, Kwesi Botchway, put pressure on a group of suspects, including Tsatsu Tsikata, to account for the whereabouts of the amount, a lack of support from Rawlings compelled him to resign. In another incident, Nigerian crooks posing as representatives of a non-existent Nigerian company came to the government with plans for an electricity-generating plant that would supplement the hydroelectric power from the Volta dam. They succeeded in duping the Rawlings government of U.S.$78 million without clearing even one square inch of project space.

A second round of parliamentary and presidential elections took place in 1996, with P.V. Obeng and others tactically dropped from the cabinet at the last minute to appease the public. The election results showed the opposition parties winning no seats in the Volta region (the Ewe region of the country), the home (it is claimed) of Rawlings's mother.[18] If the election results were really correct, then, it cannot be denied that partisan politics serves to divide and polarize Ghanaians along ethnic lines. The election results also showed that the Volta region, with a population adding up to 10 per cent of the total population, had almost the same total number of votes as the Ashanti region, with 45 per cent of the total population. Amid suspicions of rigging, the electoral commissioner (appointed by Rawlings) declared Rawlings the winner.

The behaviour of Rawlings and his wife after the elections was typical of the crazed mode of politics that had so firmly taken hold. One newspaper report about Nana Konadu (Rawlings's wife) shows the deep roots of the notion of enemy for a person belonging to another party:

> Speaking at the festival which was captured by GTV cameramen, Konadu commented on the people's appeal to the government for development projects and remarked, "You want development. But you did not vote for us. You see, the left hand washes the right and vice versa." Shorn of all its idiomatic colouration, The Ghanaian Chronicle believes Nana Konadu was telling the nation that constituencies which voted against the NDC should not expect any government projects.
>
> In other words, this would be their punishment for rejecting the NDC at the polls. Besides, it was also a veiled warning that they should not expect any government projects should they continue to vote against the party.... The Ghanaian Chronicle posits that Nana Konadu's statement has the support of her husband, who is the President of Ghana and leader of the NDC and it reflects the psychology of the men and women who hold the reins of power in

Ghana today. These are the people who came to power on the wings of accountability but refused to be accountable. They burst on the political scene preaching modesty but are now engaged in ostentation and conspicuous consumption. They rapped the wealthy whose children were educated abroad yet with their scanty salaries have their children in expensive universities abroad.[19]

Despite his own and his party's open lack of political discipline, disrespect for the provisions of the constitution, and confused politics, Rawlings hypocritically urged Ghanaians to desist from acts of indiscipline. In apparent frustration, Anthony Obeng-Sarfo, a concerned Ghanaian nationalist, wrote in *The Ghanaian Chronicle* in February 1998:

> The President, Flt. Lt. J. J. Rawlings, has urged Ghanaians to desist from indiscipline and lead decent lives. One will ask, what is the guarantee that the President himself who behaves like a chameleon has turned over a new leaf? The President organized junior ranking soldiers to overthrow his counterpart in 1979, is that not indiscipline? The President again organized military men to overthrow a democratically elected government in 1981; is that also not indiscipline? The President allows his daughter, Ezenator, to fly an airplane without licence. Is that not indiscipline? The President allegedly beat his Vice, Mr. Arkaah, at a Cabinet meeting and he has the guts to accuse others of indiscipline? The President continues to celebrate 31st December which the Supreme Court, the highest court of the land, has ruled not to be celebrated. Is that not indiscipline? President Rawlings rejected the Commission of Human Rights and Administrative Justice (CHRAJ's) findings on his ministers when evidence showed clearly that they had acquired property illegally. He brought the White Paper to shield them. Is he not harbouring corruption? Is that not indiscipline? The President executed three former Heads of State without a fair trial. Is that not indiscipline? The President has practised indiscipline for the past 17 years and now with less than three years to the end of his tenure of office he is now making rhetoric on discipline. Indiscipline indeed.

Obeng-Sarfo was not alone in his frustrations about the misuse of power by a government that came to power through partisan politics. In the consensual democratic process of Ghana, no one has the chance to flout consensual decisions. Under partisan politics, with a comfortable majority and party discipline, Rawlings was able to place himself above the law.

In the 1990s the economic crisis continued to deepen, with escalating inflation. Before the surrender to the IMF and World Bank in 1983, the exchange rate was 3.5 cedis to the U.S. dollar. By the mid- to late 1990s it was over 2,300 cedis to the U.S. dollar, with the cedi still falling. High commodity prices and high levels of unemployment and underemployment explain why most Ghanaians became frustrated, considered structural adjustment a curse rather than a blessing, and suspected the surrogate colonization of their country by the IMF and World Bank on behalf of the whole configuration of Western interests.

The case of Ghana serves, once again, as a pointer that the political conditions for successful economic development cannot be achieved through the full transplantation of alien ideologies and political culture in the form of liberal democracy, socialism, or military rule. As contingency theory advised long ago, there is no best organization for the realization of human objectives. What matters is the fit between the agents, the technology that the agents employ, and the environment in which these agents operate.

CHAPTER SEVEN

NIGERIA: OIL, COUPS, AND ETHNIC WAR

Nigeria, the most populous country in Africa, was the second country in Sub-Saharan Africa to attain independence. Comprising more than 250 ethnic groups, it has a full history of the same African consensual culture. During British colonial rule and also at the time of independence, the ideological symbols of unity were not transferred from the ethnic level to the national level to enable the building of the country as one nation recognizing one Nigerian language with different dialects and with a subsequent delegation of authority to lower levels of administration in order to maintain a balance between centralization and decentralization. The consequence is a nation-state centrifugally divided along ethnic and religious lines. Although the practice of indirect rule through chiefs enabled the British to rule Nigeria as a unitary political system, independence was granted under a federal constitution that allowed only the three largest ethnic groups to each control a region: the Hausa-Fulani, in Northern Nigeria, the Igbo, in Eastern Nigeria, and the Yoruba, in Western Nigeria.

Nigeria's large population (over 107 million in 1997) affords it a relative market advantage compared to other countries in the region, but it also has other advantages: a large natural resource base, which includes petroleum and iron deposits, a high level of education of its elite, and its ethnic diversity. It was in Nigeria that the idea of indirect rule was born and first implemented under Lord Lugard. At the time of independence, in 1960, Nigeria was self-sufficient in food and, indeed, a net exporter of food to other countries in the region. While most African countries were considered not ready for industrialization because of their small internal markets, Nigeria was an exception. Its iron-ore base presented a favourable opportunity for industrialization, and the post-independence discovery of oil provided it with additional wealth. Nigeria was not among the countries that suffered greatly from the oil-pricing and monetary shocks of the 1970s and 1980s, although it did not completely escape unscathed.

The oil endowment was a source of inspiration to the rest of West Africa, where it seemed that Nigeria's success might provide forward and backward linkages to their own economies and bring trickle-down effects to the entire region. Indeed, it seemed that Nigeria's success might have become a source of pride to the whole of Sub-Saharan Africa. The post-independence experience, however, brought quite different results. The Nigerian elite proved unable to create an encompassing and committed coalition to pursue nationalist and coherent policies or to contain the stresses and strains of the development path. Nigeria was to be plagued with coups, and it went through a bitter civil war popularly known as the Biafran War. Despite its oil revenues, Nigeria fell into the trap of an external debt that had climbed to over U.S.$30 billion by the mid-1990s—and was continuing to grow. The country is, then, yet another critical case in our unearthing of the root causes of Sub-Saharan Africa's severe politico-economic problems.

The Colonial Legacy and Partisan Politics in Ethnic Garb

Nigeria's ethnic diversity, which might have been translated into a motivation for productive self-help projects and suggested the potential for a decentralizing of development activities, instead became a problem when coupled to partisan politics. Nigeria could, for instance, have gone in the direction of China, with its population of hundreds of millions. China has promoted the Beijing dialect known as Mandarin Chinese as the national written and spoken language—despite the existence of a great variety of other spoken Chinese dialects. Nigeria, with a population of less than a hundred million, could also have become one nation speaking different dialects of the same Nigerian language. The Nigerian leaders failed to take up this possibility.

The indirect-rule politics of the colonial era served to perpetuate and deepen ethnic sensitivities.[1] In addition, colonial economic policies had left Nigeria badly divided, endowing the south (Eastern and Western Nigeria) with a relatively well-educated population and the potential for diversified economic development, while limiting the predominantly Islamic North to the trappings of poverty. The British preparation of the colonies for independence involved the formation of political parties and political campaigns, and the political elite's appeals to ethnic ties and traditions in their efforts to gather political support accentuated ethnic sensitivities. Again, a party's political opposition became the *enemy*, making the Nigerian political scene an arena of intense and bitter conflict. The pre-independence elections were characterized by violence, and the parliamentary opposition in the Nigerian Parliament became the enemy rather than the legitimate adversaries of the ruling government.

At the time of independence the federal structure created its own ethnic problems, which were only accentuated by partisan politics. The country was originally divided into four states (later thirty states), with a two-chamber parliament established on the British model. The electoral system was also based on the British first-past-the-post model, in which only the majority winner in a particular district entered Parliament no matter how close the competition. The Hausa-Fulani, the Igbo, and the Yoruba held regional hegemony over substantial numbers of ethnic minorities. Furthermore, because of limited federal constitutional powers, the central government's political elites owed loyalties to their respective regional governors. Indeed, the 1960 federal structure almost seems to have been a neo-colonial ploy to keep the government of Nigeria weak enough to be dominated from outside. As in Ghana, the governments that emerged in Nigeria were wildly confused administrations that followed irrational paths, as well as divisive military regimes practising a detrimental politics. Unlike Ghana, Nigeria did not attempt to introduce socialism.

Demands for consociational political arrangements at the federal level arose after independence under pressure from Northern politicians who sought to bridge the inequities between the North and the South. The Northern politicians were encouraged by their region's population advantage to pursue the consociational arrangements of proportional representation, but the attempts were blocked by Southern politicians who feared domination by the North. Northern politicians turned to the idea of forging a strong federal coalition to govern the entire nation, calculating that this coalition would be dominated by the Northern-based Nigerian People's Congress (NPC), a Hausa-Fulani alliance. The proposed arrangement, which granted considerable autonomy to each region, received the support of Nnamdi Azikiwe's National Congress of Nigerian Citizens (NCNC), with its base among the Igbo in Eastern Nigeria, but was strongly resisted by Chief Obafemi Awolowo's Action Group (AG), a Yoruba-based party that dominated Western Nigeria at the time. Although the dream of a grand coalition within a unitary political system did not materialize, the efforts of the Northern politicians yielded the fruit of a powerful coalition between the NPC and the NCNC to challenge the influence of the AG at both the federal and regional levels.

Cracks began to emerge within the AG, which led to legislative defeats at the regional level, and with the creation of a new Midwest region the AG lost almost a third of its territory and hence a third of its former support base in the West. Despite these political developments, ethnic sensitivities arising from partisan politics became increasingly sharpened. In 1963, when the census results were announced to the effect that Northern Nigeria constituted 54 per cent of the population, Eastern and Western Nigeria refused to accept the results because the figures would have led to the allocation of more parliamentary seats to the North in the federal government. The cracks in the AG continued to develop, and a splinter party, the Nigerian National Democratic Party (NNDP) led by Chief Samuel Akintola, emerged and tactically aligned itself with the NPC. In 1964 political tension in Western Nigeria culmi-nated in the suspension of the Western Nigeria Legislature, the jailing of the minority opposition leader, Chief Obafemi Awolowo, and the appointment of a caretaker government in Western Nigeria headed by Akintola, Awolowo's arch rival.

Meanwhile, the invocation of ethnic symbols in partisan politics at the regional levels resulted in the intensification of the reaction of ethnic minorities against the domination of the Igbo in the East through the NCNC and against the domination of the Hausa-Fulani alliance in the North through the NPC. Moreover, Southern politicians from the East and West regions saw attempts by the Northern-dominated federal gov-ernment to introduce programs aimed at rectifying past inequities as unacceptable approaches by the enemies from the North to enhance their domination of the country. This behaviour is not surprising given an electoral system that was alien to the indigenous system of represen-tation at the traditional councils, served to make the losers feel alienat-ed, and increased political tensions.

The Advent of Military Rule in Ethnic Boots

Nigeria became an arena of misbegotten politics, and as this confused behaviour continued at all levels of government, the preaching by Western intellectuals of the ideology of the military as a nationalist force and an appropriate ruling organization for developing countries sank deeper and deeper into the minds of some military officers in Nigeria. In October 1965, after widespread irregularities were witnessed in regional elections in the West, the victorious NNDP government of Chief Akintola was suspected of having rigged the elections. The resulting political tensions, aggravated by the alienating winner-take-all character of the partisan electoral process, led to a breakdown of law and order in Western Nigeria. Because the NNDP was only the junior partner in the federal coalition, and because the federal government did very little to bring the crisis under control, the central government became discredited. Meanwhile the crime rate and political corruption were both on the ascendancy, and most Nigerians understandably turned their attentions to matters of personal security. In January 1966 the Nigerian government was overthrown by a group of military officers with nationalist ambitions and the ideological conviction that the military represented the best possibility for competent rule.

Despite expectations, though, the coup was organized in an unwise and hasty manner that only divided the military itself along ethnic lines and deepened the ethnic sensitivities within the country as a whole. Almost all the conspirators, including Majors C.K. Inzeogwu and E.A. Ifeajuna, who co-ordinated the coup operations, were Igbos. The political leaders assassinated, including the federal prime minister, Sir Abubakar Tafawa Balewa, and the Northern and Western premiers, as well as the military officers killed in the action were all non-Igbos. Major-General Aguiyi Ironsi, the army commander to whom the coupmakers surrendered power voluntarily, was also an Igbo. Moreover, the failure of the Ironsi government to prosecute the coup-makers in accordance with military law, and the subsequent promotion of Igbo officers in the military, accentuated the general suspicion that the coup was not only Igbo-inspired but also geared principally at Igbo domination of both the military and the nation. Despite conspicuous rising ethnic sensitivities in the military, the Ironsi government was content to maintain its great faith in the training and discipline expected of the military hierarchy, and ignored the possibility of a countercoup. In May 1966, without the consent or mandate of the Nigerian people, Ironsi issued decree number 34, intended to scrap the federal structure and return Nigeria to a unitary form of government. Northern Nigerians demonstrated their dissatisfaction by setting off riots in several cities. Ironsi, showing little if any political sensitivity towards the makeup of his own culture and the possibilities of consensual resolution conflict, expected civilians to behave like soldiers who obey commands without hesitation, much less complaining. He also neglected to take another key point into consideration: that in the Nigerian armed forces the officers and men of non-Igbo origin might react adversely to his policies. In July 1966 a group of predominantly Northern officers in co-operation with some Yoruba officers assassinated Ironsi and overthrew his government. Colonel

Yakubu Gowon, a Northern officer, assumed the leadership of the country.

The assassination of Ironsi and the overthrow of his regime did not end the ethnic strife both within and outside the armed forces, because Nigerians continued to think of themselves more as members of a particular ethnic group, as people with different destinies rather than as people belonging to one nation and sharing one destiny. The Igbo officers, of course, did not take the overthrow of the Ironsi regime lightly. Because most of the countercoup leaders were from the North, Igbo officers suspected the motive behind the coup was the North's attempt to dominate both the military and the country based on an advantage in numbers and their particular hatred for the Igbos. In 1967 Colonel Chukwuemeka Odumegwu-Ojukwu, with encouragement from prominent Igbo politicians, including Azikiwe, announced the secession of Eastern Nigeria under the new name of Biafra. Several years of civil war characterized by much destruction followed, with resources on both sides diverted from economic and social needs to support for the war effort. Before the conflict finally ended, in 1970, and Biafra ceased to exist, thousands of Nigerians had lost their lives.

The behaviour of the various military regimes that governed Nigeria over the following decades left much to be desired. In changes to the 1963 constitution, the federal government assumed control over important areas, including education, university administration, petroleum production, and the direction and co-ordination of development plans.[2] Petroleum-generated wealth encouraged concentration of financial power in the hands of the federal government. In the absence of consensual guidance to control federal decisions, excessive import bills drove Nigeria into a debt trap. Between 1969 and 1979, federal outlays increased from about 548 million Naira to about 18 billion Naira, with federal government spending rising from about 60 per cent of total state government spending in 1968/69 to about 87 per cent in 1980/81. The more the federal government spent, the more were the demands placed on it by different ethnic groups for recognition and attention. In the absence of an African consensualism that diffuses tensions and rivalries, the federal government responded to these challenges by means of a structural differentiation, in which the number of states increased from three on the eve of independence to nineteen.

Before the development of the oil industry began in the 1960s, Nigeria was an agricultural country that was not only self-sufficient in food production but also a net food exporter to West Africa. The military government's economic policies, geared principally towards the balancing of internal political forces, turned the internal terms of trade against agriculture and encouraged food importation. After excessive borrowing to finance ambitious projects, Nigeria became a net food importer, with an economy dependent mainly on oil revenue. Once the oil boom of the 1970s was over and oil prices plummeted, Nigeria found itself saddled with a debt burden, with a balance of payments problem putting great strain on its oil revenues and undermining growth. With their slice of the national cake shrinking, the military officers involved in politics turned to corrupt practices, attempting to enrich themselves before handing over power to a civilian government. But divisions within the military arising from these practices and bitterness surrounding the apparent affluence and corruption of fellow officers in political appointments led to the 1975 overthrow of the Gowon regime by General Murtala Mohammed, who was later assassinated by an officer sympathetic to Gowon. In short, like their Ghanaian counterparts, the Nigerian generals and colonels confirmed that the military is not necessarily the most disciplined, nationalist, and appropriate organization to rule a country.

The Second Coming of Partisan Politics

After thirteen years of military rule, civilian rule resumed in 1979 under Shehu Shagari in a second republic, but Nigerians remained divided on ethnic and sub-ethnic lines. The new administration reintroduced partisan politics with its attendant incompatibilities and tendencies to divide Nigerians. Like the first republic (1963-66), the resulting government followed a confused and irrational trail of policy. To arrest the centrifugal forces of ethnic origin, the constitution of the second republic mandated the president to appoint at least one cabinet minister from each of the nineteen states. However, the stresses and strains of the incompatible partisan politics prevented the emergence of consensual arrangements.[3] Furthermore, political tolerance and coalition-building were undermined by the formation of the Progressive Parties Alliance, which had the main purpose of unseating Shagari despite a keen rivalry among its leaders, Awolowo, Azikiwe, and Wazari.[4] Complicating this political intolerance was the existence of a group of bureaucrats, politicians, and businessmen who had amassed wealth during the oil boom and were united in preserving their collective interest through organized electoral misconduct and violence.[5] Given these prejudices and the priorities of preserving interests, partisan politics in Nigeria only became more vindictive and violent.

Aware of the potential harm that centrifugal forces could play in Nigerian politics, the constitutional architects ensured that the constitution of the second republic injected consociational elements in the federal political affairs and administrative machine by stating: "The composition of the Government of the Federation or any of its agencies and the conduct of its affairs shall be carried out in such a manner as to reflect the federal character of Nigeria ... ensuring that there shall be no predominance of persons from a few ethnic or other sectional groups."[6] Pressure to enforce this consociational provision in the arena of partisan politics created unforeseen problems. In response to criticisms in the federal legislature that appointments in the federal ministries and state corporations had favoured the Yoruba ethnic group, Shagari embarked upon a process of dismissing key Yoruba civil servants, which turned the Yoruba against his government.[7] The consociational provision of the constitution suggested that the combination of consociational principles and partisan politics was itself not well understood. The constitution did not provide for proportional representation based on the predominant and sensitive ethnic and religious issues.[8] If representation had been properly and adequately mapped, and some attempt had been made to transfer the ideological symbols of unity from all ethnic levels to the regions and from the regions to centre, followed by an appropriate decentralization to ensure that centralized power was balanced by decentralized power, the proper intrastate, ethnic, religious, and professional structures might have been constructed.

Consociational resource allocation also became a severe headache because the constitution did not specify responsibility for that area of activity. The Nigerian political parties outside the federal coalition realized that if the federal government were to use its discretion to allocate resources directly, then the parties forming the federal coalition could manipulate the allocation to their political advantage. Legislators from the more populous regions perceived that the equal allocation of resources to the states would be unfair per head. The petroleum-producing states demanded a larger share of the national cake, because their regions provided the greater proportion of federal revenue and were disproportionately polluted in the process.

A problem of representation and rule-bending occurred in the elections of 1983, when the Nigeria Advance Party (NAP) was approved to participate in the elections despite its disqualification under the constitutional provisions. The NAP drew its support from anti-Awolowo Yoruba groups, which implied a potential ally of the ruling National Party of Nigeria (NPN) government, and so the NPN was accused of using its office to meddle in electoral affairs, with the hidden agenda of tactically drawing votes away from Awolowo's Unity Party of Nigeria (UPN). Later it was also revealed that administrative secretary of the Federal Electoral Commission (FEDECO) had revised the 1979 voters list in his home district from 48,216 to 214,500 in preparation for the 1983 elections. All of this suggested a partisan manipulation of electoral politics. Other irregularities reported included the registration of under-age children in the state of Borno, pre-stuffed ballot boxes in the states of Plateau and Niger, the bribing of police and polling officials, and the hiring of thugs to keep people away from voting booths.[9] Furthermore, the elections were so characterized by acts of carnage and destruction of property that when Shagari was declared a landslide winner very few onlookers gave the elections any credibility. In an interview with *West Africa* magazine, Awolowo reportedly said, "It is the first time that elections have been won in such a massive manner and nobody rejoices."[10] As in Ghana, elections results in Nigeria depended not so much on who voted appropriately, but on who controlled registration, the ballot box, counted the votes, and announced the election results.

Partisan politics undermined other provisions of the federal constitution. The constitution provided for the establishment of independent legislatures for each of the nineteen states, which were also each given complete control over education, infrastructure development, health, housing, chieftaincy affairs, and operating budgets. But to win political support, state governors and state legislatures co-operated to suspend the collection of local taxes and shift funding responsibility to the federal level. Meanwhile, heavy expenditures at the federal level coupled with mismanagement of foreign loans and an attendant rise in foreign debts and debt-servicing obligations meant the shrinking of federal transfers to the states. In 1979 the federal budget showed a surplus of N.2.75 billion; in 1982 it had a deficit of N.3 billion. The external debt was N.8.5 billion in 1979; in 1983, it was N.62 billion. At both the federal and the state levels, the politicians were more interested in garnering votes at the next election than in addressing these problems.

It soon became obvious that if the ruling party were to meet the demands of opposition parties at the state level, however just, it would only be ensuring those parties of votes at the next election. Under the circumstances, the Shagari government's interest lay in bypassing the politicians of opposing parties by directly funding public welfare projects. That way the efforts of the NPN would be conspicuous and appreciated by the local people and thus attract their votes. But for partisan reasons the state governors of the opposition states attempted to frustrate the efforts of the federal government—not because the federal projects were not needed by their constituencies, but because of their fears that Shagari's party would become popular enough in the states to attract votes during the federal elections. Their tactics included delaying and withholding co-operation in the implementation of the projects, with the view of discrediting the promises of the federal government. In Oyo state, this kind of partisan sensitivity encouraged the UPN governor, Bala Ige, to go so far as ordering the demolition of two housing projects with the excuse that his office had not authorized the use of the land. Similarly, the NPP (Nigerian People's Party) governor of Anambra state, Jim Nwobodo, halted a road construction plan on the grounds of improper use of funds earmarked for the state government. In Bendel state, the UPN governor Abrose took the federal government to court for undertaking projects and services that constituted an encroachment upon state powers guaranteed under the federal constitution.[11] When the Shagari government responded by appointing presidential liaison officers in each state capital, the opposition governors became more offended.

Meanwhile, ethnic sensitivities were putting pressure for the creation of more states as provided in the constitution of the Second Republic, and to an extent that implied an ultimate conversion of all the 450 federal electoral districts into states. Because the constitution gave state legislatures the power to create new local government constituencies, or to dissolve councils created by the military government as well as supervise local council elections, state governments were habitually encouraged to use these provisions as channels for building political support. Between 1979 and 1983 the number of local government areas rose from 301 to 850.[12] As the struggle for political support continued, Shagari's NPN thought it politically wise in May 1982 to win political support in the Igbo area by granting amnesty to the former Biafran leader, Odumegwu-Ojukwu, to make him a member of the NPN, and to adopt a conciliatory attitude towards former Biafran civil servants. This political manoeuvre and a noted preference for the police were resented by the armed forces. When in the midst of economic difficulties the general elections of 1983 were characterized by dishonest practices, the military staged a coup to remove Shehu Shagari from office.

The Second and Third Coming of Military Rule

Major General Muhammad Buhari assumed power, applying policies that were biased towards the Northern states and both incited ethnic tension and disrupted unity within the armed forces. Buhari embarked upon austerity measures, taking tight fiscal control and introducing cutbacks in most sectors of the economy, including the military and excepting only agriculture. To enable them to withstand the resulting stresses and strains, these kinds of austerity measures require an encompassing and committed nationalist coalition that enjoys the support of all sections of society. The Nigerian military did not represent that kind of coalition, nor could civilian governments based on partisan politics. Strangely enough, Buhari did not attempt any reduction in the debt-service burden, which stood at 44 per cent of export earnings. The cutback in defence spending antagonized Major-General Ibrahim Babangida, the military chief of staff, who also saw Buhari's refusal to reduce the debt-service burden as anti-nationalist. In August 1985 Babangida overthrew Buhari in a military coup and assumed power.

After several years of military rule, pressures from both inside and outside Nigeria compelled Babangida to hand over power to a civilian government. When the Social Democratic Party (SDP) candidate Moshood Abiola won the presidential elections in May 1993, the military refused to hand over power, suspending the results, alleging fraud. Later Abiola, who had launched a civil disobedience campaign, was jailed for treason. The military elite had clearly decided that Abiola was not the right person to rule Nigeria—which brought into question the whole purpose of partisan democracy in Nigeria. In August, under great pressure, Babangida stepped down, to be replaced by defence minister General Sani Abacha, who held power until his death in June 1998.

Before his sudden death, Abacha had been selected to stand as the only presidential candidate in an election that would presumably return Nigeria to civilian rule. Nigerian groups opposed to military rule legally challenged Abacha's nomination and the legitimacy of the parties that had nominated him, but to no effect. The unprecedented nomination of Abacha as the only presidential candidate by the contesting political parties might be an indication that a new brand of politics was developing in Nigeria—one in which the same party appears under different names to give an impression to the outside world that a multiparty regime rather than a one-party type was in place.[13]

The case of Nigeria confirms, once again, the incompatibility of both Western democratic practice and an imported ideology of military rule with the African political environment. In contravention of the African cultural practice of nation-building, the ideological symbols of unity were not transferred to unite Nigeria into one nation-state and one ethnic society speaking different dialects of the same Nigerian language, followed by a delegation of authority to the lower levels. As a result development was undermined by competing and centrifugal political forces.

CHAPTER EIGHT

KENYA: SETTLER IDEOLOGY AND THE STRUGGLE FOR MAJIMBO

After British rule came to Kenya following the Berlin Conference, the completion of the Ugandan Railway in 1901 provided an opportunity for commodities to be exported through the port of Mombasa. The land was not rich enough in mineral or other natural resources to provide the necessary freight for the railway, but the Kenyan Highlands had the potential for large-scale farming, including an appropriate climate. In pursuit of this economic logic, and given the suitability of the climate for European settlement, the colonial government embarked upon luring European visitors and settlers to Kenya by offering land cheaply to anyone interested in settling to farm there. Among those who were attracted was Lord Delamere, whose enthusiasm encouraged him to sell all he had in England and invest the results in farming in the Highlands. His success attracted more settlers, which led the British to take more land from the African populations for allocation to the relatively few European settlers. As settlers poured into Kenya, a settler ideology supported by both the British and colonial governments developed to the effect that Kenya was to be the country of the white man. This ideology was expressed in a biography of Lord Delamere written by Elspeth Huxley and titled *White Man's Country*. In conformity with this ideology, the British encouraged the settlement of European veterans of World War I, and allocated to them the fertile lands in the Highlands. The defenceless Masai chief Lenana was compelled to sell the Masai rights to land, and the Kikuyu were confined to reserves. Despite African resentment, a hut tax system ensured local labour for the white settlers. In an equally resented colour differentiation practice, immigrants from Asia were accorded more respect and received better education than the indigenous people and became the economic mediators between Europeans and Africans.

The end of the First World War saw an increasing number of Africans, especially the Kikuyus, working in Nairobi and being exposed to urban life. Several political associations emerged, including the Kikuyu Central Association (KCA), of which Jomo Kenyatta became the leader. An association called the Kikuyu Independent Churches sprang up to fight against what the Kikuyu perceived as European missionary imperialism. As the political activities mounted, along with the resentment of oppression and exploitation, the colonial government decided in March 1922 to arrest and detain a young Kikuyu activist, Harry Thuku. The news of his arrest led to massive demonstrations, the police opened fire, and twenty-one Africans were killed. This eruption of violence marked the beginning of the long road to independence, won only after much shedding of Kikuyu blood in the Mau Mau uprising of the 1950s.

In Kenya the levers of political power changed hands from white minority Kenyans to black majority Kenyans, but economic power remained in the hands of the white minority. The transfer of political power was a product of struggle between the entrenched ideology of white settlers, according to which Kenya remained a white man's country, just like Australia and New Zealand; and, on the other side, the view of some British civil servants and politicians that Kenya was an African country. The latter view was expressed by Winston Churchill after an official visit to Kenya in 1907 and reaffirmed in a government White Paper in 1923: "Primarily, Kenya is an African country.... The interests of the African native must be paramount."[1] While the transfer of political power from the white minority to the black majority was in itself a fulfilment of the nationalist cause, that did not mean that the "white tribe" of Kenya would be entirely excluded from participating in the country's affairs. Although rivalry between the two major ethnic groups, the Kikuyu and the Luo, afforded the minority ethnic groups such as the Kalenjin a relative political advantage, the white minority Kenyans (the white tribe) who commanded economic power were apparently left out of the political structure after independence—despite the seemingly democratic need for participation based not on the colour of skin but on legality and commitment.

The bloodshed experienced in the struggle for Kenyan independence could have been avoided if the white settlers, the British government, and the Kikuyu had exercised restraint and controlled their emotions. The events of the Second World War accentuated Kenyan nationalism, which had formed as a matter of course as Kenyan ethnic groups were robbed of their lands. During the war Kenyan soldiers were exposed to the strengths and weaknesses of other races and became convinced that they were equal to any other soldier, but on their return home they found themselves largely excluded from the systems of rewards or medals meted out to Europeans and Asians. They were expected to retire to their previous rural lives, in which the commodities and protections of barracks life were non-existent. Under such circumstances, the veterans and their families faced bleak opportunities for a better future. When this experience was compounded with a general resentment arising from the loss of their fertile lands to whites, strikes and riots became common and the bloody Mau Mau uprisings followed. Apart from the violence of those uprisings, the nationalist aspirations evident in the independence struggle raised expectations that given the chance, Kenya might be a case of successful development. Indeed, partly because of its white settler population and high proportion of educated elite, and partly because during the Cold War Kenya under Jomo Kenyatta avoided the socialist path, the country did receive more aid than most African countries, and achieved a relative stability. Despite these advantages, Kenya's economic performance turned out to be not as bright as expected, and the political scene became unpredictable and characterized by assassinations and attempted assassinations, with an attempted coup along the way as well.

Like most non-oil producing countries, Kenya was hurt by the oil-pricing and monetary shocks of the 1970s and 1980s. But the country's economic problems showed up even before that time. Kenya's balance of payment position had begun to weaken in the 1960s, and it depended on Britain and other sources for the grants, loans, and technical assistance so necessary to economic growth. As early as the 1960s Kenya had become a beggar-state or an economic Lazarus going with cap in hand to beg for the crumbs allowed to fall from the master's table. Something had gone wrong despite the nationalist fervour and optimism that had animated the independence struggle.

Kenya became yet another example of the failure to create a united nation-state with a balance between centralization and decentralization to check abuses of power. The divide and rule tactics of colonial rule had deepened ethnic sensitivities. Moreover, colonial restrictions on political activity prevented the formation of a trans-ethnic political organization or movement with one leadership.

Partisan Politics in Ethnic Garb

As in other African countries, partisan politics, introduced long before independence had come, tended to divide Kenyans along ethnic lines instead of uniting them into one strong nation. In 1944 Eliud Mathu, the first African appointed to the colonial Legislative Council, formed what would become the Kenya African Union (KAU). Although the KAU was heavily dominated by the Kikuyu, it aimed at the formation of an encompassing coalition of Kenyan elites. Its members included Oginga Odinga from Kisumu, Ambrose Ofafa from Nyanza, Tom Mbotela from Cape Province, and Paul Ukambani, all of them not Kikuyu. Like the UGCC of Ghana, therefore, and like the KCA before it, the KAU respected the African consensual culture. In 1946 Kenyatta arrived in Kenya from a long stay in Britain and by the following year had assumed the leadership of the KAU, which soon found itself engulfed in problems. The conservative colonial administration was not prepared to cooperate with the African party. The KAU leaders had promised to fight for land reforms—a promise that had established their base of support among the Kikuyu in particular. But these hopes were dashed, and a split developed between the radical and moderate elites within the KAU.

A radical group of mainly ex-servicemen called the Forty Group within the KAU derived support from unemployed Kikuyu in Nairobi and Kikuyu villagers who wanted more land. This group, acting independently of the KAU executive, organized a Land Freedom Army, which saw violence as a means of delivering the only message that the colonizers, their stooges, and moderate Kenyans could understand, and as therefore an appropriate tactic for realizing the aspirations of the Kikuyu. Their independent action itself revealed a lack of understanding of partisan politics, which calls for party discipline. The slogan of the radicals was "Uma! Uma!"—"Go Away! Go Away!" which was a call for the colonizers to go back to Europe so that Kenya might be free from the yoke and tutelage of imperialism and colonialism. The colonizers called the Land Freedom Army the Mau Mau, a name without any apparent meaning except the one it acquired with usage over time.[2]

The Land Freedom Army secretly organized the raiding of shops for firearms, cattle maiming on the white settler farms, the undermining of the authority of local chiefs and village headmen, and the assassination of moderate chiefs (such as Waruhiu of Kiambu in 1952) considered imperialist stooges. In their gross ignorance of partisan politics, they did not foresee any action that the British government might take against the KAU leadership. For its part, the British government, with its culture of partisan politics and its expectations of discipline within political parties, would not accept that the KAU leadership knew nothing about the activities of the Land Freedom Army or the Mau Mau. On October 20, 1952, the governor, Sir Evelyn Baring, declared a state of emergency during which Kenyatta and other KAU leaders were arrested and detained. In 1953 Kenyatta and other KAU leaders were tried and sentenced to seven years' imprisonment with hard labour, and the KAU and all local African political organizations were banned. Although the KAU was multi-ethnic, with its divide and rule tactics the British government targeted only the Kikuyu for detention, followed by the dismissal of Kikuyu civil servants and their replacement with members of other ethnic groups. The strategy worked, for instead of recognizing the clever British tactics, the Kikuyu felt betrayed by the other ethnic groups. The Land Freedom Army turned its attention specifically to the assassination of non-Kikuyu members of the KAU, including the vice-president, Tom Mbotela, and Ambrose Ofafa. These Kikuyu acts, in turn, set Kenya's two largest ethnic groups, the Luo and the Kikuyu, against each other, devastated the KAU beyond salvaging, and led to the later emergence of new parties. Partisan politics had failed in its mission to mobilize and unite Kenyans, decolonize the country, and introduce the Western type of democracy to the Kenyan cultural environment.

The state of emergency lasted seven years (1952-59) and during that time the rebellion was ruthlessly crushed by British forces. According to Mike Mason, "Africans were arrested, interrogated, terrorized, tortured, and murdered in astonishing numbers; according to some estimates, as many as 25,000 Africans (but just over a hundred Europeans) were killed."[3] The colonial government portrayed the Mau Mau as a satanic and savage organization and, to serve as a deterrent, sentenced more than one thousand Africans to death by hanging.

The rebellion, however, was not entirely an ill wind that blew no good. The British government did receive the message that the Africans of Kenya would not compromise on majority rule, and the white settlers got the message that without the intervention of the British government, they might not be able to dominate the African population and continue to control the situation in Kenya. After the rebellion, the British government changed its policy of "Kenya, a white man's country," embarked upon land reforms, and increased the representation of Africans in the Legislative Council. However, with the emergency still in progress, the KAU banned, and leaders either killed or in jail, African political activity was officially restricted to the district level, with individual candidates aspiring for membership in the Legislative Council constrained to mobilizing support in their own ethnic societies. These candidates and the ethnic localities they represented had different interests and aspirations, and when the British finally did legalize the formation of political parties, it became difficult to articulate and integrate all these interests and aspirations to form one national organization. Subsequently, in 1960, two parties emerged, each supported by ethnic configurations and with differing interests: the Kenya African National Union (KANU) and the Kenya African Democratic Union (KADU). It became even more difficult to transform the ideological symbols of unity not only from the ethnic level to the nation-state level, but also with a consciousness that would recognize Kenyans as one people speaking the same Kenyan language, but in different dialects.

KANU derived its support mainly from those ethnic groups, districts, and special-interest organizations (especially from ethnic minorities, including Asians) that had supported KAU before the emergency. Thus, it was the party of the Kikuyus, the Luo, the Kamba, the Gusii, the Embu, and the Meru, which, apart from constituting about 60 per cent of the total Kenyan population, also comprised the most politically mobilized and richest members. Among the ranks of KANU were its president, James Gichuru (who was tactically to hold that appointment until the release of Jomo Kenyatta), its vice-president, Oginga Odinga, and its general secretary, Tom Mboya, a trade-union leader. KANU aimed at uniting all Kenyans in a mass movement that would favour the control of power and authority by a strong central leadership.

KADU derived its support from ethnic groups and interest organizations who feared that a one-party Kenyan state would be dominated principally by the Kikuyu and the Luo. Its support came from districts and organizations located in the relatively undeveloped areas inhabited by ethnic groups of smaller sizes, including the Abaluhya of the Western Province, the Kalenjin of the western Rift Valley Province, the Mijikenda of Coast Province, and the semi-nomadic populations of the sparsely populated southern Rift Valley and northeastern Kenya. KADU was opposed to the idea of a strong central government, which it thought would place too much power in the hands of the Kikuyu and Luo. Included among its ranks were Ronald Ngala (a former treasurer of KANU who resented the dictatorial tendencies of some KANU leaders and left to join KADU), and Daniel Arap Moi. Thus, KANU and KADU were both multi-ethnic but non-encompassing parties that essentially divided Kenya into two camps with different interests and political aspirations.

In 1961 elections, KANU demonstrated its majoritarian composition by winning 67 per cent of the vote, which translated into nineteen seats. KADU got 16 per cent of the vote, translating into eleven seats. In the

European reserved seats, the votes were four seats for the New Kenya Party (NKP), which favoured co-operation with an African majority, and three seats for the Kenya Coalition (KC). The translation of percentage votes into seats showed that in the type of Western democracy being introduced to Kenya, it was not so much who voted that mattered, but who controlled the gerrymandering allocation of electoral districts. Despite KANU's overwhelmingly high percentage of the vote, the resulting configuration of seats called for the formation of a coalition government. KANU's condition for participating in any coalition government was the release of Kenyatta, a condition the governor was not prepared to accept. With the support of Asian members of the Legislative Assembly and twelve members appointed specially by the governor, KADU was able to form a coalition government in co-operation with the NKP. Oginga Odinga, the KANU vice-president, commented, "The Governor has manufactured a deadlock over Kenyatta to get KADU in government, in the hope that KANU, in frustrated opposition would splinter into quarrelling factions."[4]

KANU's recognition of the governor's divide and rule tactics helped to keep its ethnic alliance together, and Kenyatta was subsequently released in August 1961. Aware of KADU's opposition to a strong central government, at the first Lancaster House constitutional conference the settlers were able to convince the KADU leadership to support and promote a federal form of government called *majimbo*, with six regions, each with its own legislature, financial and executive power, and control over land, police, and administration, and with a weak central government comprising a lower house and a senate.[5]

In this respect, partisan politics encouraged KADU to forge an alliance with the same European settlers who had usurped African lands and were privileged by the colonial system.

The Attempt at a Nationalist Coalition under Partisan Politics

In April 1962, after a second Lancaster House constitutional conference, and concessions made by KANU to KADU on the subject of *majimbo*, the two parties formed a coalition government, but with the provision that the constitution might be changed to one reflecting a strong central government if KANU won a landslide victory in the coming 1963 general elections. In those elections, with the revised structure of seats under the *majimbo* constitution, KANU won eighty-three seats in the House of Representatives against a total of forty-one for the opposing parties.

The Senate saw a tie, with KANU and KADU obtaining three seats each. However, the character of the political process was one in which each party struggled to build ethnically charged clientele organizations as a means of political support. On June 1, 1963, Kenya attained internal self-government, or *madaraka*, with Kenyatta as prime minister. Full independence was granted on December 12, 1963, and a year later Kenya became a republic with Kenyatta as president.

Policies pursued by the Kenyatta government systematically weakened the federal character of the *majimbo* constitution and KADU.[6] Eventually, with the spirit of *majimbo* dead, KADU decided to join KANU to form one nationalist party. The Kenyan elite failed to realize at that time that the formation of one party would polarize Kenyan society conspicuously into those who belonged to the party and those who did not belong to it. In accordance with the alien one-party logic, in 1965 the government passed an Amendment Act that downgraded regions to provinces and the regional assemblies to councils. In 1967 the final death of *majimbo* was pronounced when a new constitution formally abolished the regions and the Senate. However, the death of *majimbo* and the folding of KADU into KANU did not bring an end to ethnic sensitivities. The ethnically charged clientele organizations remained, so that KANU was essentially a loose coalition of local and regional clientele organizations that did not transfer the ideological symbols of unity entirely to the centre.

The seeds of partisan politics began to haunt Kenya in various ways. Some members of the Senate and the House of Representatives were concerned with the slow pace of land reforms and believed that Kenyatta and KANU had betrayed the fundamental objectives of the independence struggle. Concluding that what Kenya needed was a party that could offer a socialist alternative, the dissidents, led by Oginga Odinga, crossed the floor to form the Kenya People's Union (KPU), which provided strong opposition to Kenyatta in Parliament. To silence these dissidents, and aware of his general popularity with the public, who respectfully called him "*Mzee*" (wise leader), Kenyatta called for a special election in 1966 to compel the dissidents to renew their electoral mandate. Of the twenty-nine dissidents, twenty lost their seats. In 1969 the KPU was banned and Kenya again became a one-party state.

Kenya as a one-party state was still not free from the dangers of partisan politics. The interparty competition and violence of multiparty systems were simply converted into intraparty competition and violence fuelled by ethnic sensitivities. In July 1969, through the activities of

Kikuyu conspirators within KANU, Tom Mboya, a Luo and the heir apparent to Kenyatta, was assassinated. His assassination invoked suspicion and enmity between the Luo and the Kikuyu. Tensions increased in March 1975, when Josiah Mwangi Kariuki was kidnapped and murdered by senior police officers. Contrary to what a number of African political elites sometimes suggest, the Kenya cultural environment confirmed that a one-party regime might not necessarily ensure national unity or cohesion among elites.

Subsequently Kenyatta embarked upon an electoral policy that was to some extent African in content, but still enshrined in the European culture of partisan politics. The sizes of the constituencies were reduced, and any adult KANU member who refrained from challenging the policies of the government could contest. This kind of democratic practice came closer to African democratic practice, except that the ideological symbols of unity were still not transferred from the ethnic level to the nation-state level, and the indigenous democratic system had no party and the traditional councils allowed free expression of views. The affinity of this practice to the methods of indigenous political culture helped to strengthen Kenyatta's regime by compelling parliamentarians to be more attentive to their constituents so that they could renew their mandates—a provision similar to the indigenous democratic practice of deposing incompetent chiefs. The system insulated Kenyatta from politics at the local level, thus providing him with the reserve political energy required to attend to the more pressing demands of the state as a whole.

The accountability of parliamentarians to their constituencies encouraged the proliferation of self-help organizations, called *Harambee*, committed to providing basic infrastructure and welfare services to their localities. Their activities included the construction of school buildings, health clinics, water systems, bridges, and feeder roads. In many cases they provided staff for the schools and health clinics. The funds for the *Harambee* projects were obtained mainly through local contributions in which all adult members of the local community participated, with the relatively rich or affluent contributing more. This funding process was similar to the original African fundraising system called *susu* in West Africa and in the Caribbean. It thus reflected African cultural values and behaviour.

Kenyatta's death in August 1978 and his succession by Vice-President Arap Moi in accordance with Kenya's constitution served to reveal not only some of the discontinuities in policy and political direction, but also the dangers of partisan politics both in Africa in general and in Kenya in particular. The polarized convictions of KADU—rural nationalism and federalism—and KANU—strong central leadership—did not simply vanish when the two parties had merged into one. When Kenyatta was alive, Arap Moi suppressed or controlled his KADU convictions to work alongside the first president. After Kenyatta died, Arap Moi's policies turned to largely reflect KADU's approaches to the nation.

Coalition-Building and Partisan Politics in the Moi Era

Moi assumed the presidency with policies aimed at crippling the wings of the corrupt members of the Kenyatta regime, which implied dismantling the domineering network structures of the privileged Kikuyu. In a series of policies called *Nyayo*, government resources were to be directed increasingly to the relatively poor regions, which had once provided KADU with political support, and away from the predominantly Kikuyu and other ethno-regional bases of the original KANU party. In theory, Moi's government presented *nyayo* ("footsteps to freedom") as a reflection of love, peace, and unity in which the poor were to be adequately cared for. In practice, they did not gear their approaches to alleviating the suffering of the general poor, including those in the city slums, but to addressing only spatial inequalities involving regions. Parliamentarians who challenged Moi's policies were labelled disloyal and expelled from the National Assembly, from KANU, or from both. In May 1982, to consolidate his position and arrest any danger of a new party emerging in opposition to his rule, possibly with Oginga Odinga (the former KPU leader) as its head—as had occurred under Kenyatta in May 1982—Moi introduced a constitutional amendment to render Kenya a de jure one-party state. When the press criticized these Moi policies, Moi responded by taking repressive measures to silence them. The crackdown on the press and a general resentment against his policies led to an attempted coup by the air force in August 1982. Moi responded to the coup by working systematically to eliminate prominent KANU members perceived as rivals, an effort that revealed the extent of intraparty rivalry within the one-party state. These people included National Assembly members Charles Njojo, the minister of constitutional affairs, and G.G. Kariuki, the minister of state in the office of the president. Prominent Kikuyu leaders eliminated included Mwai Kibaki, the former vice-president, Kenneth Matilba, and Charles Rubia, the former mayor of Nairobi. In other developments, the Moi government replaced the secret ballot system with a system that had voters, in a first stage, lining up behind pictures of the contestants in open fields, followed, in a second stage, by a secret ballot. The new electoral system discouraged voters to the extent that in the 1988 elections, participation dropped to 23 per cent of eligible voters—making fully apparent the failure to achieve the most basic democratic principle of government with the consent of the people. Moi responded to both internal and external pressure for multiparty elections with the excuse that multipartism would lead to ethnic conflict—forgetting that ethnic conflict existed in his own one-party state, in which large numbers of Kikuyu district commissioners and administrators of other ethnic groups were replaced with Kalenjin belonging to Moi's own ethnic group.

Moi's policies also undermined the effectiveness of the *Harambee* self-help organizations. A policy of District Focus required all local projects needing government assistance to be reviewed by the District Development Committee, thus undermining the autonomy of the *Harambee* and the support that local electoral candidates derived in assisting these self-help organizations. In this way, Moi delinked the *Harambee* from electoral politics and killed the spirit that animated and compelled parliamentarians to be responsive to their constituencies and alert to renewing their mandates. Foreign Non-Governmental Organizations (NGOs) became required by law to register with the government and comply with a code of conduct. A Co-ordination Board (CB) began to monitor NGO activities closely, with the power to register or refuse to register them. The need for these clampdowns in itself confirms that intraparty conflict characterized the one-party regime in Kenya, and that a one-party regime went against the grain of democracy in the Kenya cultural environment. The political elite, again, were not able to constitute a strong and encompassing coalition capable of attaining the political conditions for successful economic development. The total effect of this political deficiency was the diversion of resources to the building of clientele-based political support.

By the 1980s Kenya was being praised as a success story—as an African country that respected the operation of market forces and had achieved a certain growth. If development means the mere attainment of favourable macroeconomic indicators on paper, perhaps Kenya was really a success story; but if development means an improvement in the living standard and dignity of humans, and the emancipation of the greater proportion of the population from poverty and misery, Kenya was a total failure. Given that the second conception of development had initiated and animated the independence struggle, it must be the yardstick for measuring the degree of Kenya's success. Presumably, because of the white settler population in the country, Kenya was highly favoured in the flow of funds from outside for development. Despite this favour, though, in 1990 the World Bank admitted that most Kenyans were no better off than most Haitians (who are often considered among the poorest people in the world).

Kenya's pattern of income distribution remains one of the most distorted in the world. At the very top of the ladder are the wealthy elite with black skins but of Western culture, mentality, and taste, who, though located on Kenyan soil, live like the affluent of Western Europe or the United States. This affluent elite comprises business people, landowners, professionals, and politicians. They are the owners of the expensive bungalows and expensive cars, and the players of golf and tennis, while the majority of Kenyans earn less than U.S.$50 per month. In Kenyan society, where women perform most of the farming work, the illiteracy rate of women is about 33.2 per cent compared to 15 per cent for men. Meanwhile, corruption is endemic in the state bureaucracy. In 1991 the auditor-general admitted that the funds that were supposed to be used for administering Kenya's development had disappeared, and no one knew where they had gone.[7]

The political scene continued to be characterized by violence, with elections characterized by charges of rigging and intimidation by KANU thugs. The murder in February 1990 of Minister of Foreign Affairs Robert Ouko, considered to be a political rival of Arap Moi, riots in July 1990, the subsequent emergence of a new political party with Oginga Odinga as its founder, the resignation of several cabinet ministers in 1991 as a protest against Moi's refusal to call for general elections, and food riots in 1992 all confirm that KANU's long stay in power had not brought real political stability. Behind the mirage of stability was a serious play of centrifugal political forces arising from ethnic sensitivities and accentuated by partisan politics. Instead of bringing the authoritative allocation of Kenyan values to the majority of Kenyans, politics in Kenya has delivered, to some extent, the authoritative allocation of macroeconomic indicators on paper and, to a great extent, the allocation of Western values to a privileged few.

In a scandal popularly known as the Goldenberg frauds, over U.S.$100 million was siphoned out of the treasury and the Central Bank of Kenya sometime between 1992 and 1993. The amount was supposed to have been paid to a company as compensation for gold and diamond exports, whereas Kenya produces very little gold and has no diamonds. In another development in 1997, Parliament's Public Accounts Committee seriously indicted the government for irregular expenditure of public funds. These kind of scandals continued despite government promises to crack down on corruption and straddling (an attitude whereby a civil servant pretends to support government policy but in reality acts to undermine it in various ways including misuse of position to divert human and material resources for personal gain). Given that partisan politics requires financial resources to build political support, and to meet campaign expenditures, the scandals are not surprising. Public reactions to them included demonstrations demanding political reforms, which led to clashes with the riot police in June and July 1997. In a move to take some of the steam out of the political tension, Moi promised political changes before the presidential and parliamentary elections of 1997, although he did not give any details about those intended reforms. Meanwhile, international pressure on his regime continued to mount. The IMF decided to halt a three-year aid program of $205 million, which compelled the Moi government to warn in 1997, the election year, that it might have to cut spending and raise taxes. While foreign investors believed that the IMF's action might force Moi to tackle the problem of corruption in the country, some opposition leaders reasoned that because the country's corruption involved many people at the top, the government might not have the political will to change direction.

Moi responded to both internal and external pressures by diverting attention to imaginary guerrilla groups, inter-ethnic violence, and the double standards of the West in their dealings with Kenya and Uganda. He accused Uganda of training a guerrilla army to invade Kenya and accused the donor countries of putting pressure on Kenya to make sweeping political changes while ignoring Uganda's recent ban on multi-party politics for five years. Moi's behaviour shows that the confused and crazed politics springing from the adoption of an alien ideology might have influences outside national boundaries and could carry the dangerous potential of pitching one African country against another.

CHAPTER NINE

TANZANIA: UJAMAA, COMPULSION, AND THE FREEDOM OF ASSOCIATION

Historically, given its geographic position, Tanzania experienced a strong Arab influence—like the whole of the East African coast and the Horn of Africa—as well as the standard pattern of European intervention. The British act of 1833 that abolished slavery in the British Empire did not end the slave trade in East Africa, where slaves continued to be exported by the Sultan of Muscat, Seyyid Said. The island of Zanzibar, once controlled by the Portuguese, became a British Protectorate in 1890, a status it held until 1963. The mainland territory of Tanganyika was a German colony from 1844 to 1914, when it fell to Britain during the First World War; and after the war it came under British rule. Although Tanganyika, the largest country in East Africa, was close to Kenya, it was not at any time in its history settled heavily by Europeans and was thus never thought of as a "white man's country." Tanganyika attained full independence on December 9, 1961, with Julius Nyerere as president. On May 1, 1964, the mainland of Tanganyika united with Zanzibar (and the island of Pemba) to constitute the United Republic of Tanzania. In 1965 Tanzania adopted a constitution that made it a de jure one-party state and at the same time granted Zanzibar a degree of autonomy. The historical incorporation of Arab words into an African language produced a language called Kiswahili, and Tanzania injected a sense of national pride, unity, and identity into the country's people when it adopted Kiswahili as the national language.

Tanzania's economy has traditionally been based on subsistence agriculture, which in the 1990s still constituted about 40 per cent of the gross domestic product. The combination of the nature of the vegetation and poor soils has placed limits on both agriculture and population density. The principal export crop is coffee, which replaced sisal after the increased use of synthetics led to the decline of sisal sales in the world market. Zanzibar is one of the world's major sources of cloves.

Other agricultural exports include cotton, tea, sisal, tobacco, and cashew nuts. Gold is found in several areas of Tanzania, and the potential for diamond mining exists at Mwadni, where production began in 1950 but later closed down. Natural gas was discovered offshore and in several inland areas.

Tanganyika had a rich pre-colonial social structure comprising ethnic groups, some of them led by kings and others by clan elders. Although ethnic groupings had different cultures, the consensual decision-making process prevailed in clan government as well as in the various councils of kingship groups. The Hehe of the Southern highlands developed a political system in which several kings served under a single emperor who, in colonial times, was relegated to the status of paramount chief.

About one hundred thousand Tanzanians fought for the Allies in the Second World War and became exposed to the weaknesses and strengths of other societies, living customs, and urban life and became convinced that Tanzanians were as capable as people of other nations. That spirit of conviction was what animated the struggle for independence. In the postwar period Tanzanians believed that, given the chance, they could move their country forward economically and socially. Egalitarian concerns combined with the desire to catch up with the industrialized world encouraged Tanzanian leaders to declare socialism as their ideology of development—again without paying enough attention to that ideology's real possibilities in the local cultural environment and to the stage of development of the country's productive forces. In the process of establishing socialism, the country would have its losers and winners, and losers again.

The losers were understandably tempted to react to defend their interests, which led, for instance, to an attempted coup in 1964, which was quickly foiled with British help and led in turn to the consolidation of a one-party state. The internal threat was followed by an external danger from just across the border. Milton Obote's government in Uganda, which had very friendly relations with the Nyerere government, was overthrown by General Idi Amin. During the 1970s Nyerere refused to recognize the Amin government in Uganda. As the animosity between the two countries escalated, the Kagera border region west of Lake Victoria became a disputed area, and tensions escalated as Tanzania showed sympathy for the Ugandan rebels poised to restore Obote to power. After a series of serious military provocations by the Amin regime, Tanzania was compelled to enter into a costly war with Amin's Uganda. Tanzania emerged victorious, and its one-party state became stronger. However, despite Nyerere's philosophy of *ujamaa* (a Kiswahili word meaning "family" and implying an emphasis on local village co-operatives—but which amounted to compulsory villagization) and pan-territorial pricing policies in support of the socialist drive, the resulting performance of the economy and general social conditions were so disappointing that after the mid-1980s the country had to swing back to a free-market system in which the one-party state gave way to a multi-party politics.

Independent Tanzania went through a series of economic crises and year after year made the United Nations' annual listing of the poorest countries in the world. Various reasons have been advanced to explain the poor performance of the Tanzania economy after nearly thirty years of political efforts to make an alien socialist democracy possible and realize the objective of *ujamaa*. These reasons include unrealistic social-ist policies, corruption, a series of droughts and flooding, a decline in terms of trade, the demise of the East African Community, maladminis-tration, and the oil-pricing and monetary shocks of the 1970s and 1980s. However, these explanations fail to go to the root of the problem or to explain why other countries in Asia with almost the same starting con-ditions have succeeded where Tanzania failed—given that they also faced similar natural disasters and shocks from the international envi-ronment. The problems the country faced demanded the existence of a strong nationalist coalition, compatible with the indigenous culture, to absorb the resulting stresses and strains without compromising the nationalist aspirations that had animated the independence struggle. Unfavourable terms of trade also demanded the existence of such an encompassing coalition. But the roots of Tanzania's economic problems ran deep. The substantial amounts of international assistance received—with Sweden and other Nordic countries the most important donors—had little positive effect on economic conditions, and by the 1980s it was clear to donors and critics alike that the country had to make major structural changes in its economy, and that Nyerere's social-ist approach had in essence failed. By 1986 Nyerere himself was declar-ing that he had underestimated the amount of time necessary for achiev-ing socialism.

The adoption of Kiswahili as the national language provided Tanza-nia with the very rare advantage of a nation united by a common lan-guage in which the ordinary citizen could speak and communicate. This is in sharp contrast with less fortunate countries such as Ghana and Nigeria, where the majority of the population did not understand the inherited national language of English. After independence Tanzania made large investments in education to provide it with the elite seemingly required for development. Educated Tanzanians have also distinguished themselves at the international forums of the United Nations and the Commonwealth. Tanzania also has the unique history of two independent African societies, Tanganyika and Zanzibar, coming together to realize common nationalist objectives and thereby providing a signal that a united Africa is possible. Indeed, Tanzania served as an inspiration to committed African nationalists who believed that a united Africa was the solution to Africa's problems of underdevelopment. Despite these high expectations and rare advantages, the development performance of the country stands in sharp contrast to the nationalist aspirations that justified the independence struggle and united Tanzania.

The Advent of Partisan Politics

In Tanzania a common language was not only forged but the ideological symbols of unity were also almost completely transferred from the ethnic level to a voluntary organization at the centre. Later, this voluntary organization was converted into a political party into which divisive centrifugal forces gradually entered to disrupt the motion towards successful development. The development of Kiswahili as a common language for the whole country served as a catalyst to unite the various ethnic groups of the Tanganyika mainland. The dispersed nature of the population combined with a lack of concentration of wealth weakened ethnic cleavages and suppressed competition along ethnic lines. When the struggle against colonial rule eventually surfaced and expressed itself early on in the Maji Maji rebellion of 1905 to 1907, it was completely a non-ethnic resistance against colonialism, and all the ethnic groups learned from the ruthless crushing of that rebellion that they had a common destiny that might be achieved through active but non-violent means.

After the First World War, Tanganyika was administered by Britain under the trusteeship of the League of Nations. Several self-help organizations, including the Tanganyika African Association (TAA), sprang up in response to the welfare and needs of the people. After the Second World War most of these organizations folded into the TAA to constitute a united front against the prejudices of the colonial administration towards Africans, including representation in the Legislative Council and in the composition of its executive. The TAA became more popular among the African population of Tanzania when, in 1947, it protested against the idea of a Closer Union in East Africa designed by the colonizers principally to strengthen the political role of the white settlers of Kenya, and when it successfully organized a strike of the low-income group of teachers, dockers, sisal workers, and salt workers. As it gained strength, the TAA succeeded in organizing local producer co-operatives to fight against the privileged position of Asians, which had enabled some Asians to dominate and control the marketing and pricing of cash crops produced by Africans.

Support for the TAA expanded further when, in 1947, the colonial administration decided to evict about three thousand members of the Meru ethnic group and hand over their lands to white settlers. The Meru traditional leader not only petitioned the United Nations in 1952, but also toured the whole of Tanganyika to educate and alert Africans about the impending danger of land being taken from African ethnic communities to satisfy white settler interests, and the need for all Africans of Tanganyika to rally behind the TAA to fight for their rights. Support for the non-ethnic TAA grew among civil servants, traders, clerks, and peasants. In July 1954 the TAA was transformed into a non-racial party, the Tanganyika African National Union (TANU), with Julius Nyerere, then a teacher, as its president. TANU's primary objective was to achieve independence under an African government. Nyerere derived much of his political tactics from the experience of Ghana's Convention People's Party (CPP) led by Kwame Nkrumah. He emphasized the expression of grievances through the non-violent activities of positive action.[1]

The colonial government responded to TANU with the usual divide and rule tactics, but in this case, given the unity of purpose among the various ethnic groups and the perception of Tanganyikans of themselves as one nation with a common destiny, that approach proved ineffective. The Tanzanian experience confirms the view that when the ideological symbols of unity and solidarity are transferred to the centre, it is possible to form an effective national coalition capable of challenging and withstanding imperialist tactics. The divisive tactics of the imperialists included the banning of TANU in various districts of Tanganyika and the introduction of a policy of multiracial district councils in the provinces, which, even though TANU was non-racial and open to both Africans and non-Africans, made it mandatory for the exclusively African district councils to include Asians and Europeans in their membership. The African populations perceived the introduction of this multiracialism as a ploy by the colonial government to allocate district lands to Asians and Europeans. As the policy was greeted with riots, both the African and non-African membership of TANU swelled, and the majority of TANU members advised a boycott of the 1958-59 elections. Nyerere succeeded in convincing a TANU conference that the party should take part in the elections to prevent the white-dominated United Tanganyika Party (UTP), with a probable hidden agenda of delaying both independence and the transfer of control of the economy to Africans, from assuming the reins of government.

Subsequently, TANU won all the seats allocated to Africans under the policy of multiracialism, together with some of the seats allocated to Europeans and Asians. In 1960, following a new constitution that provided for fifty open seats, eleven Asian seats, and ten European seats, TANU won seventy out of the seventy-one seats, with one seat going to an independent candidate, who was also a TANU member. Nyerere became the chief minister of the TANU government, which achieved internal self-government on May 1, 1961, and full independence that December. Thus, in Tanganyika, the emergence of one African political party was a consequence of the transfer of the ideological symbols of unity from the ethnic level to, first, a voluntary self-help organization (the TAA) at the centre, followed by a transfer of these symbols intact to a political party, TANU. There were no ethnic divisions or competition that justified the formation of another African party. Furthermore, the non-racial character and openness of TANU so encouraged non-Africans to join its ranks that TANU won the elections in the non-African constituencies as well. However, the very existence of a party suggests, again, that there were those who belonged to the party and those who did not. It only required the emergence of ideological differences to give rise to the formation of opposing political parties. That ideological flame was ignited when Tanzania declared socialism as its development route.

The Advent of Socialism

In the middle 1970s, following a revolution in Zanzibar, Tanganyika and Zanzibar became united into Tanzania, with socialism declared to be the ideological basis of its future development. In 1977 the Afro Shirazi Party of Zanzibar and TANU merged to form the Chama Cha Mapinduzi (CCM) party. As it was in Ghana, socialism was introduced into

Tanzania at a time when the productive forces had not been sufficiently established to enable a transition from the capitalist stage of development to a socialist state. A statement by Martinique politician and writer Aimé Césaire in 1956 attests to the lack of seriousness with which African leaders, in general, have applied themselves to the socialist ideology: "I think I have said enough to make it understood that it is neither Marxism nor Communism that I renounce, but it is the use that certain people have made of the use of Marxism and Communism of which I disapprove. What I want is Marxism and Communism to be placed in the service of the black peoples and not the black peoples in the service of Marxism and Communism."[2]

As Césaire indicates, African leaders may have learned about Marxism and communism, but they were not prepared or desirous to abide by its tenets. What they wanted was a blend of socialist and other ideas, including African traditional values, that would satisfy African conditions and address African problems. In Ghana this blend was called Nkrumaism; in Egypt it was Nasserism. In Tanzania Nyerere perceived of socialism as the guiding ideology, as a new theology, but warned of the danger of being blindly obsessed with it.[3] What the Tanzanian politicians had in mind was essentially a form of African communalism with an egalitarian expression, but by labelling this kind of development strategy socialism, they invited suspicion from the West and set in motion economic and political forces with an ideological base.

The logic of the Cold War suggested that Tanzania could not realistically expect Western countries (Tanzania's major trading partners, and the likely source of most of its development aid) to assist wholeheartedly and effectively in its establishment of socialism. Tanzanian politicians overlooked the possibility of the West acting through its domination of the international economic system to frustrate the country's efforts to establish socialism. If Tanzania had declared African communalism as its development strategy, that approach might have proved more acceptable in the West; but not socialism, a pill too bitter for the West to swallow. Furthermore, because of the historical experience of socialism in China and the Soviet Union, where the rich and affluent had gone under seige, the relatively affluent people in Tanzania preferred capitalism and liberal democracy to socialism; they quickly became suspicious of the government and understandably feared for the safety of their property. Under the circumstances it appeared wise for them to seek safe havens abroad to deposit their money, leading to substantial capital flight. Socialist policies led to the nationalization of the banks, chief industries, including sisal plantations, agricultural marketing associations, and the export-import trade. Those who had previously benefited from these nationalized concerns could not be expected to lend their support to the government or party. Furthermore, in African political culture, individuals and families had the freedom to own whatever they could manage to take over through their own ingenuity, effort, and creativity. Socialism, with its one-party politics, was alien to the Tanzania cultural environment. Because those who belonged to the party could easily be identified, Tanzania society became polarized into two camps: those who supported the party and those who did not. The prevailing stress of ideological differences made it likely that another party would eventually be formed—a probability that the ruling party was aware of even on the eve of independence.

Policies adopted by the TANU government without the consensus of the political elite as a whole intensified the tensions. The ruling party was aware that TANU was a product of ethnic voluntary associations, other independent social unions and movements, and local governments that had united to form the TAA. The evolution of the TAA and TANU suggests that independent associations and local governments are not necessarily divisive, and their role in African culture and history shows that, in times of crisis, they can be resilient instruments for survival. However, instead of delegating authority to these organizations at the lower levels of the social order in accordance with African culture, after independence the government embarked upon policies that would frustrate or eliminate those possibilities. The government moved to centralize power and social activities in the hands of the party.

In 1972 Nyerere's administration abolished local governments. Many independent social organizations were absorbed into the party, some were eliminated, and others had their activities curtailed. TANU created new independent organizations as its own organs, while not permitting the formation of new voluntary organizations. These actions suggest that the government and party perceived independent organizations as potential threats to political and social order. Eventually Tanzania became a duplicitous state. On the one hand, in 1973 Nyerere wrote, "Indeed as far as we are concerned, the people's freedom to determine their own priorities, to organize their own ... welfare, is an important part of our objective ... because only through this participation will the people develop."[4] On the other hand, his party and its governmental control undermined the ability of the people to organize themselves. People were not free to organize themselves except through the party, and in the party independent initiative was controlled and curtailed.

The process of concentrating power in the party progressed with the constitutional declaration of Tanzania as a one-party state in 1965; the banning of the Ruvuma Development Association (RDA), which emphasized democracy and self-reliance, in 1969; a decentralization program, which shifted the accountability of local governments from the people to the central government and the control of those organizations to the party, followed by the abolishing of local governments; an amendment of the constitution in 1975 to subordinate Parliament to the party; the bringing of co-operatives in the rural areas and the trade unions in the urban areas under direct state control; and an amendment to the constitution of the party to the effect that "all activity of the organs of the state of the United Republic shall be conducted under the auspices of the party." With these transformations, appointed officials of the party assumed more power and authority than elected officials.

The policies directed against the independent organizations stifled the private initiative and creativity required to follow a successful development path. At the same time, to prevent any loss of legitimacy the government stance meant the party had to assume the functions and responsibilities of those independent organizations in Tanzanian society that it was crowding out. The assumption of these functions, in turn, required high levels of revenues and resources, which the country's weak economy could not provide. Moreover, history has shown the indigenous organizations to be resilient instruments that absorb shocks and enhance survival in crisis situations. By suppressing or eliminating them, the party and the government placed themselves and the nation at risk in times of crisis. In addition, the self-reliance potential was being undermined at a time when the government propaganda machine professed self-reliance as an integral part of, and central to, its socialist ideology.

Socialism, Ujamaa, Villagization, and Voluntary Organizations

Despite the rhetoric of a freedom to organize, after the Arusha Declaration of 1967 the party and government embarked upon a policy of *ujamaa* as central to its socialist development of agriculture. *Ujamaa* was supposed to embrace the communal concepts of African culture such as mutual respect, common property, and common labour. In practice the party violated these cultural practices. The party seemed to have soon forgotten that one of the principal reasons that ethnic conflict was relatively absent in Tanzania was the dispersed nature of the population, which encouraged rural Tanzanians to concentrate more on solving their local problems. TANU encouraged and put pressure on people in rural Tanzania to move voluntarily from their homesteads or scattered huts to form *ujamaa* villages. Apparently and presumably, the scattered pattern of settlement made it difficult to provide the necessary support to the peasant producers, and a village settlement scheme in 1964 proved slow in arresting the problem. However, while the official policy of TANU and the government remained settlement by voluntary means, on the implementation side, party and government officials wishing to be seen as effective agents resorted to manipulation and coercion to accelerate the rate of formation of *ujamaa* villages. The people were in essence so conservative that in spite of all these manipulative and coercive tactics, between 1967 and 1969 only about eight hundred *ujamaa* villages were formed.

Given the reluctance of the peasants to change their way of life, Nyerere launched a plan to move everyone in the central Dodoma area to *ujamaa* villages, and party and government officials became increasingly militant about moving peasants to form villages. The intensity of coercion was such that between 1970 and 1972 the number of *ujamaa* villages increased from 1,956 to 5,556.[5] Opposition to these coercive movements led to clashes, including the assassination of Wilbert Klerruu, a senior party official. Still not satisfied by the pace of villagization, on November 6, 1973, President Nyerere introduced a new policy of compulsory villagization, with a statement to the effect that although he could not make all Tanzanians socialist he would ensure that by 1976 all Tanzanians lived in *ujamaa* villages. What this meant was that in contravention of the consensual culture with its voluntary posture to association, compulsion had replaced freedom of association.

In spite of its relatively weak economy, Tanzania embarked upon the greatest mass movement of people in Africa (involving about six million people), stretching the limits of the army, police, and civil service, as well as the party. Middlemen in trade and commerce were accused of being responsible for the slow progress in the villagization program. Under a new operation, *maduka*, private shops were replaced by cooperatives to enable officials and *ujamaa* shops established in the cooperatives to distribute goods directly to the villagers. Operation *maduka* introduced unexpected shortages of essential commodities, including kerosene, sugar, and soap, with attendant general discontent. In the end, *ujamaa* failed in its central objective of increasing productivity. Furthermore, the *ujamaa* villages were planned originally to have their own democratic local governments, but the policy of centralization of power in the party and the shifting of accountability from the people to the government in effect placed the local councils under the government and party control. The intended localization of democracy at the village level was stifled. The behaviour and ideology of party officials, government officials, and the executive belied the very tenets of socialism.

The oil-pricing and monetary shocks of the 1970s and 1980s were to teach Tanzania some lessons. The government revenues could no longer support the enormous responsibilities assumed by the party and government when they suppressed the independent voluntary organizations. Fortunately, some informal and unregistered voluntary organizations survived, and these voluntary organizations, including the rotational fundraising organizations called *upato* and various informal self-help organizations, were able to provide significant alternatives to meet the demands of Tanzanians. The impressive performance and accountability of these organizations placed pressure on the state to reconsider and retreat from the policies that were undermining the efforts of the voluntary wing.

The local voluntary policing organizations popularly known in Tanzania as *sungusungu* (biting ants)[6] gradually resurfaced, and with the blessing of the government were formally recognized in the districts of Dar es Salaam. Prior to their resurfacing, the rate of crime was high, and Tanzanians so suspected the police to be aligned with the criminals that even when they knew who the criminals were, they considered it futile and dangerous to expose them to the police. On January 1, 1991, the *Daily News* reported that not long after the patrols of the *sungusungu* began, the crime rate dropped dramatically, confirming suspicions about the police. The events also confirmed that the voluntary organizations of African culture might be indispensable in an African democracy.

The policies of the Tanzanian party and government towards voluntary organizations before the oil-pricing and monetary shocks did not conform to African cultural values. The ruling powers simply assumed that the organizations might pose a political threat. At the same time that the party emphasized participation by all Tanzanians in decision-making, it considered participation by independent organizations as sources of potential centrifugal forces that might break up the state. The right of the Tanzanian people to free association was usurped, and compulsory villagization that, in the end, did not improve productivity was imposed from above.

The Tactical Retreat of the Tanzanian State

The economic crisis of the 1980s sent a signal to both government and party to be more cautious in their dealings with the independent cultural associations. This was buttressed by the state's retreat from its former policies that either attacked or ignored the organizations.

Public policies are government actions intended to address problems of society, but they can also be, in effect, inactions. An example of a government inaction is when a government deliberately turns a blind eye to an ongoing practice or activity. In the retreat from its repressive policies, the Tanzanian government judiciously applied both the action and inaction aspects of public policy. For example, banned independent newspapers and publications continued to be sold openly without any repressive action on the part of the state. In some instances, the state encouraged the independence of existing organizations. For example, it gave the green light to trade unions and co-operatives to draw up their own constitutions and appoint their own leaders without any interference from the party. In other instances, the state legalized and protected some previously informal organizations. For example, the state legalized and protected the *sungusungu* and the Tanzania Traditional Healers Association. These new policies show that the Tanzania government came to realize that the voluntary organizations had a greater potential of acting as allies of the government than as its enemies.

Despite this retreat, the Tanzanian elite failed to realize that partisan politics was not a sufficient condition for democracy and not democracy's sacred definition. Multiparty politics was introduced in 1995, with attendant accusations of electoral rigging and a tendency to divide Tanzanians and, thereby, weaken the Tanzanian state. The requirement of party discipline might suppress the free expression of views so conducive to development. Can the Tanzanian state retreat to the situation similar to the one when the TAA symbolized the unity of all social groups under one umbrella and acted in the interests of the whole nation? That would be the re-expression of compatible cultural democracy in Tanzania. It will be the realization of a type of democracy compatible with the Tanzanian cultural environment, and one that does not need any tactical retreat of the state in the face of a crisis, because the means of cushioning the stresses and strains of development and crisis will always be present, resilient, and reliable.

CHAPTER TEN

SOMALIA: EXPERIMENTS WITH DEMOCRACY, MILITARY RULE, AND SOCIALISM

Somalia has had a long history of colonial rule, and an equally long history of resistance to that rule. By 1885 Somali society had come under five different types of rule, by the British, French, Italians, Ethiopians, and colonized Kenya in the Northern Frontier District. The British controlled the north-central area; the northwest (Djibouti) was under the French; the Italians administered the south; the Ogaden in the west had become part of Ethiopia; and the southern part had virtually become part of Kenya.[1]

This historical division of Somali society against their wishes is the source of the irredentist spirit of shifting coalitions of Somali politicians. For the first two decades of this century, and under its great resistance leader Mohammed Abdullah Bin Hassan, Somalia courageously resisted colonialism and finally defeated the British. During the Second World War, in reaction to the British occupation of Italian Somaliland, and drawing inspiration from their previous heroic leader, Hassan, the radical and nationalist Somali Youth Club (SYC), which changed its name later to the Somali Youth League (SYL), was formed with the objective of uniting all Somalis to decolonize the nation by peaceful means, unify all Somali territories, and oppose clannish attitudes. After the war the hopes of the SYL for immediate independence for Somalia were dashed when Italian Somaliland was returned to Italy to administer as a United Nations Trust Territory. The SYC, led by its president, Haji Mohammed Hussain, responded with riots in the towns, compelling the UN to exert pressure on Italy to prepare the Trust Territory for independence. In the process, and like Tanzania's Tanganyika African Association, the SYL developed into a political party. Other political parties emerged, but the SYL remained the dominant political party and, in the 1956 elections, won forty-three out of the seventy seats. Meanwhile, in the colony of British Somaliland, the Somali National

League (SNL), led by Mohammed Ibrahim Egal, emerged as the dominant political party with twenty out of the thirty-three seats in the 1960 elections. Through pressure from Egal, the British agreed to grant independence to British Somaliland on the same date—July 1, 1960—as Italian Somaliland to facilitate the unification of the two Somalilands into one independent country, the Somali Republic.

The different colonial experience of the two entities that united became the source of political forces tending to divide the republic. However, the political leaders were wise enough to introduce the Somali language in education and administration. The common Somali language served as the binding tie. Pan-Somalism, which included an element of irredentism, was also advanced as a unifying force. Its ambitions stretched beyond seeking to unite all former Somali colonies into annexing areas of other African states that contained Somali minorities. This spirit of irredentism preceded the grant of independence. Thus, on the day of independence, the flag of the Somali Republic had five stars, representing the intention to bring British Somaliland, Italian Somaliland, the Ogaden and Haud provinces of Ethiopia inhabited by Somalis, and the Somali-inhabited northern region of Kenya into one Republic of Somalia. The *shifta* war of 1960 to 1967 with Kenya and the Ogaden war of 1967 with Ethiopia were both products of the Somali policy of irredentism.

Despite the costs of these wars, Somalia's economic prospects remained encouraging. According to an assessment by the International Co-operation Administration of the United States (Inter River Exploration, January 1961), "Resources now completely uncultivated can be brought into productivity by irrigation, dry farming methods and improved grazing. Standards of income can be raised by much work and judicious improvement."[2] The report, *Somalia: A Divided Nation Seeking Reunification*, stated: "Many basic conditions for progress prevail: (1) Plentiful and relatively flat land; (2) Excellent climate for plant growth; (3) About 5 million acres in 20 to 24 inch average annual rainfall zone; (4) Two rivers which flow a good volume eight months of the year; and (5) a large grazing area."[3]

Somalia also had a rich endowment in mineral resources, which if exploited wisely could contribute effectively to successful development:

Those known to be in commercial value and others whose quantity is yet unexplored include: Iron ore, Tin Gypsum, Limestone, Sandstone, Bauxite, Meerschaun (Sepiolite), Titanium, Salt, Anhydrate and Feldspar.

Rhodemites, Lead Platinum, Mica, Beryl, Columbite, Tantalite, Copper, Florite Galena, Talc, Emery, Asbestos, Coal, Lignite, Kaolin, Graphite, Rutile, Vermiculate, Manganese and petroleum are known to exist but the quality and quantity of these have not been finally explored.[4]

Further research confirmed that Somalia had the potential for resource-based industrial development.[5] But despite this seemingly bright future, the country degenerated into a state of anarchy.

During the early part of the twentieth century Somalia had been able to come together under one leader supported by an encompassing coalition of clan leaders who operated within the consensually democratic culture of the *shir* (assembly). By the end of the century, after experimenting with Western democracy, military rule, and socialism, it had become a divided country, with an economy in shambles and a bleak future. Like all non-oil-producing countries, it was seriously hurt by the oil-pricing and monetary shocks of the 1970s and 1980s, and its irredentism resulted in a war with Ethiopia. Still, these factors alone cannot explain the breakdown into anarchy or the collapse of the state and the continuing economic chaos. The root causes, as usual, go deeper.

Somalia in the Garb of Partisan Politics

Irredentism is not the only or most effective means of achieving the aims of pan-Somalism. Indeed, it is the most expensive and ineffective way. Peaceful coexistence with the neighbouring states where Somalis reside might ensure a better spirit of pan-Somalism, one in which Somalis would move freely across national boundaries to socialize and help one another. The Somali policy of irredentism therefore falls into the larger context of partisan politics, in which the struggle between different parties and the subsequent building of political support led to promises that accentuated Somali nationalism. Once made, these irredentist promises, which also raised the expectations of Somalis elsewhere in the region, became difficult to ignore after independence. Breaking those promises might have been translated into a loss of confidence and legitimacy within Somalia and could have antagonized Somali populations outside the country. The ruling forces ignored the alternate path of federating with the neighbouring states to bring Somalis together in one country, primarily because that goal was outside the range of election promises and also because of fears that a federation of neighbouring

African states would not necessarily lead to what could be called a United Republic of Somalia.

Partisan politics was soon to prove incompatible with Somalia's complicated clan structure. Unlike most African countries, which consist of different ethnic groupings, each of them containing different clans, most Somalians are members of the same ethnic group, while still belonging to different clans. Somali society includes six major clan-families, four of which (the Dir, Darood, Isaaq, and Hawiye, which together constitute 70 per cent of the population) are predominantly pastoral. The other two clans (the Digil and Rahanwayn, about 20 per cent of the population) are predominantly agricultural.[6] Each of the clan-families branches into several levels of patriarchal sub-clans. The lower the level of a sub-clan, the more the members cling together.

Allegiance within the clan structure is such that there is always a potential for interclan as well as intraclan struggle at all levels. However, solidarity at the lowest level of the structure is the strongest. Although the clan structure tends to produce centripetal forces at the lower levels, the interclan and intraclan forces are centrifugal, so that the net effect of clanism at the macro-level tends to be centrifugal. The centripetal forces tend to predominate when a common external enemy exists and centrifugal forces tend to predominate when some delicate internal event disturbs the interclan or intraclan equilibrium beyond limits.

Not all Somalians belong to the major clan-families, for in the valley systems of the Shabeelle and Juba rivers of Southern Somalia pockets of Bantu communities constitute a minority group in Somali society. But clan consciousness is deeply rooted in Somali society, with attendant problems, and the pastoral and nomadic Somalis also tend to look down upon the agricultural Somalis. Despite these divisions, however, the relative homogeneity of Somali society enabled it to preserve its basic unity under its traditional rule of co-operating and encompassing clan leaders. The democratic *shir* is the traditional polity in which every adult male of a clan participates.

Superimposed on the centrifugal character of clanism is the ideology of Islam. Almost all Somalis are Sunni Moslems, who believe in saint veneration, the mystical powers of holy men, and the Sufi brotherhood. While the centrifugal forces arising from the lineage segmentation of clanism tend to divide the Somali, Islam tends to unite them. The net effect is that Somalis can unite to fight a common external enemy but remain divided among themselves. The Somali themselves tell a joke that recognizes the peculiar character of their society. According to this joke, in which God is assumed to be masculine, when God decided to create human beings He first created the family of the Prophet Mohammed, and given the impressive behaviour of that family He was pleased with the nobility of his handiwork. Next, He created the rest of the world, excluding the Somali, and He was moderately pleased with their behaviour. Finally, God created the Somalis, and when He observed their behaviour He burst into laughter.

Historically, the semi-nomadic and mainly pastoral Somali were able to govern themselves in their own culturally democratic way. In their particular democracy, liberal democracy as a balance between individual right and majority right does not make sense. Although the Shaffite code of Islam teaches that the person who deliberately commits homicide is alone responsible for the crime, the Somali Moslems do not practise that belief. Instead, in accordance with their own clan culture, they hold responsible the kinsmen of the murderer, at the lowest level of the clan structure, and those kinsmen are collectively responsible for the payment of the traditional *diya*, or blood money, to the collective kinsmen of the victim. This practice implies that, if the murderer escapes Somali society or goes into hiding, in retaliation any innocent member of his *diya* group of kinsmen could be murdered by any member of the victim's kinsmen. The Somali clan system thus lacks the principle of individual culpability or rights, and the basic tenet of liberal democracy stressing individualism, therefore, does not hold.

The Somali devised their own form of democracy, then, one compatible with their own cultural values, and they were satisfied and happy with it. Those cultural values comprised blood ties established through a common male lineage called *tol*, marriage ties called *Hidid*, a general code of conduct that guided both interclan and intraclan relations called the *Heer*, and the *Quanoon*, which guided the behaviour of all believers.[7] These values together provided the basis for democratic decision-making by elders within clans and between clans. The Somalis did not have a central state that exerted its power and authority everywhere in society, but at the same time their common cultural values provided them with a democratic and moral commonwealth. Thus, Somali society might be described not only as partially stateless, but also as a democratic commonwealth that could unite to fight a common external enemy, and within this commonwealth interclan and intraclan rivalries were prevalent. The intervention of colonialism disturbed the delicate balance between the centrifugal and centripetal political forces, and the introduction of partisan politics before and after independence tended to increase the interclan and intraclan centrifugal forces to a point beyond what the balancing centripetal forces could bear. Military rule, which was also alien to Somali culture, divided the society along clan lines and finally returned Somalia to the stateless society that it had been before the advent of colonialism.

Despite Somalia's cultural homogeneity, independence did not lead to political stability and the achievement of the political conditions for successful economic development. The game of partisan politics was played along clan lines as party competition translated into interclan and intraclan competition. Clan-based political parties proliferated to the extent that Somalia had the highest number of political parties per capita in the world. In 1969, in a population of barely five million, Somalia had as many as sixty-four political parties, representing the total number of sub-clans. In the absence of party discipline, which was alien to the culture, debates in the National Assembly were almost endless, as each member of the Assembly pressed for his voice to be heard and political issues were interpreted along clan lines. This was by no means the Western practice of representative democracy, in which about two or three political parties compete, but, rather, reflected the confusion of elites as to the meaning and practice of Western democracy. It was not a polyarchy in which interest groups guided by party discipline competed through elites representing them, but it was, rather, elites competing along clan lines without regard to any party discipline.

Immediately after independence the legislatures of British Somaliland and Italian Somaliland met together and elected as president Aadan Abdullah Usman, a member of a Hawiye sub-clan and of the popular Somali Youth League. The president, in turn, recommended the appointment of Abdirashid Ali Shermarke of the Majeerteen sub-clan of the Darood as the premier. Taking clan sensitivities into consideration, the president and prime minister worked together to create a clan-balanced cabinet to arrest any feeling of alienation by any of the principal clan-families. Thus the Digil, Hawiye, Darood, Isaac, and Rahawayn of the United Republic all had their share of cabinet posts. However, encouraged by his electoral success in 1964, Usman decided to drop Shermarke as prime minister in preference for Abdiriqzaaq Haaji Huseen, who also hailed from the Majeerteen sub-clan, the same clan-family as Shermarke. Despite this continuity, the decision generated so much of a stir that it took six months for the new appointment to be constitutionally approved. What Usman seriously overlooked was the interclan and intraclan character of clan conflict. He also made the mistake of underestimating Shermarke's popularity and organizing abilities.

These two mistakes were to cost him and Somalia a great deal. Because of the clan structure and its allegiances, a cabinet reshuffle or ministerial replacements had potential misinterpretations and misgivings, and this one in particular created tension within the Majeerteen sub-clans of the Darood clan-family. At the same time, it created the impression that a member of the Hawiye clan-family, Usman, had acted with the intention of creating confusion within the Majeerteen, and the Darood clan-family as a whole became offended.

In June 1967, when the National Assembly met to elect a new president, Usman paid for his mistakes. Shermarke was able to combine his popularity and organizing abilities to defeat Usman and assume the office of president. To keep the SYL united, Shermarke nominated a previous party defector, Mohammed A. Egal, as prime minister. These new developments did not heal the intraclan conflict within the Majeerteen, and Egal's foreign policy moves proved unpopular. Contrary to the election promises of irredentism, Egal adopted a new approach towards Somalia's neighbours in which co-operation rather than confrontation was the strategy aimed at bringing self-determination for those Somalis living in Kenya and Ethiopia. Egal also restored diplomatic relations with Britain, which had been broken over the irredentist issue. Political rivals saw these policy actions as a betrayal of the Somali cause, and demonstrations against them took place in many parts of the country.[8] Intraclan tension within the Majeerteen sub-clan also increased. The 1969 general elections, with sixty-four parties participating, were characterized by violence and rioting, with many people losing their lives. The SYL, led by Shermarke and Egal, emerged as the dominant party once again, winning seventy-three seats amidst accusations of rigging and heavy spending aimed at courting political support.

Still, to foster their respective clan interests, when the National Assembly convened all but one of the opposition deputies crossed the floor to join the SYL. The only opposition member was Huseen, the former prime minister under Usman. The crossing of the floor, however, did not stop the intraclan conflict within the Majeerteen. Some four months after the elections of 1969, with Premier Egal away on a visit to the United States, Shermarke was gunned down by one of his bodyguards, who was a soldier of a Majeerteen sub-clan whose candidate had lost to Shermarke. This was a case in which centrifugal forces arising from partisan politics within the Majeerteen far outweighed the centripetal forces tending to keep the Majeerteen together. After Shermarke's assassination Egal was compelled to return quickly to the country to participate in the choice of a new president.

The Advent of Military Rule and Socialism

The choice of a president became difficult as parliamentarians and ministers without any sense of party discipline quarrelled among themselves. Meanwhile, due to its inability to honour its irredentist election promises coupled with the ongoing quarrels in Parliament and within the cabinet, both government and Parliament lost the confidence of Somalis in general. Into this state of political confusion and lack of legitimacy, the military intervened on October 21, 1969, with General Siad Barré seizing power as the chairman of the Supreme Revolutionary Council (SRC) amidst a popular rejoicing and celebration that Somali society was later to regret.

Military rule, like partisan politics, was also totally incompatible with the Somali culture. Again contrary to the theories and expectations of certain Western scholars, the Somali military leaders became so divided along clan lines that the whole military appeared to have lost touch with reality. Like its civilian predecessor, the military regime failed to ensure the transfer of the ideological symbols of unity from the various clans and sub-clans to the centre to build a strong nation, a move that needed to be followed by the delegation of authority and devolution of power to the clans and sub-clans to promote state-building and maintain a balance between centralization and decentralization.

Military rule began with the banning of political parties and, for the purposes of legitimization, an irredentist rhetoric. The military declared socialism as a development philosophy at a time when the capitalist phase of development had not yet been set in place.[9] Like the attempt to establish socialism in Ghana, what resulted was a form of mixed economy within which clans, led by their elites and not classes, struggled among themselves for pieces of the national pie. At the same time as it preached a socialist ideology, the military regime emphasized a Somali cultural revival, indicating that its leaders were aiming at a Somali brand of African communalism, with an emphasis on self-help programs in which the state would play a significant role. In 1972 the revolutionary government of Siad Barré, after adopting a Latin script for the Somali language, nationalized the education system and declared Somali to be the only official language and only medium of instruction. The regime introduced a crash program of free, mass education, succeeding within a few years in providing an estimated 60 per cent of the population with rudimentary and writing skills.

This crash program was not, however, Somali in content, in the sense that it was not geared towards an ideological education to rid the country of clanism and thereby facilitate the transfer of the ideological symbols of unity from the clan level to the centre. This failure to seize the opportunity at that particular time to create a new Somalia free from clanism and identifying with nationalist aspirations would later come back to haunt the Barré government.

Barré's government succeeded in two other matters. He was able to attract a supply of arms from the Soviet Union and to simultaneously antagonize the West. He also combined a skilful manipulation of clan politics with the suppression of critics, detention of opponents, and use of cash to silence opposition groups to maintain a false impression of political stability. His own means of political support derived from his membership in the Marehaan of the Darood sub-clan and from the army, which was dominated by the Ogadeenis sub-clan of the Darood clan-family, to which Barré's mother belonged. As a result of these clan games, thousands of the Majeerteen sub-clan of the Darood and the Isaaq clan-family were either killed or victimized in various ways.[10] The domination of the army by the Ogadeenis encouraged Barré to embark upon his 1977-78 irredentist ambition of snatching the Ethiopian portion of the Ogaden by force.[11] This action angered the former Soviet Union (Somali's chief supplier of arms at the time), which saw Colonel Haile Mengistu of Ethiopia as a communist brother. When the Soviet Union, using the Cubans as surrogates, openly supported Ethiopia militarily, Barré switched his allegiance to the United States.

Clan Manipulation under Military Rule

Despite all these setbacks, Barré was able to rule Somalia for twenty-one years, combining manipulation of clan politics with ruthless repression. However, his regime's stability was only in appearance, not reality. He was assisted in the maintenance of this apparent stability by the enormous amount of economic aid and arms received from both the Soviet Union and the United States, which competed for control of the strategic Berbera port. Given the effects of military rule and clan games, only an appropriate spark in time was required to expose the inherent instability of the regime. After all, the existence of a politically stable equilibrium means that after a political disturbance a state's political system will return to its former situation and status. A politically unstable situation means that when a political disturbance occurs, the political system is unable to return to its former status and the situation continues to deteriorate. Political stability, then, is not a matter of the number of years that a government is in power, but of the ability of the political system to absorb shocks and challenges and remain essentially effective. Developments in the international arena provided the litmus test for the stability of the military regime.

The oil-pricing and monetary shocks of the 1970s and the 1980s hit Somalia very hard. The economy was undermined, and the national debt grew with rampant shortages of essential commodities. Meanwhile, a massive influx of Somali-speaking refugees into Somalia after the Ogaden war carried heavy costs. The situation required the existence of an encompassing and committed coalition capable of absorbing the shocks while simultaneously enjoying the support of all clans—and this the manipulation of clan politics was not capable of achieving.

The economic hardships translated into a Somali perception of an incompetence surrounding the military regime. Barré's manipulation of clan politics no longer worked, with clan rivalry only becoming intensified through his efforts. Moreover, his clan politics fragmented and turned many of his own clan-family members against him. By 1989 Somalis held a widespread resentment against Barré and his Marehaan sub-clan. The suppression of critics and nepotism were fragmenting the political system as a whole, and alienated Somalis were engaging in growing insurgency operations. Moreover, because of Barré's loss of the Ogaden war, both the military and the government administrative machinery suffered from a general loss of morale.

Between 1989 and late 1990 political authority broke down to the extent that nobody seemed to be in control of Somali affairs. The Western ideology touting the competence of the military failed miserably to materialize in Somalia. Discipline and loyalty among the high-ranking officers of the military broke down to the extent that three clan-based opposition groups, led by three former generals under Barré, arose in Somalia: the United Somali Congress (USC), which derived its support from the Hawiye clan-family; the Somali National Movement (SNM), which derived support from the Isaaq clan-family of the former British Somaliland of the North; and the Somali Patriotic Movement (SPM), which derived support from the Ogadeeni sub-clan of the Darood clan, from which Barré's mother hailed. The Ogadeeni rebellion against Barré shows both how strong intraclan forces can be and what can happen when high hopes are suddenly dashed. But because these generals hated one another almost to the same extent that they hated Barré, they could neither unite nor co-ordinate their actions against their common enemy. Superimposed upon this situation were influences from the international arena.

The Impact of the End of the Cold War

The end of the Cold War translated into a relative Western neglect of Africa, including Somalia. Events in Eastern Europe, including the war in Bosnia, and in the Middle East, including the Gulf War, shifted attention further away from Africa. The relative neglect of Somalia meant a slowdown in the arms supplies that had enabled Barré to maintain military supremacy over the insurgents fighting against him, especially the USC led by General Mohammed Aidid, the most popular Somali general. Not surprisingly, therefore, in January 1991 the USC succeeded in toppling the Barré regime. However, because the three generals leading the opposing forces fighting against Barré hated one another, the resulting deepening of the crisis plunged Somalia into the chaos of a country without government, a turn of events that took on something of the character of the Hobbesian state of nature.

The confused state of affairs was aggravated by controversial actions taken by a number of concerned Somalis. Without the approval of the warring factions or a consensus among the USC leaders who toppled the Barré regime, in January 1991 a group of Somalis appointed Ali Mahdi of the Abgal sub-clan of the Hawiye clan-family as president. His appointment was challenged not only by the SNM and SPM but also, and most vehemently, by the faction of the USC that supported General Mohammed Aidid. Even though Aidid belonged to the Haber Gedir sub-clan of the Hawiye clan-family, which implied that he and Ali Mahdi hailed from the same clan-family, the two could not resolve their differences. Fighting, therefore, continued among the SNM, SPM, and the USC, as well as between two factions within the USC. As the fighting went on, the innocent Bantu-speaking people of Somalia who did not belong to any of the clan-families of Somalia were trampled upon and victimized by the fighting clan-groups. In complete contravention of the teachings of Islam, the atrocities of these fighting groups included intensive rape in the fertile Juba Valley, where the pockets of Bantu-speaking people lived. Thus, as J. Predergast points out:

> During the latter part of 1992, the Bardera-Baidoa-Lug triangle degenerated into the most acute famine belt in the country. The people of the fertile Juba Valley had been repeatedly victimised by the scorched-earth tactics of the Somali National Front (SNF), the Somali Patriotic Movement (SPM) and the United Somali Congress (Haber Gedir) militia as their forces looted livestock, seeds,

tools and grain, destroyed water resources, raped women and killed men.[12]

Given this apparent state of anarchy, the United Nations decided to intervene in the Somali crisis under Operation Restore Hope. By labelling the generals "warlords" (a label not applied, for instance, to the generals fighting in Bosnia), the United Nations offended the Somali warring parties and made them suspicious of the world body's intentions. In particular, General Aidid and his faction were insulted on racist grounds. General Aidid reportedly stated, angrily, "I know I am a properly trained General by Western standards. When I became a warlord, I do not know."[13] To those who understand the impact of insult in African culture, it was no surprise that delay and impediments were put in the way of the deployment of the UN troops. For example, in July 1992 General Aidid complained that a UN landing of food to Somalia had included military equipment destined for his rival, Ali Mahdi.[14] Subsequently, Aidid agreed to the deployment of only five hundred Pakistani troops. In addition, the reconciliation moves by Mohammed Sahnoun, the special representative of the UN Secretary General in Somalia, proved fruitless.

The U.S. government's resort to force, which led to the deaths or wounding of several hundred Somalis in Mogadishu, finally ended in a disaster in which the bodies of U.S. troops killed in combat were dragged in the streets while other captured soldiers were humiliated in televised interviews. Finally, the UN troops were withdrawn amid accusations of inhuman acts against some Somalis involving Canadian troops. With the withdrawal of the UN troops in March 1995, Somalia's state of anarchy continued. The assassination of Aidid in August 1996 did not bring an end to the anarchy of interclan and intraclan struggle.

Many Somalis admit and accept that partisan politics as a democratic process failed to work in Somalia and might not work within the current Somali culture. Military rule was also a failure. However, where both partisan politics and military rule failed, the indigenous Somali democracy has proved effective. This is not surprising given that the indigenous democracy was practised for hundreds of years before it was replaced by the colonial administrative apparatuses of Britain and Italy. Recent years have seen a re-emergence of the authority of traditional elders as part of indigenous democratic practice. About twelve out of the eighteen regions of Somalia recognize the council of elders as the highest administrative body. These councils also have the final word in disputed matters so that, practically, they are recognized as the highest court of appeal. In Northern Somalia, the Isaaq clan-family declared a unilateral secession from Somalia and were opposed by the Dhulbahante sub-clan of the Darood. In the days of partisan politics and military rule such a declaration might have been a sufficient justification for bloody military action to end the secession. The indigenous democracy of Somalia demonstrated its capacity and ability to handle such crisis situations when the council of leaders of the Isaaq and the Dhulbahante found a common ground for peaceful coexistence without any resort to violence.[15] Furthermore, the two councils of elders found it wise to condense centrifugal political forces by agreeing through the traditional consensual means not to recognize the authority of any government declared in Somalia until the political problems of Somalia as a whole have been solved.[16] As a result, the North is enjoying relative peace and stability, and Somalia as a whole appears to be returning to its own indigenous democracy.

CHAPTER ELEVEN

SENEGAL: FROM FRENCH COLONIALISM TO THE FAILURE OF PARTISAN POLITICS

Senegal has, perhaps, been in longer and more continuous contact with Europe than has any other country in Sub-Saharan Africa. Its exposure to French partisan politics goes back to the eighteenth century. It was the territory that France used as a springboard for its colonialist expansion in the region. Unlike many African countries, in which the imaginary boundary lines drawn during the Scramble for Africa had little or no relation to the ethnic structure of society, Senegal has boundaries that coincide roughly with the traditional boundaries separating different cultures and ethnic groups. Its borders separate off the Moors to the north, the Sudanic people to the east, and various ethic groups to the south from the bulk of Senegalese.

The country therefore does not face the irredentist and family separation problems prevalent in the Horn of Africa and elsewhere in Sub-Saharan Africa. This is not to deny that the ethnic groups of Casamance are distinct from the rest of the Senegalese people. It is to emphasize that the Wolof, Lebou, Severe, Tukulor, and Fulani, who constitute the majority of the Senegalese population, are closely related in language and culture.

During the colonial period Senegal was the political and economic centre of the Federation of French West Africa. As the country in which the Western practice of democracy first arrived, Senegal occupies an important place in the political history of Sub-Saharan Africa. Saint-Louis (the former capital) and Goree are reputed to have had African mayors as far back as the days of the French Revolution and to have elected a deputy to the National Assembly in Paris in 1848.[1] Before colonialism each of the ethnic groups of Senegal society had its own organized form of politics, so that the concept of politics as a means of realizing the aspirations of society was nothing new. What colonialism brought was a different mode of political organization—one alien to the cultural environment and forced down the Senegalese throat.

French colonialism brought along with it changes in the indigenous social and political structures. In the enforcement of French rule powerful traditional rulers were deposed, and in achieving their colonial objectives and interests the French appointed or created their own chiefs as they deemed convenient. Wesley Johnson writes:

> The French retained the institution of local chiefship only because they found it essential for the smooth running of the colony. Where a French official might bog down in his dealings with the Africans, a traditional authority could accomplish a great deal. Moreover, the great moral authority of a respected local chief soon associated itself with his French superior as well. But most chiefs were aware that their real power derived from the French administration.[2]

Traditional rulers had limited power and legitimacy under the French. The French appointed as chiefs African commoners who had worked for them as interpreters, messengers, or clerks—people who had no experience in traditional rule and sometimes could not even speak the local language. The process led to the disappearance of several traditional power roles and distorted general behavioural patterns within Senegalese society. The French-appointed chiefs, with no local legitimacy, were seldom successful in leading their subjects through the harsh adjustments to French rule. In difficult times the Senegalese would naturally look to their chiefs for help and encouragement but found little of what they expected because most of the legitimate chiefs had been deposed, imprisoned, or transformed into the puppets of the French. It was under these conditions that the French first introduced partisan politics in Senegal, which became dominated by the Bordeaux merchants and Creoles.

The introduction of Western education had its own problems, indicating, among other things, the discriminatory attitude of the French towards the African population. Despite the Western ideals of individual advancement according to merit, in their admissions to schools in the urban centres the French colonialists gave preference to their own students. Qualified African teachers received far less pay than their French peers, and French graduates were preferred in appointments within the colonial administration. In addition, because of a tendency to replace Africans in the administration with new arrivals from France or young French graduates from the local schools, the few Africans in the administration had no assurances of job security. There were spatial inequalities in the standard of education as well. The urban school programs to which the French were exposed were almost identical to the programs in France, but the education that African students received in the regional and rural schools was substandard. The disparities and discrimination in education fuelled the growing discontent against French rule.

Compared to other countries in Sub-Saharan Africa, Senegal has had the longest exposure to the Western brand of partisan politics. Surely, then, if that brand of politics were at all compatible with African culture it is in Senegal that it should have been most effective in leading to successful development. Economically, Senegal is one of the world's major producers of peanuts. It has a relatively well-developed transportation network, including railroads linking the principal cities. Dakar, one of Africa's major ports, is connected by rail to Bamako, the Mali capital. Apart from the international airport in Dakar, several cities and towns have airports that can service domestic flights and raise the potential for commercial activity.

French assimilationist policies were implemented early in Senegal, and Africans in Senegal so sought assimilation to French political institutions that the country may be said to be a critical test case for the effectiveness of the policy of assimilation in the context of African development. The tension between the assimilation to French culture on one hand and maintaining their Islamic identity and African culture on the other had an impact on the attitudes and orientations of Senegalese Africans. A paradoxical dualism developed: the African elite had to rely on assimilation to gain entry into the French colonial political space, but at the same time a complete cultural assimilation would leave no place for the nurturing of African culture. In the process, some Senegalese Africans became assimilated, others rejected assimilation in favour of their African heritage, and still others pursued a dualistic balance. Those who were assimilated became aliens in their own land—sometimes becoming more French than the French themselves. Those who were opposed to assimilation became extremists or radicals. Those who maintained a dualistic balance became moderates. As a result, the Senegalese slowly fashioned a capable African elite that was not homogeneous in attitudes and orientations. Some of the capable leaders, including Léopold Senghor, the country's first president, commanded international respect and participated in the National Assembly in Paris.

Despite its earlier exposure to Western democracy, its close relationship with France and the Western bloc, and its well-trained elite, Senegal's post-independence development experience was not overly successful. While it became the most industrious country in French West Africa, after it gained independence in 1960 its economic prospects, which seemed excellent to that point, increasingly deteriorated. The removal of a French subsidy for peanuts and drought conditions continuing into the 1970s placed great stresses and strains on the country's economy. Like all non-oil-producing countries, Senegal was hurt by the oil-pricing and monetary shocks of the 1970s and 1980s, and unfavourable terms of trade also had their impact. The peanut farmers responded to a 20 per cent drop in prices by planting fewer acres in peanuts, which weakened the economy further and contributed to labour disturbances in the major cities and to student rebellions after 1968. A Sahel drought in the 1980s, coupled with the declining price of peanuts in the international market, translated into political unrest, including a secession bid by the ethnic groups of Casamance.

The First Coming of Western Politics

Senegal has had a long exposure to partisan politics. Western politics took root in Senegal as far back as the eighteenth century, and deputies to the French National Assembly were elected from Senegal as far back as 1848. But this transplanted partisan politics was an adulterated version of the French practice. The political scene was dominated by the French, particularly the Bordeaux merchants and the Creole. Voters did not cast their ballots as supporters of the indigenous Africans, who were excluded from running, but for the French or the Creole. Vote-buying through the bribing of indigenous Africans was the norm. Johnson describes the scenario:

> The Bordeaux merchants were at their most cynical during the campaigns. African voters were looked upon as objects to be bought—or more precisely, to be rented for elections. French agents distributed sacks of flour, rice, sugar, and tea to neighbourhood chiefs as electoral insurance; in time, this practice developed into open bribery. Lavish campaign promises and flattery were commonplace. Some firms even transplanted their African workers from one Commune to another for voting under assumed names. There is no doubt that the electoral scandals uncovered by Verrier in 1905 were not entirely African in origin.[3]

Certainly, this was not the kind of democracy practised in France, and the French in Senegal themselves must certainly have been aware of the discrepancy. The exclusion of African voters from the list of eligible candidates meant that the French and Creole minority were to represent African interests, which they knew very little about, and probably cared about even less. The Africans, for their part, did not understand the alien political system. To them, voting was a festival in which the French and Creoles provided free commodities for some pieces of papers to be cast into some boxes on their behalf. Thus, true Western democratic practice was undermined from the eighteenth century until 1900.

Gradually, by 1900, African voters began to show greater interest in participating directly in political decision-making. That awareness posed a new threat to the privileged position of the French, who were quick to react. The French colonial authorities decided to kill the policy of assimilation, which was continuously creating black voters. They began to think that assimilation had gone too far and was setting a dangerous example for the newer French colonies in Africa. The Bordeaux merchants launched a campaign to deprive Senegalese Africans of political rights, but miscalculated and underestimated the resolve of the African political elite, who assigned to themselves the name of *originaires*. The campaign set the stage for struggles between the French colonial officials, the French colonists, the Creoles, and the indigenous Africans to decide who would dominate the colony's political space and control its levers of political power. The political ideology of the *originaires* was to adapt European ideas to an African cultural base in the same manner that Islamic ideas had in the past been adapted to African culture. Their approach, then, was not a total rejection of French culture in a fanatical way but was a question of adapting to that culture and blending it with African and Islamic culture. The approach was not without its problems and confusions. It was difficult for both the French and the *originaires* to specify the dosage of assimilation required by Africans. In 1912 the French, who wanted Africans to behave just like Europeans, defined requirements for those Africans who desired to advance to the prestigious position of being certified as French citizens. It was this struggle that brought the African writer Blaise Diagne to the political stage in Senegal in 1914.

The desire by the *originaires* to adapt and blend European ideas with the existing blend of Islamic ideas and African culture came up against the influence of Islamic marabouts, who had responded to the repressive character of French rule. As the French deposed the powerful chiefs and replaced them with their puppets who had little legitimacy, the general morale of the African populations declined. Because the Africans could not trust the chiefs, they had no effective leaders to serve as sources of encouragement and consolation in the harsh environment of French colonial rule. The Islamic marabouts arose to fill this vacuum and succeeded in attracting the attention of both urban and rural Senegalese. The marabouts were clever enough to adapt Islamic ideas to African culture. Because most Africans could not read the Koran, the teachings and words of the marabouts became more important than the Koran. Among the most popular marabouts were Amadou Bamba M' Backe, the founder of the Mourides Islamic brotherhood, and Al Haji Malick Sy of the Tijaniya sect. By winning the hearts of the Africans, the marabouts eventually came to control the voting behaviour of the enfranchised Africans, particularly in the rural areas. If the *originaires* were to win and control political space, it became increasingly evident that they could not ignore the support and influence of the marabouts. Furthermore, because the *originaires* were not as rich as the French and could therefore not buy as many votes, winning the support of the influential marabouts became an indispensable alternative. To work towards their goals, in 1912 the *originaires* founded Senegal's first African political group, the Jeunes Senegalais, in Saint-Louis. The organization derived its inspiration not only from the marabouts but also, as their role model and a symbol of determination that wins in the end, from Booker T. Washington.

Despite the support of the marabouts, the *originaires* did not find an easy path to the levers of political power. The French were suspicious of the activities of those who identified with the *originaires* or any person who showed any propensity for African nationalism, and they resorted to character assassination and demonology to discredit influential members of the *originaires*. Blaise Diagne, for example, was described as an undisciplined and dangerous fellow. When he was serving with the military in the French Congo, for instance, his superior officer had reported: "Monsieur Diagne, the Senegalese *originaire*, has tried to play the role of emancipator of the African race here in the Congo. All his remarks exhibit a burning hostility toward the white race. At election time certain of his compatriots in Saint-Louis yell, 'Senegal for the Senegalese!' In the same way, he seeks to implant in this colony the doctrine of 'Africa for the Africans.'"[4]

The French, like all colonizers, claimed that the colonization of Africa was a civilizing mission. If that claim were genuine, the French should not have been at all disturbed by slogans such as "Africa for

Africans" or "Senegal for the Senegalese." After all, Europe is for Europeans, and France (for the most part) is for the French. What should have been decided upon were the definitions of "Africans" and "Senegalese," and surely that definition would not depend upon the colour of the skin but on a commitment to the aspirations of the country or Africa as a whole. Furthermore, during the early political struggles at the beginning of the twentieth century, because the aspirations of the *originaires* were to gain equal treatment within the French empire, the question of "independence" was not at issue. By being openly troubled by these slogans, the French were sending signals to the indigenous Africans that people of French descent born in Africa or Senegal or even living there for a long period of time did not consider themselves as Africans but as French citizens, as people who were not prepared to identify with the aspirations of the indigenous African populations, give up their racial prejudices, and accept the equality of the races as a guiding principle in the territory's growth.

The flames of discontent among the indigenous populations continued to burn brightly. As Senegal was the centre of French Equatorial Africa, the discontent there became infectious and spread to other areas of that region. Into this situation of general discontent, Blaise Diagne arrived in Senegal to contest the Senegalese elections in 1914, marking the first time an indigenous African contested the vote. The French colonists, relying on the power of vote-buying, and out of touch with the indigenous populations, were so confident of winning the elections that Governor Cor wrote to Paris that Diagne had no chance of success. Cor was in for a shock, because the Islamic marabouts had introduced their own political technique that proved a match for the detrimental politics of the French colonists: the marabouts dictated whom their faithfuls should vote for.

The new marabout countermeasures proved effective. Several candidates competed for the elections. With the support of the marabouts who had thoughtfully integrated Islam with African cultural values to bring African nationalist aspirations to the fore, Blaise Diagne, although a Catholic, won by a large margin in the first round and proceeded to win the second round of voting despite French vote-buying efforts. The *originaires* and the African masses rejoiced. According to one writer, Blaise Diagne's victory "profoundly affected" the masses:

Blaise Diagne ... personified the realization of their wildest dreams—a black man who wasn't afraid to attack the whites, who often spoke to them with disdain, who declared (quite truthfully) that he was superior to most of them. Diagne had his newspaper, he campaigned mightily.... He spoke in public on a platform. He exalted the most secret African desires: "Today him, tomorrow me." He opened a door through which all hoped to pass. They dreamed of the public offices they would have. The General Council, the municipal councils—all of it would fall into their hands.[5]

Diagne lived up to the expectations of the marabouts and the indigenous populations. Under his leadership, and even before 1945 when African nationalist movements acquired significant political momentum, the *originaires* won a series of election victories and succeeded in replacing the French and Creole actors in the Senegalese political arena. The political opening in Senegal, though, was the result of a combination of factors, including nationalism, assimilation, the urbanization that brought the *originaires* together, and religion through the mediation of Islamic marabouts. The indigenous Africans tended not to vote out of a sense of individual volition but according to how they were bought by the French or dictated to by Islamic marabouts. Despite these shortcomings, the *originaires*' success laid the foundations of political development in French-speaking Africa. It raised the potential for putting pressure on France to make Africans French citizens and voters and provided the impetus for the development of nationalist movements in French Africa.

The Second World War, in which many Africans fought for France, acted as a catalyst to the African aspirations previously demonstrated by the *originaires*. African soldiers brought home stories of how events of the war convinced them that the African was in no way inferior to the French or indeed any other European or any other race. In response to pressures after the war, the French extended citizenship to all inhabitants of French West Africa, making the colonies overseas territories of France, but this change came too late. By that time the political wind blowing in Africa carried a clear call for independence. The nationalist movements had developed into political parties with various branches in the colonies.

Partisan Politics after the Second World War

Senegal is another example of an African country in which the ideological symbols of unity were almost[6] completely transferred to the centre to constitute a nation-state, and still the introduction of partisan politics succeeded in dividing the country along urban and rural lines. As the political and administrative centre of French West Africa, Senegal has been closely connected in its development experience to other former French colonies in the region. Unlike the previous era, postwar political development in French West Africa began not with a leader from Senegal but under the leadership of Felix Houphouet-Boigny of the Ivory Coast with the formation in 1946 of the Rassemblement Démocratique Africain (RDA) in Bamako of present-day Mali. The party adopted an anti-colonial posture with the objectives of uniting the French colonies in Africa to fight for reforms to the colonial system and of gaining independence for political parties from parties in France. It drew the support of thousands in most of the French colonies and became the main political party of the Ivory Coast, Mali, Upper Volta, Guinea, and Niger.

Meanwhile, in Senegal another political party, independent of the RDA, was formed with Léopold Senghor as its leader. The RDA was not effective in Senegal, where the Bloc Démocratique Senegalais (BDS) led by Senghor was strong. Like the RDA, the BDS desired a strong West African Federation. The Cold War was in progress, and France and its allies were diametrically opposed to communism, doing all they could to halt its spread. The RDA did not seem to be sensitive enough to the realities of the ideological struggles of the Cold War, and it made a serious political and ideological miscalculation by aligning itself with the French Communist Party. That miscalculation was to cost it a great deal, leading to a loss of its principal objective of uniting the French territories.

The RDA had started as a pan-regional and multi-ethnic party that invested much energy to overcome ethnicism and posed a serious threat to France's strategy of divide and rule. Despite pressure from the United Nations for self-determination for all peoples of the world, France would not permit any of its territories—and their enormous resources, necessary for postwar reconstruction—to go communist. The French initiated mass arrests of RDA members, and banned all pro-RDA newspapers and publications. When the RDA resorted to demonstrations, the French responded by opening fire on the demonstrators. When the RDA resorted to strikes and boycotts of French firms, the French responded by using the army to crush the workers.

Given that Houphouet-Boigny derived much support from the Ivory Coast, and especially from his own Baule ethnic group, the French resorted to the ruthless killing of his supporters in the Korhogo and Dimbokro areas. The sympathies aroused by those killings drew multi-ethnic support, encouraging Houphouet-Boigny to organize non-violent resistance, including strikes by railway workers, hunger strikes in the prisons, a boycott of French firms, and protest marches by women. The French responded by financing the formation of ethnic parties to counter the RDA influence. Elections held in 1951 were rigged by the French, who declared the ethnic parties the winner. The French also instigated and encouraged Moshi nationalism in Upper Volta (now Burkina Faso) and used that as the basis for severing that territory from the Ivory Coast. The French colonies—far from being ripe for communism—did not understand the basic tenets of communism, which was confused with African communalism, in which co-operative labour and communal ownership of land played a role. By misconceiving African communalism as communism, and aligning with a communist ideology that was alien to African culture, the RDA unnecessarily antagonized France, in particular, and the West as a whole. It invited upon itself the ruthlessness of France, which was understandable given the logic of the Cold War. As the French attitude towards the RDA hardened, Houphouet-Boigny was compelled by the prevailing objective situation to forsake the communists and to become a puppet of France working for the recognition of the former French territories as separate entities. In this way, he began to act against what he originally stood for when the RDA was formed. He now aimed at becoming a leader of the Ivory Coast instead of a leader of the proposed West African federation, where he perceived Senghor as a challenger from a relatively poor territory. This change in political direction did not please Senghor, who maintained consistently that the interests of the French colonies might be served more effectively within a strong West African federation. Subsequently, the RDA broke up into territorial sections that made it weaker and exposed each territory to the rise of the same ethnicity that the party initially sought to eliminate.

The French political strategists had another hidden agenda. The French did not want to see the proposed West African federation, which was the initial vision of the RDA, come to fruition. The French political strategy was to have the territories remain separate entities rather than be united under the umbrella of a strong federation. Their political calculation was that a strong federation would be more effective in challenging French domination. Thus, in 1947, when the French perceived that the RDA's power base was in the Ivory Coast, they detached Upper Volta from the Ivory Coast administration to weaken the RDA. When Houphouet-Boigny shifted to align with the French strategists,

France became encouraged to pursue its hidden agenda more effectively and was assisted by events in the international arena. The price of coffee rose in the 1950s, at a time when the Ivory Coast production of coffee had also risen. Houphouet-Boigny did not want the Ivory Coast to share this boom with the other relatively poor French colonies, and his desire and the hidden agenda of the French became fused.

The Entente and Mali Federation Experience

The French, with the support of Houphouet-Boigny, set up elected assemblies in each colony, with the Federal Council in Dakar now limited to advisory functions only. However, within the French territories there was a strong feeling for federation. In 1958 representatives from Senegal, Soudan (now Mali), Upper Volta (now Burkina Faso), and Dahomey (now Benin) met in Dakar to consider the federation issue. A constituent assembly met in 1959, and a constitution was proposed for a new federation of Mali. That did not please the French and Houphouet-Boigny, who, acting together, were able to use economic threats to pressure Upper Volta and Dahomey not to join the Mali federation. To counteract any further influence of Senghor, Houphouet-Boigny worked for a loose association called the Sahel-Benin Union or the Entente, which would comprise the Ivory Coast, Niger, Dahomey, and Upper Volta—an association that had nothing to offer the participants, and broke up in 1960. Thus, partisan politics succeeded in creating a rivalry between Houphouet-Boigny and Senghor to render the West African Federation nothing but an illusion. Meanwhile, Senegal and Soudan went ahead to form the Mali federation, which lasted only from 1959 to 1960.

The Mali federation was short-lived not because it was something the peoples of the two countries did not want, but because the political parties of the two countries had different foreign ideological postures and agendas. At the time of the federation in 1959, Senegal was a multiparty state while the Soudan was a one-party state of the Soudanese branch of the RDA led by Modibo Keita. Although the two dominant parties claimed to be socialist, their interpretation of what constituted socialism was different. The more radical Keita favoured a strong unitary government, rapid Africanization of the civil service, expulsion of the French army from African soil, and nationalization of all foreign firms. His posture was understandable given the ruthless behaviour of the French towards the RDA. The Bloc Démocratique Senegalais (BDS) had not been subjected to the same kind of hostility by the French, and Senghor favoured a federal structure that would be loose enough to enable other states to join, as well as a slower pace of Africanization conducive to a smooth running of the public service without loss of effectiveness or efficiency. He was opposed to the nationalization of foreign firms and regarded the presence of French troops as an economic necessity. In addition, Senghor was married to a French woman and could not be expected to embrace a radical policy that might paint his beloved wife as an enemy. Keita's posture was not sensitive enough to Senghor's marital situation. Indeed, the French were proud that Senghor was married to a French woman, as one writer indicates: "Senghor's marriage to a white woman caused no ripple, no negative excitement at all in France. His fellow deputies in the French National Assembly and the French Public reacted to his marriage positively. It was as though the French had expected all along that Senghor, as a fine self-respecting Frenchman, albeit an African ancestry, would marry a French woman."[7]

Problems also arose in the federation about how federal jobs were to be allocated, and how to unite their two political parties into one to be called Parti de la Fédération Africaine (PFA). Despite these differences, the two countries became independent in June 1960 under the name Mali, with Senghor as president and Keita as prime minister. Differences between the two political parties escalated so rapidly that on August 20, while the two populations were still rejoicing over their federation and independence, and without warning or mandate from the people, Senghor ordered the police to arrest Keita and all the Soudanese ministers with him in Dakar and deport them to Bamako, the Soudanese capital. William J. Foltz explains, "The Senegalese political leaders felt that the continued existence of the Federation threatened their domestic political base and, therefore, their opportunity to continue to play a significant role in African political life."[8] However, considering the popularity of the Mali federation in the African political scene of those days and that it had the mandate of the peoples of the Soudan and Senegal, its short life might be attributed more to the problems related to difficulties associated with the partisan democratic process.

Partisan Politics in Senghor's Senegal after the Mali Federation

Senghor turned from his federalist stance to concentrate on Senegal's internal politics. In Senegal a number of factors—Wolof as a common language, a long history of interaction and intermarriages between the ethnic groups, the unifying influence of Islam among the majority of the population, and the common French assimilationist policies—had drowned ethnic sensitivities and enabled an almost complete transfer of the ideological symbols of unity from the ethnic level to the centre to constitute a nation-state. In addition, Senghor's cultural nationalism, which emphasized African values, in conjunction with the earlier work of the Islamic marabouts in fusing African culture with Islamic values to bring the aspirations of the indigenous Senegalese to the fore, served as a unifying force. As a result, although he was a Christian Senghor enjoyed the support of the Moslem majority in the same manner as Blaise Diagne did in 1914. His massive victories in the 1951 and 1956 elections, in which he won almost all the seats except in a few urban areas, confirmed the multi-ethnic character of his support. The relative support he derived from the rural areas signalled the rural-urban polarization of Senegal through partisan politics. His political rival in Senegal, Lamine Guéye, enjoyed the support of the urban areas, while Senghor, hailing from the rural area, enjoyed the support of the rural populations.

The breakup of the Mali federation meant Senegal had to pursue its own development strategy. Senghor proceeded to create a de facto one-party state with centralized administration and a rapid establishment of parastatals, which saw the creation of about seventy-five corporations between 1970 and 1975. Penetration of the party in society was through clientele-based networks that linked communities to patrons, and patrons to the president, which rendered almost impossible the organization of any meaningful opposition. The state of affairs was not in conformity with African cultural practice, in which voluntary organizations and freedom of association are so predominant that clientele networks are unnecessary. The resources invested in the clientele networks might have been directed to productive ventures to satisfy the basic needs and legitimate demands of the people.

The oil-pricing and monetary shocks of the 1970s demanded the existence of a nationalist and encompassing coalition capable of absorbing the shocks while simultaneously maintaining both internal and external legitimacy. The de facto one-party state found itself wanting, and the ruling party sought to maintain international legitimacy and to vent internal political steam by reintroducing multiparty politics. The party seemed to have forgotten that the pre-independence elections and the post-independence elections of 1963 had been greeted with allegations of fraud that tended to divide Senegalese society along both partisan and rural-urban lines. In 1977 it drew up plans for a return to multiparty politics and changed its name to Parti Socialiste (PS). To discourage any resurfacing of ethnicity or religious sensitivity, the plan placed certain restrictions on the number of parties—allowing only three—and the political perspectives to be tolerated.[9] One of the parties was to campaign on liberal-democratic principles, the second on social-democratic principles, and the third on Marxist principles.

The electoral law also introduced a new system of proportional representation. Meanwhile a new political party, Rassemblement Nationale Démocratique (RND), had been formed by Cheik Anta Diop, a moderate socialist with strong support among the urban intellectuals and educated youth. The RND posed a serious threat to the PS, and to eliminate this opposition the PS allocated the social-democratic slot to itself. The liberal-democratic slot went to the Parti Démocratique Senegalais (PDS), led by Abdoulaye Wade, and the Marxist slot to the Parti Africain d'Indépendance (PAI), led by Majmout Diop. The RND was left with no slot, and with only three parties allowed to compete, it was automatically eliminated.

The elections of 1978 were characterized by resentment against the system. At the local level, officials appointed by the ruling PS treated the opposition parties with intolerance, as if members and supporters of those parties, though Senegalese, were enemies of Senegal. In addition, the clientele-based network built by the ruling party, PS, placed it in an advantageous position. Because of a lack of confidence in the political system and a resulting apathy, only about 37 per cent of the registered voters participated.[10] When the election results were announced, with the PS winning 82.02 per cent of the vote, very few people in the urban areas rejoiced.

Partisan Politics after Senghor

A change in the political leadership of the PS when Senghor stepped down at the end of 1980 did not alter the political behaviour of that party. In January 1981, as the economic problems for non-oil-producing countries deepened, Senghor was succeeded by Abdou Diouf, who decided to legitimize his regime both internally and externally by removing the restrictions on the number of parties. Within a year or two the system recognized sixteen parties, including six Marxist formations that could not unite to present a common front; eight of these parties competed at the legislative level. If in partisan politics the number of parties was the measure of democracy, Senegal was more democratic than any country in the West at that time.

Long before the 1983 elections the opposition parties declared the electoral code to be biased and unacceptable. Even with the removal of the limitation on the number of political parties, the electoral provisions favoured the ruling party and restricted the effectiveness of the proliferating political parties. Among other things, the ruling party allocated to itself half of the total time on the state media—leaving some sixteen other political parties to share the remaining half. The provisions of the electoral code made it difficult to verify the identities of voters, and because secret balloting was not mandatory, voters sometimes felt threatened by the presence of government officials at the polling booths, especially in the rural areas. The PS government's attitude was to see multiparty political participation as at best only some kind of favour extended to the opposing parties. Drawing lessons from the French colonial political practice—characterized by vote-buying and the provision of essential commodities—Diouf and the ruling party resorted to pledging a supply of goods and local amenities. Under the circumstances, the opposition parties became suspicious that the government had a hidden agenda of rigging the elections. When the PS, led by Diouf, was declared the winner, the populations of the urban centres were particularly displeased.

The next elections, in 1988, were also a mockery of democracy. They accentuated the rural-urban polarization and pointed to the dangerous consequences of setting down partisan politics in the cultural environment of Senegal. Despite protests by the opposition parties, the system applied the same electoral code that the opposition had declared to be biased and unacceptable in 1981-82. Again, the government attitude was as though multiparty political participation was only some kind of favour bestowed on the opposing parties. Initially seventeen parties contested the elections, but some were eliminated through new requirements. The smaller parties, for instance, were automatically eliminated by requirements that every party should submit a full candidate list and that parties were not to form electoral coalitions. Eventually only six parties were able to compete at the legislative level, and four in the presidential elections. Again the opposition parties protested against provisions of the electoral code, which among other things still allocated half the time on the state media to the PS alone, but their protests fell on deaf ears.

Secret balloting was again not mandatory, and again voters, especially in the rural areas, were threatened by the presence of the government officials at the voting stations. Although the newspaper *Le Soleil* was financed from the coffers of the state and should have given every party equal attention, it violated the fundamental democratic principle of equality by focusing its coverage of the campaign almost entirely on the PS and providing very little space to the opposition parties. What was even more disappointing was the responsibility assigned to the Supreme Court to monitor over three thousand polling stations, with the government and the Court both knowing very well that it did not have adequate staff to do the job.[11] Sensing an impending electoral fraud, the opposition parties advised and encouraged their supporters to monitor the elections themselves and to be prepared to confront the police. Opposition supporters were advised to occupy government offices in protest should their attempts to monitor the election process or fraudulent irregularities be challenged.

The registration process itself had its grave problems. The rural populations were expected to travel long distances to specified centres to register and obtain voting cards, and then on the voting day they had to go back to the same centres to cast their votes. The PS was aware not only that the youth between ages eighteen and twenty-one wanted to register and cast a vote on the affairs affecting their lives, but also that youth were mostly against the government because they had been hit hardest by the high rate of unemployment arising from the government's structural adjustment programs. By keeping the voting age at twenty-one the government deliberately disqualified a large section of Senegalese youth from voting.

Legislation limited the campaign period to three weeks in February 1988, and the election code also provided for a five-day delay before results could be announced, which was aimed at ensuring that voting behaviour in one area did not influence voting behaviour in another. As if it was above the law, the PS, whose government had approved the code, decided not to honour either of these two provisions. In 1987, several months before the campaign period had started, Diouf visited some regions and took pains to pledge a supply of desired amenities. The opposition parties, fully aware that Diouf and PS were violating the electoral rules, with the support of students, teachers, and intellectuals challenged aspects of the electoral code in the PS-dominated courts, but with little success. Tensions, with accompanying threats, mounted, especially towards the end of the campaign period. The voting took place on a single day, with the Supreme Court and its allocated staff of about twenty attempting to monitor the over three thousand polling stations.

Reports on the conduct of the elections were disappointing. About 41 per cent of Senegalese registered voters showed their lack of confidence in the electoral process by refusing to vote. More than 150 polling stations declared flawed reports, and over forty thousand votes were disqualified.[12] In areas with strong support for the opposing PDS, including Dakar and Thies, the voting station heads refused with impunity to sign the voting report and thus disqualified those votes. In other areas, local PS officials fraudulently distributed bundles of electoral cards to their clientele to enable them to vote even though they were not registered. In the end, in determining the election victory it was not so much who registered to vote and then got out to vote that mattered, but who was allowed to vote, which votes were approved by the voting station heads appointed by the government, and who announced the results of the vote.

In open defiance of the electoral provision of a five-day delay before the announcement, on the eve of the election day the government started releasing results that portrayed a landslide victory for the PS. The opposition parties responded immediately with charges of widespread fraud, which won the support of the youth. Riots erupted in the university in Dakar and quickly spread to most areas of the city. The violence included attacks on municipal buses, overturning cars and burning them, and the ransacking of government offices.

The PS responded by declaring a state of emergency a day after the elections. Several leaders of the opposing parties were arrested, quickly tried, and convicted. But the behaviour of the government before and after the trials and convictions pointed to an inner guilt and associated damage control strategies. First, even before the trials, to ease tensions the government reduced the prices of essential commodities. Second, soon after the trials it convened the National Assembly to vote on an amnesty law covering every infraction of the electoral law. To ease tensions further, the Assembly voted on freeing some of the Casamance separatists who were then in jail. Third, PDS leader Wade and members of the other political parties were invited to a roundtable conference to discuss the electoral problems. It seems in the face of a crisis, the government recognized the power of African consensualism in maintaining national unity. However, the opposition stood firm on their demands for new elections or a coalition government.

Tensions were mounting between the two sides when, in 1989, two Senegalese were shot on the Mauritania border. Senegal blamed the incident on the Mauritania border guards, but that country flatly denied the allegation. Indeed, there was no apparent reason why Mauritanian guards would attack the Senegalese, and no sufficient evidence that they did. Nevertheless, Senegalese in Dakar responded by attacking shops owned by Mauritanians. Mauritanians responded with attacks on Senegalese residents in Nouakchott, in which several Senegalese were killed. Violent attacks on Mauritanians everywhere in Senegal followed. As tensions increased, the two countries decided to repatriate their nationals resident in each other's country to prevent further bloody violence. In Senegal the troubles convinced the two sides of the political conflict to forget their differences and unite behind President Diouf to confront Mauritania. The emotions of nationalism buried any possible suspicions that the Diouf government might have initiated the conflict as a means of uniting the country around a common cause. Whatever the origin of the crisis, both poles of the Senegalese political divide apparently recognized African consensualism as the means to national solidarity, security, and survival.

Once the crisis was over, partisan politics succeeded in again dividing the Senegalese. The 1993 elections, scheduled for March 15 (presidential) and May 9 (legislative), had their own problems, including violence. In March the opposition parties aired their concerns about fraudulent registration by the PS, and opposition leader Wade claimed election fraud when Diouf was officially declared the winner of the presidential elections. Diouf's election victory was greeted with violence. The radio station Libreville Africa No.1 described the prevailing situation by offering advice to tourists:

> You already know that President Diouf has been declared the winner with a little more than 58 percent of the votes. You also know what followed: several clashes and violent acts in the streets of Dakar where supporters of the opposition are rejecting the validity of the votes. In any case president Abdou Diouf, who has been re-elected for the third time as president of Senegal, first must tackle the demands of the Casamance separatists whose actions have led to more than 400 deaths over the past six months. The situation in that southern region of Senegal may even worsen as separatists of the Movement of the Casamance Democratic Forces (MFDC) have warned foreign tourists against trips to Casamance.[13]

Foreign observers and Senegalese scholars alike have long maintained that Senegalese politics is free of ethnic considerations. As partisan politics marches on amid a situation of growing economic classes, spatial inequalities, and strains, the ethnic strands of the national fabric have been gradually unravelling.

The activities of the Casamance separatists, who feel underrepresented in and alienated from the national political and economic structures, show the dangers of the prevailing politics. Casamance, a highly fertile area popularly known as the breadbasket of Senegal, is separated from the rest of Senegal by the Gambia River. The conflict with the Casamance rebels began in 1982 after the Senegalese government ordered mass nationalization of Casamance lands to facilitate the issue of oil licences for oil exploration in that area. As a political strategy of divide and rule, the Senegalese government had claimed that the conflict arose out of demands and rights pursued by the Diala ethnic group in the area. But given that the Diala is only one of many ethnic groups in the area and that the rebels are not solely Diala, the government's explanation is difficult to accept.

With their views repressed in the interests of party loyalty and discipline, and with the history of election frauds, the Casamance have resorted to violence in their campaign against the Senegalese government; and it is surely no coincidence that the Casamance intensified their violent activities some months before the 1993 elections. They were drawing attention to their cause, and they were aware that one more set of fraudulent elections could not possibly address their concerns.

Diouf had to take action to calm the troubled political waters and draw attention away from the Casamance. On April 16, largely to court international legitimacy, and especially to gain Western favour, Diouf announced cosmetic revisions to the electoral code, among other things requiring three magistrates to approve the election results before they were announced, a measure that would apply to the upcoming legislative elections. The revision failed to satisfy the opposition, and they had valid reasons for their scepticism. The magistrates were all appointees of the ruling PS government, and in the past the judiciary had consistently turned a deaf ear to opposition charges of election fraud. The opposition parties had not forgotten the failure of the Supreme court to monitor the elections of 1988 properly. Even before the new procedure had been introduced, Wade openly expressed his mistrust of magistrates: "The problem lies not so much in the number of magistrates as in the confidence that one can have in these magistrates. So it is not so important that the government might propose that this time there should be three magistrates instead of one, or 10 magistrates—it is all much the same, because if the government can find one magistrate devoted to its cause, it can find 10, 20, 30 or 40; this is not the problem."[14]

The mistrust of the judiciary itself reflects a deeper issue: a lack of trust for Western democratic practice and its administrative machinery. Given that the elites themselves did not trust the democratic system set in place, it was not surprising that others greeted the election results with violent demonstrations, and that security forces had to be called in to disperse the demonstrators with tear gas.

The 1996 elections also revealed problems with partisan politics. The campaigning for the regional, municipal, and rural elections, slated for November 24, 1996, began on November 2. Before the campaign began, in September, Africa No.1 radio, Libreville, reported that allegations of pre-election fraud were generating controversy. In October the Pan African News Agency (PANA) in Dakar reported that Wade was complaining about the hoarding of voter cards by the ruling party. The opposition parties called upon international observers to monitor the local elections, an appeal that by itself was not only another indication of lack of confidence in the system, but also an open demonstration of a colonial mentality that places undue trust in foreign observers and looks to outsiders to solve internal problems. For one thing, a few foreign observers could not possibly monitor over three thousand voting booths. In any case the foreign observers would well turn out to be more interested in the pay they expect to earn than in the welfare of Senegal. Wade apparently forgot that nobody can love Senegal more than the Senegalese themselves and that, rather than subject themselves to the harsh life of the African interior, foreign observers would prefer to monitor events from air-conditioned hotel rooms. How many Western countries have ever invited African countries to monitor their elections and pass judgement? The use of outside mechanisms such as foreign observers passing judgement means sovereignty falls into outside hands and, again, reflects badly on the attempted practice of partisan politics.

Despite what this means for the violation of a country's sovereignty, it has become fashionable for some so-called international observers drawn from the West to monitor African elections and pass final judgements. Invariably, not wanting to offend the party declared the winner, these observers usually comment that, despite a few anomalies here and there, the elections are generally fair. In reality the foreign observers are not able to monitor even one-thousandth of the voting booths. If they found a few anomalies at these few voting booths, logic would indicate that thousands of such anomalies occurred. Their general declaration that the elections are fair is therefore a mere demonstration of diplomatic hypocrisy. However, given the mistrust arising from fraudulent allegations against the ruling party in the past, and the inability of the

Supreme Court to provide adequate resources for monitoring, Wade's approach to the problem is understandable.

On November 24, Radio France International reported that election chaos had caused the voting period to be extended in Senegal. Reports followed that elections had been postponed in twenty centres and that the opposition had called for annulment of the local elections, all of which made it difficult for onlookers to deny the confusion surrounding the conduct of the elections. The confusion developed to the extent that on January 11, 1997, the ruling party declared its intention to sue the opposition parties.

The post-independence election results in Senegal have always been disputed, largely because of a grave misunderstanding of the nature of partisan politics as a democratic practice. The people's mandate as reflected through the electoral process has not been seriously respected—as evidenced, for example, by Senghor's behaviour towards Keita after the people of Senegal had voted massively in support of the Mali federation. When he decided to dissolve the federation, Senghor did not seek the people's mandate at all. Elections in Senegal have been characterized by gerrymandering efforts aimed at maintaining the government in power. Elections became increasingly violent as election fraud and irregularities failed to be effectively checked. As in Ghana and other African countries, the election process in Senegal has fallen far short of reflecting any established fundamentals of democracy.

Partisan politics has succeeded in dividing Senegal along rural-urban lines but has not succeeded to the same extent in dividing the country along ethnic lines. However, the Casamance secession bid and the importance attached in 1988 by Diouf to easing tension by releasing a number of these separatists from jail suggest that partisan politics might be a welcome ally for fomenting ethnic tension in the future. The Casamance secessionist operations in 1993, resulting in hundreds of deaths, point further to the unsuitability of partisan politics given Senegal's present stage of development. Rather, Senegal needs a brand of democratic practice that all Senegalese, including the Casamance, can understand and that might enable the formation of a strong and encompassing coalition of elites to meet the challenges of the development path.

CHAPTER TWELVE

RWANDA: FROM SUCCESS STORY TO HUMAN DISASTER

The case of Rwanda demonstrates, once again, how partisan politics—when superimposed upon a European-created history, colonial legacy, church interference in politics, international political and economic forces, and IMF and World Bank stabilization and structural adjustment conditionalities and policies—can ruin an African nation. The Belgians, who ruled Rwanda first under a League of Nations mandate and later under a United Nations Trusteeship, were aware of the confusion they had helped to create in the country, and predicted nothing but impending doom when the country attained independence in 1962. Thus, Catherine Newbury writes that on the eve of independence, "Expatriate experts ... assumed that this small, landlocked, densely populated country was destined to remain forever a backwater of poverty—'a museum-piece of postcolonial underdevelopment,' as one Rwandan specialist put it." But, as Newbury points out, twenty-five years later Rwanda had a "bustling economy" that disproved the outsiders' "gloomy predictions."

A 1989 World Bank report singled out Rwanda as a "successful case of adaptation," where government policies had successfully encouraged growth in agricultural production: "Rwanda avoided the urban bias so common in Africa. Government remained attentive to the farming majority in determining pricing policy, exchange rate policy, fiscal priorities, and effective rural institutions." The report praises the Rwandan government for providing an "enabling environment" that encouraged growth in agricultural production, by allowing market forces to determine food prices and by trying to insure that coffee producers received a substantial share of the export price.[1]

The World Bank, in 1989, saw Rwanda as a success story that other Sub-Saharan African countries would do well to emulate. To the World Bank experts, Rwanda had demonstrated the superiority of the market theory of value as a guiding ideology in development. Alas, these appraisals proved to be badly mistaken. In less than a year the onlookers, including the so-called experts of the World Bank, were in total shock. The success theory had become a mirage and a disappointment leading to one of the most disgraceful genocides of the twentieth century. What went wrong?

The case of Rwanda demonstrates starkly that development is a more complex matter than simply getting the price of goods laid down correctly through market forces, having government policies that encourage growth in agricultural production, avoiding urban bias, or having a government that is attentive to the farming majority in determining pricing policy, exchange rate policies, or proper fiscal priorities. It confirms that an "enabling environment" capable of sustaining successful development cannot be achieved without due regard both for culture and for the historical forces constituting that culture.

Rwanda had cadres trained in the high institutions of the developed world, and those cadres succeeded for a quarter of a century in creating the impression that the country was on the road to successful development. Colonialism reduced Rwanda, like most developing countries in Sub-Saharan Africa, to a mono-crop country. In its case its economy was dependent on coffee. As a price-taker on the world market, Rwanda had an economy that was vulnerable to fluctuations in the world market price of its key commodity. That vulnerability alone suggests that Rwanda required a government of committed elites in an encompassing coalition capable of absorbing the stresses and strains of the development path while simultaneously enjoying the confidence and support of all sections of society. As a non-oil-producing country, Rwanda was also hurt by the oil-pricing and monetary shocks of the 1970s and 1980s, which again demanded the existence of a committed government capable of absorbing those shocks. In the absence of such a coalition, Rwanda resorted to reliance on foreign aid and foreign-funded projects, with a high administrative cost ratio in their implementation—projects that were often ineffective.[2] Through these projects and aid, Rwanda was able to avoid the temptation of going for the petrodollar loans of the 1970s, which had trapped many developing countries into debt. However, it could not apply the same strategy when the prices of tea and coffee began to decline sharply after 1986, because, unlike in the 1970s, donors were now less willing to provide funds. With no encompassing and committed coalition forged in accordance with its own culture to contain the resulting strains, Rwanda found itself caught in a web of complex problems. When, in response to pressure from the United States, the International Coffee Agreement was abrogated in 1989, the threshold was reached where the political fabric could no longer withstand the social pressures and it tore apart, leading to chaos and one of the most shameful genocides of the twentieth century. The complexity of the Rwandan case affords an opportunity for understanding the multidimensional development problems of Sub-Saharan Africa, and the dangers involved in transplanting the alien and competitive partisan politics of the West into a cultural environment in which sensitive historical forces prevail.

The Origin of the Historical Forces

The pre-colonial history of Rwanda was not written by Rwandans but by foreigners with European mentality and prejudices. What these Europeans wrote in the name of research or investigation is full of contradictions and fantasies that, in the absence of an alternative written history, later generations of Rwandans came to read and accept as their history. This concocted or "European-Created History of Rwanda" has been the source of much confusion that has led to mayhem, genocide, and the stifling of development. As the created history itself accepts: "Little is known of the origins of the present-day inhabitants. Since there was no written history before the arrival of the Europeans, information on the pre-European period is derived from investigations of popular traditions and the records of the chroniclers of the royal court."[3]

The absence of any written history provided the European writers with the opportunity to rely heavily on their imaginations in creating a history for Rwandan consumption. Their prejudiced investigations were conducted within the context of the imperialist and colonialist policy of divide and rule. In spite of the admission of a lack of knowledge about the Rwandans' origins, the account locates the Twa ethnic group as the original inhabitants, people related to the pygmies of the Congo forests. Later, supposedly, came the Hutus, followed by the pastoral Tutsis. The historians paid little if any attention to the undeniable fact that for thousands of years before the advent of Europeans, Africans, like all other peoples, could freely roam the land from one place to another. Hence it is difficult, if not impossible, to determine the original inhabitants of any part of Africa. The European-recorded historical narratives about the Hutus and the Tutsis are a combination of fictions, legends, and fantasies, as the following account shows:

Hutu life centered about small-scale agriculture, and social organization was based on the clan, with petty kings ruling over limited domains. These kings were called Bahinza, "those who cause things to grow," and their strength was based on the popular belief that they controlled fertility. The Bahinza were believed to be endowed with magical powers by which they could cause rain to fall and seeds to germinate and could protect crops from insects and cattle from disease.[4]

The kings or Bahinza were human beings, who, like all human beings, were not capable of causing things to grow. As Mosca argued in his elite analysis, rulers always advance some myth or ideology to justify their rule, and the Bahinza were no different from other rulers in that regard. Assuming that the Bahinza could indeed protect cattle from disease (another ideological dimension), it follows that the Hutus would have been pastoralists. In a twist of history, however, it is the Tutsis, who came to the area sometime between the fourteenth and fifteenth centuries—long after the Hutus—whom historians described as pastoral. In a fictional or ideological twist, the Tutsis were supposed to be the descendants of two brothers, Kigwa and Mututsi, and their sister, Nyampundu, who lived in heaven and somehow fell down to the earth. Kigwa married his sister and later generations produced Bami (the plural of Mwami—King). One of these powerful kings, Gihanga, designated his son Kanyanruanda (hence the name Ruanda or Rwanda) as the heir and commanded all descendants to submit to his rule. When the Tutsis migrated to Rwanda, despite their minority status, they succeeded in militarily subduing the Hutus and became the rulers of the territory. A patron-client relationship called *ubuhare* developed between the Tutsis and the Hutus, whereby the Hutu obtained the use of Tutsi cattle and, in return, rendered personal and military service to the Tutsi.

The European creators of Rwandan history were perhaps unaware of elite theory, which explains how the elites or leaders of societies arise out of a struggle for pre-eminence, and so it was quite possible that the Twas, Hutus, and Tutsis might have originated from the same area at the same time. The struggle for pre-eminence, in combination with adaptation processes, might have been at the roots of the evolution, within the same society, of Twas, Hutus, and Tutsis.

Africans derive humour in answering fantasy-inducing questions with legends, leaving strangers to apply their own wisdom to sift the chaff from the wheat. The Rwandan experience was not the first time that

Europeans received legends in response to their questions about origins. When Europeans asked the Ashantis of Ghana where they came from, the Ashantis replied that they came out of holes in the ground.[5] The subtext of this answer was that the Ashantis did not take seriously this concern about where fellow human beings originated when they had to contend with more important and pressing human problems and issues.

The historical origins of the Bahutu, Batutsi, and Batwa clans are certainly complicated, but it cannot be denied that, in pre-colonial times, a clan society emerged in Rwanda that was culturally integrated and shared a common language. Unlike many African countries comprising different ethnic groups with entirely different languages, Rwanda saw the emergence of one ethnic group speaking the same language and with the same cultural practices, though differentiated by the kind of profession practised. In the course of human development, the Batwa, who depended upon gathering and hunting and were not engaged in settled agriculture, became a clan of very short people generally known as pygmies. The Bahutu were mainly engaged in settled agriculture but were not protein-rich meat and milk consumers; they developed, on the average, into a clan of people of medium height but very stocky. The Batutsi were the pastoralists of Rwandan society, people who fed on a protein-rich diet and developed into one of the tallest peoples in the world.

This classification of clans in Rwanda became misleading because of intermarriages between the three clans. Moreover, it was possible for a Bahutu, for example, to become a Batutsi by changing his or her profession to that of a pastoralist. This social mobility through intermarriages and changes in profession continued to the extent that it became difficult to identify the Bahutu and Batutsi clans just by height or to draw a line between where a Bahutu ancestry ended and Batutsi ancestry began.

However, the Batutsi, as an identified clan, emerged as the main ruling class within a kingdom headed by a *Mwami*. The *Mwami* ruled from the centre, with the assistance of an administrative council called the Biru, whose members were given land as incentive. Authority was delegated to the provinces in the hierarchical order of military chiefs, cattle chiefs, and land chiefs. In the provinces, cattle and land chiefs were responsible for collecting cattle dues and land rents respectively. Authority was further delegated from the provinces to hill chiefs at the district level. Most of these chiefs were Batutsi, but some were Bahutu chiefs. Interclan, intraclan, as well as interprovince rivalries existed, and these forces prevented the various chiefs from uniting against the *Mwami*. Within the Batutsi clan itself, the wealthy owned the cattle and the poorer tended the cattle. Similar stratification existed among the Bahutu. To consolidate *Mwami* rule, the majority of the Rwandan army was Batutsi, though some Bahutus and Batwas served within the military ranks. Although the Bahutu constituted over 80 per cent of the Rwandan population, through a system of indirect rule within the provinces they accepted the rule of an aristocracy comprising Batutsis, who constituted less than 20 per cent of the population. This Batutsi aristocracy, then, ruled a Rwandan clan-society comprising Batutsis, Bahutus, and Batwas. Not all Batutsis were aristocrats; some Batutsis were even poorer than the average Bahutu. This is not to deny that the Tutsis, in general, prided themselves in seeing their clan as the clan of the aristocracy in Rwanda. Moreover, there were variations in *Mwami* control of the various regions of Rwanda. Control was strongest near the capital, Nyanza, but decreased in proportion to distance from the capital. The Northwest, which was never brought completely under *Mwami* rule, remained Hutu-controlled despite continued hegemonic struggle in Rwanda's history. As a consequence, the Northwest naturally became the strongest centre for a Hutu nationalism that continues to haunt Rwanda.

The European-Created Hamitic Thesis

The processes of social mobility were still going on when Europeans established contact. The prejudiced Europeans, who thought that the African "negro" was not capable of any sophisticated political organization and who knew little about the ancient African empires of Ghana, Mali, Songhai, and Zimbabwe, propounded a so-called Hamitic thesis to explain the sophisticated political organizations of the general area. The British explorer John Speke rationalized the Buganda kingdom in terms of the descent of the Buganda people from the Galla Hamites of Ethiopia. According to this flawed Hamitic thesis, physical characteristics are related to mental capacity. The Hamites are supposed to have had the same physical characteristics as Caucasians, except for the colour of their skin, which was first tanned before it became black. The Hamites are thus supposed to be essentially Caucasians in black skin.

The Europeans identified the Tutsi as Hamites and, therefore, as Caucasians or Europeans in black skin. A story was created to the effect that they migrated from the Horn of Africa and specifically from Somalia, a land of Hamites. History shows that it is normally the conquerors who impose their language upon the conquered and not the other way round. If the Tutsis were the conquerors, the Rwandan language should have been a derivative of one of the languages of the Horn of Africa and, specifically, similar to the Somali language. The fact that all Rwandans speak the same language, which is not similar to any language spoken in the Horn of Africa, suggests that the Tutsis might not have migrated from that area and exposes the flaw in the Hamitic thesis. Strangely enough, this Hamitic thesis was not applied to societies in West Africa—the Fulani, Madingoes, or Tuareg—some of whom, as pastoralists, ate similar food and had similar characteristics as the Tutsi.

The Hamitic thesis was boosted and buttressed by colonialism. As Caucasians in black skins, the Tutsi were considered the section of Rwandan society with whom Europeans could easily work. When colonialism intervened, through first the Germans and later the Belgians, the colonial authorities and the Catholic Church supported the Hamitic thesis and implemented it in their dealings with the Rwandan society. The thesis was compatible with the colonial logic of divide and rule. In conformity with the Hamitic thesis and Pareto's ideas about the elite, the Germans considered the Tutsi to be endowed with the required biological residues and capacity to govern, and they therefore imposed a policy of indirect rule in Rwanda, making full use of the existing political system of *Mwami* rule.

The Belgians, who replaced the Germans, also accepted the Hamitic thesis and continued with the policy of indirect rule, but with a marked distortion of the social relationship between the Tutsi and Hutu. The pre-colonial system had been founded on a mutual obligation between the Tutsi aristocracy and the Hutu, which promoted a harmonious relationship. The Belgians abolished this mutual obligation and established a forced-labour system in which the Tutsi supervised the Hutu. In so doing the Belgians set in motion a continuously deepening enmity between the Hutu and Tutsi. The Belgians were encouraged in their social policy by the attitude of the Catholic missionaries, who openly supported the Hamitic thesis. A letter from Monsignor Leon-Paul Classe, the Vicar Apostolic to Rwanda, written on September 21, 1927, to the Belgian Resident Commissioner, Georges Mortehan, revealed the Hamitic mentality of the Catholic mission in Rwanda:

> If we want to be practical and look after the real interest of the country, we shall find a remarkable element of progress with the MiTutsi youth.... Ask the Bahutu whether they prefer to be given orders by uncouth persons or by nobles and the answer will be

clear: they will prefer the BaTutsi, and quite rightly so. Born chiefs, the latter have the knack of giving orders.... Here lies the secret of how they managed to settle in this country and hold it in their grip.[6]

The colonial government was slow to implement the policy suggested by the Vicar, and so in 1930 he sent a warning letter to suggest an end to what he perceived as foot-dragging by the colonial administration:

The greatest harm that the government could possibly inflict on itself and on the country would be to do away with the MuTutsi caste. Such revolution would lead the country straight into anarchy and towards a viciously anti-European communism. Far from achieving progress, this will annihilate any action taken by the government for the latter would be deprived of auxiliaries who are born capable of comprehension and obedience.... As a rule, we cannot possibly deny who'd be better, more intelligent, more active, more capable of understanding the idea of progress and even more likely to be accepted by the population than the Batutsi.[7]

The Vicar's attitude explains why many African countries today are suspicious of the intentions of missionaries and especially of Catholic missionaries. As a consequence of his advice, the colonial government pursued Tutsi supremacist policies, replacing Bahutu chiefs with Batutsis. The regime abolished the threefold hierarchy of chiefs categorized as military chief, cattle chief, and land chief. To facilitate the identification of individuals by clan, identity cards were introduced in 1933. Meanwhile, the predominantly Catholic educational system openly favoured the Tutsis. In this way the colonial government, in alliance with the Catholic mission in Rwanda, set Hutu and Tutsi and the country as a whole on a course of bitter antagonism.

The identity card requirement, whereby a child's clan was patrilineally determined, meant that clan became fixed at birth and could no longer be altered through any change in profession. Thus, in later Rwandan society there were pygmies of the Batwa clan who were six-feet tall and owned cattle; and Batutsis who were less than five-feet tall and engaged in farming. Profession and physical appearance no longer determined the clan; the identity card did.

Colonial policies proceeded to divide Rwandan society even further.

The Belgian colonialists, with the Catholic mission acting as the ideological apparatus of the colonial state, continued to align themselves with the Tutsis (Batutsi) and discriminate against the Hutu (Bahutu) majority. Although a few Bahutus received some education, the educational system established by the Germans, the Belgians, and the Catholic missionaries provided the Tutsis with a virtual monopoly in formal schooling and, subsequently, a monopoly in the administrative jobs that required some level of Western education. To facilitate political control over the Hutu majority, the colonialists ruled through the *Mwami* political establishment and ensured that Tutsis dominated the military establishment.

The colonial privileges extended to the Tutsi enabled their aristocracy to control the allocation of lands and act as agents through whom the Belgians could extract rent, in the form of forced labour, from the Hutus. Although this system of enslavement was abolished in 1954, it created a lasting tension between the Hutu majority and the Tutsi minority, for the Hutus saw the aristocracy, and principally the Tutsi, as the exploiters. As the population increased the Hutus found themselves with less land to live on, and the relation of hatred between the two clans was aggravated by the onset of a series of famines in the colonial period during which Tutsi cattle freely grazed on Hutu farms.

The Advent of Partisan Politics

The mounting tension of hatred required only a spark to ignite it into a violent explosion. In February 1957, in its "Statement of Views," the High Council of Rwanda, which was entirely Tutsi, called for self-government through an accelerated preparation of the Rwandan elite.[8] Because the Rwandan elite in government was predominantly Tutsi, the Hutu leaders saw in that call a Tutsi machination to perpetuate their dominance in an independent Rwanda. In March of the same year the Hutu leaders came out with the "Manifesto of the Bahutu," recommending the continuation of Belgian Trusteeship until such a time as the Tutsi domination of the political, economic, and social spheres of Rwanda was corrected. The manifesto was a landmark in the history of Rwanda, because it represented the first organized Hutu opposition. It was followed by the creation of a series of Hutu organizations opposed to Tutsi rule. The Hutu Social Movement was formed in June 1957, and the Association for the Social Betterment of the Masses (Association pour la Promotion Sociale de la Masse—APROSOMA) was formed in

November 1957 by Joseph Habyarimana Gitera. APROSOMA was vocal in its condemnation of the system of Tutsi domination. During 1958 the Hutu leaders attempted to convince the *Mwami* and his High Council of the gravity of Hutu-Tutsi relations and the need for reform, but to no avail. In reaction, the APROSOMA newspaper came out boldly with a statement doubting that there could be any hope in the Tutsi leadership for Bahutu emancipation.

On July 24, 1959, *Mwami* Matata III died, leaving no heir to succeed him. The vacuum created by the king's death seemed to encourage the formation of new political parties, and September 3, 1959, witnessed the formation of the Rwandan National Union Party (Union Nationale Rwandaise—UNAR) with a call for immediate self-government under a constitutional, but hereditary, monarchy. It took the strong nationalist stance that Belgian administrators and missionaries had divided Rwandans. On September 14, 1959, the formation of the Rwanda Democratic Rally (Rassemblement Démocratique Rwandaise—RADER) was announced. The party called for a constitutional monarchy, but with a major difference: chiefs were to be elected through universal suffrage. To the members of UNAR, RADER was nothing else but a tool of the Belgians. In October 1959 the former Hutu Social Movement became a political party, the Party of the Hutu Emancipation Movement (Parti du Movement de l'Emancipation Hutu—PARMEHUTU). Its goal was to put an end both to Tutsi hegemony and the feudal system.

The Belgians saw the death of the king as the opening of an opportunity for the establishment of a republic in Rwanda, but they were mistaken. With the Tutsis occupying high positions in the colonial administrative machine, it was clear who would be best positioned to take power. Meanwhile, under heavy postwar pressure from the United Nations for independence and self-determination for all colonized peoples, coupled with the push towards the implementation of Western democracy, the Catholic Church and the Belgians considered it in their best interests to switch allegiance from the minority Tutsi to the majority Hutu. Acting on the basis of this general frame of mind, in the late 1950s Archbishop Andre Perruadin of the Catholic mission circulated a letter complaining that the Hutu-Tutsi inequality established earlier by the Belgians and Catholic missionaries was in contravention of Christian morality and had to be corrected. The Belgians had begun preparing Rwanda for Hutu majority rule, including the replacement of some Tutsi chiefs by Hutu chiefs and by encouraging the formation of political parties in the 1950s.

The Tutsi aristocracy saw these new political developments as threats to the privileged positions they had long enjoyed—from even before colonial rule—and which they believed were ordained by God. But this frame of mind was not entirely a Tutsi creation. In compliance with the Hamitic thesis created by the historical forces of colonialism, the Catholic mission, and the Belgians, the Tutsis had come to believe in an ideology of Tutsi supremacy over Hutu. They were determined to reverse the reforms. At the burial of the *Mwami*, the Belgian resident-general was forced by armed Tutsis at graveside to approve the half-bother of Matata, Kigeri, as the new *Mwami*. The installation of Kigeri did not end the political struggle. When the Belgian administration attempted to discipline three chiefs for aligning themselves openly with the UNAR and engaging in activities considered detrimental to the administration, the *Mwami* caused strained relations with the Belgian administration by declaring its action illegal. This move encouraged the Tutsis to attack Hutu leaders suspected of supporting the republican and reform ideas. An attack on a Hutu party leader in November 1959 led to a bloody Hutu uprising in which several Tutsi homes were burned down.

The Tutsis retaliated by killing several Hutu leaders, which, in turn, resulted in bloody fighting between the two clans. Although Belgian troops were called in to restore order, the fighting continued with such intensity and ferocity that hundreds of Tutsis lost their lives, and over twenty thousand of them sought refuge in the neighbouring countries. On June 29, 1960, *Mwami* Kigeri left the country on an official visit to attend the independence celebrations of Congo (Kinshasa) with an intention to meet the Secretary General of the United Nations to protest the elections. The high-handed Belgian administration refused to permit him to return to Rwanda. With the Belgians as the dominant power in both Rwanda and the Congo, it was not surprising that the *Mwami* could not come back to his country, and his body was never again seen. What really happened to him at the hands of the Belgians remains a mystery. Meanwhile, because the Belgians did not prosecute those responsible for the massacres in Rwanda, a precedence was set for a culture of genocide with impunity that would long haunt the country. Against this background, the year 1960 saw the holding of partisan elections in which the Tutsis (because of their disadvantage in numbers) were expected to lose almost everywhere.

If a modified African democratic practice (see chapter 5) had instead been set in place, the Tutsis would not have had to fear that they would suffer from their minority status, because each Tutsi would have been represented by clan and by profession at the council, and with consensual decision-making the dictatorship of the majority would have been tempered. Its principle of merit might also have enabled a Tutsi to hold any level of political appointment, and the *ajina* process would have enabled quick decisions to be made. Under majoritarian partisan democracy, as favoured by the Rwandan Hutu elite and imposed by the colonizer as a condition for independence, the Tutsi experienced a feeling of exclusion and a sense of alienation from a system they had dominated for centuries, and they naturally sought to resist and possibly reverse the reforms.

Rwanda required a democratic practice in which no clan would feel left out or dominated and in which there would be an authoritative allocation of Rwandan values to Rwandans irrespective of clan. Indeed, what Rwanda required was a type of democracy compatible with its culture and capable of factoring sensitivities arising from the European-created Hamitic thesis into the political equation to unite all Rwandans irrespective of clan—a Rwandan brand of Africanism capable of uniting all Rwandans to achieve the political conditions for successful development. Instead, what was introduced was a system that was capable only of the authoritative allocation of Western values to Rwandans, and which constituted a total misfit in the Rwandan cultural and historical environment.

By the time of independence a number of parties had formed to contest the country's political affairs: Le Parti du movement de l'emancipation Hutu (PARMEHUTU), a Hutu party, with a following in the central and northern areas; APROSOMA, a predominantly Hutu party, with a following in the south and southwest; UNAR, a Tutsi party; and RADER, another Tutsi party, with support among the younger educated Tutsis. This partisan politics immediately divided Rwandans along clan lines. PARMEHUTU, as its name suggests, was an anti-Tutsi radical party that aimed principally at fostering Hutu interests.

PARMEHUTU produced the Bahutu Manifesto, which called for Hutu emancipation and democratization. To further its interests, the party interpreted the Hamitic thesis to mean that the Hutus were the only legitimate nationals of Rwanda and that the minority Tutsi were some few Hamitic foreigners from the Horn of Africa resident in Rwanda only as immigrants. This rationalization implied that only the Hutu were qualified to rule Rwanda. Initially, APROSOMA aimed at fostering the interests of the Rwandan poor, including both Tutsis and

	1961 Election	
Party	Percentage Vote	Number of Seats
PARMEHUTU	77.7	35
UNAR	16.8	7
APROSOMA	3.5	2
Other Parties	2	—

Source: *Rwanda: A Country Study*, Library of Congress, 1983, p. 24

Hutus, but because it was predominantly Hutu it soon became more oriented towards Hutu interests. UNAR, as a radical and anti-Hutu Tutsi party, aimed at the preservation of the monarchy and crushing any Hutu resistance to that institution. It held that through conquest the Tutsi had become the rulers and superiors, and that the Bahutu were not equal citizens. RADER was a relatively moderate Tutsi party that favoured both constitutional monarchy and progressive reforms.

Following the violent acts of 1959, elections in October 1960 led to the formation of a provisional government in which a Hutu, Juvenal Habyarimana, became president and another Hutu as well as a Catholic journalist, Gregoire Kayibanda, became prime minister. The Tutsi, after occupying the top of the political hierarchy for hundreds of years, found themselves displaced entirely from the country's top leadership, with no hope of ever occupying either of the two top positions through partisan politics. A UN-supervised referendum of September 1961 led to the adoption of a republican constitution that prepared the way for pre-independence elections in October, from which PARMEHUTU emerged with an overwhelming victory. Its leader, Kayibanda, became the president.

Given a negative vote of 80 per cent on the question of the monarchy, the Legislative Assembly abolished the monarchy on October 2, 1961. The structure of the political parties was such that the ruling party did not command the support of the Tutsi section of Rwandan society, and the enemy concept for the member of a different political party in combination with clan sensitivities led to mistrust of the Tutsis holding administrative positions in the government. Before independence in 1962, many Tutsis in political and administrative appointments were expelled. Sensing political danger and in response to the expulsions, many qualified Tutsis fled the country. The political climate was perceived by the Tutsi radicals as a situation in which the former masters had become the slaves and the slaves the masters, and they understandably found it difficult to accept that kind of democratic practice. They perceived the Western democratic practice as one that led to a dangerous dictatorship of the majority over the minority with no consideration whatsoever to merit or the capacity to achieve the country's goals. They did not accept Western partisan politics as a constructive democratic practice, but as a demonstration of a particular craziness in which a section of society who are not competent to rule assumes the reins of power by sheer majority, while those with the proper biological residues, calibre, and competence are reduced to silent spectators just because they are outnumbered. Fundamentally, the Tutsis did not understand that the Western operationalization of the concept of government with the consent of the governed through competitive elections is not rationalized on the African concept of consensual selection or appointment of well-known persons through a merit system based upon close scrutiny of character and behaviour from childhood, but on a mere counting of papers cast into ballot boxes. The outcome of competitive elections might therefore be the placement of a competent or an incompetent group in power purely by chance. Coping with that outcome demands tolerance and patience.

The retrenchment of Tutsis from administrative positions in government confirmed and aggravated their fears. For the radicals among the Tutsis, the pill of tolerance and patience was too bitter to swallow, and for them the only solution to this kind of nonsense or embarrassment was armed confrontation. Convinced by the European-created history of Rwanda that the Tutsis were militarily superior to the Hutus, the Tutsis were determined to follow the path of violent resolution of what they perceived as political injustice. In 1960 the provisional government invited the refugees to return, and it set up the State Secretariat for refugees, but the response was not encouraging. Between 1962 and 1963 the post-independence government of Kayibanda appealed to the Tutsi refugees to come back to the country, but the Tutsis did not trust the government enough to return in any great number.

Post-independence Political Struggles

Post-independence armed confrontation between the Tutsis and the Hutus began with the formation of a Tutsi guerrilla organization called the *Inyenzi*, or Cockroach, with bases in Burundi, where Tutsis were in power, and in other neighbouring countries. In December 1963

Cockroach invaded Rwanda from its base in Burundi with the aim of toppling the government. Many Tutsis in Rwanda openly expressed their support for the invasion, but in the battle that ensued Cockroach was defeated. The government declared a state of emergency, and armed with the concept of enemy for a member of another party as well as another clan, which the Cockroach invasion confirmed and accentuated, Kayibanda's Hutu government reacted against all Tutsis, and the Tutsi political leadership in particular, as though they were external enemies and not fellow citizens who deserved dignity. Tutsi leaders suspected of alliance with Cockroach were rounded up and shot. In addition, the government appealed to all Hutus to act to defend themselves. The appeal was received by the Hutus as a licence or a declared authority to kill Tutsis. Between 1963 and 1964, several thousand Tutsis were slaughtered, and many thousands more sought refuge in neighbouring countries, especially Burundi and Uganda.

The fears of the Tutsi that partisan democracy might lead to a dangerous dictatorship of the majority Hutu, in which Tutsis would be oppressed, were confirmed by Kayibanda's eleven-year post-colonial rule. Fearing that the proliferation of political parties would undermine progress, PARMEHUTU adopted policies that drove APROSOMA and the other non-Hutu political parties out of existence, thus rendering Rwanda a de facto one-party state. Some parties were eliminated through negotiations and others through arrests, intimidation, and violence. After the elimination of the opposition parties, divisions and conflicts surfaced within PARMEHUTU itself, leading to the concentration of power in the hands of a core of Hutus mainly from Gitamara in Central Rwanda, Kayibanda's region. This mode of domination and favouritism towards Hutus of a particular region introduced intra-Hutu and interregional struggles into the already volatile political equation.

Meanwhile, the Tutsis who remained in Rwanda contented themselves with their continued high representations in the educational institutions, public service, and salaried employment. Political events in neighbouring Burundi in 1972 were to disturb this delicate balance and destroy any remaining confidence that Tutsis had in the political system.

In 1972 thousands of Hutus were massacred by the predominantly Tutsi army in Burundi when they resisted the purge of Hutus from the army, police, and civil service by Colonel Michel Micombero's Tutsi supremacist regime. Because Burundi shares a common border with Rwanda, by diffusion, anti-Tutsi feelings came to the fore in Rwanda.

The government of Rwanda reacted to the purges of Hutus in Burundi with purges of Tutsis from schools, the teaching profession, and government jobs. Radical Hutus of Rwanda embarked upon attacks on Tutsi-owned shops and homes. If Tutsis in Burundi were maltreating the Hutus over there, was it the fault of Tutsis in Rwanda? The explanation to the clannish antagonism in Rwanda may be understood in the larger context of the misfit of partisan politics in the cultural environment of the country. The invocation of ethnic symbols in the election campaign to win votes combined with the clan structure of the political parties and the particular clan structure of the ruling party to lead to a perception of the members of other parties and clans as enemies. The campaign platform was an arena for inciting war between clans and clan-parties.

As the interclan struggle continued, intra-Hutu struggles surfaced in which Hutus originating from Central and Southern Rwanda, perceived as having been favoured by the ruling government, were forced to leave the North, especially the Musanza area. The other Hutus saw those Hutus favoured by the ruling government as having the same domineering characteristics and holding the same privileged class position as the Tutsi. The alien partisan politics, then, gave the political struggle a class twist. At the same time, Northern Hutus driving Central and Southern Hutus away irrespective of their status meant partisan politics had given the political struggle an interregional character.

The situation required some agency to bring an end to the confused state of affairs, and the Rwandan army, dominated by Northern Hutus and under the leadership of General Juvenal Habyarimana, provided that agency by staging a coup in 1973. In 1997 the *Journal of Humanitarian Assistance* explained the events leading up to the coup:

> Faced with expressions of discontent, especially on the part of politicians and military from the north, Gregoire Kayibanda's government eventually tried to resort to "ethnic" tactics. In 1973, violence—initially of an ethnic nature—erupted in the schools, in the administration and in business enterprises. Psychologically, these events were certainly influenced (and facilitated) by the bloody events in Burundi, where the Hutu were the victims of genocidal killings.... It remains to be emphasized, though, that the impulse aimed at expelling Tutsi found its origin within the center of power, which tried to detract attention from other issues.... However, the politicians from Gitarama lost sight of the dynamism

such a policy could provoke in a situation where complete control became rather precarious. Thus, the population began to attack the rich (and not only Tutsi); Hutu of the north began chasing those of the central region; politicians of the north shifted their attention from the schools—where everything started—to the ministries and the enterprises where they felt underrated or ostracised. As certain politicians from the north, especially the National Defence Minister, Major General Juvenal Habyarimana, felt in danger of being physically eliminated, he finally decided on army intervention; an army in which, historically, the north had always been dominant.[9]

The constitution was abrogated after the coup and PARMEHUTU was banned. That banning itself suggests an identification of the political party as a major part of the problem, but the identification of the problem did not go deep enough to identify partisan politics as a whole as a root cause of the problem.

Habyarimana's handling of political prisoners after the coup left much to be desired. A secret court martial of June 1974 sentenced Kayibanda and seven other members of his regime to death. Others were sentenced to long years of imprisonment. Harsh conditions in the so-called special session of the Ruhengeri prison led to the death of scores of former dignitaries. Kayibanda himself died under house arrest in Kavumu in 1976, where he was denied medical care. These events deepened intra-Hutu dissension. Despite the tendency to interpret the Rwandan problem solely in terms of the country's clan structure, in this case a Hutu general, in co-operation with a Hutu-dominated army, overthrew a Hutu government and proceeded to execute and maltreat Hutu dignitaries. The country's fundamental problem has been the misfit between the alien partisan politics, the elites, and the cultural environment—with clan, history, and the Hamitic thesis acting as catalysts that accelerated the political reaction and consequences.

Planned Liberalism

Habyarimana proceeded to introduce strategies aimed at organizing an encompassing coalition to ensure a strong state. It was in conformity with this political strategy that in July 1975 the Mouvement Révolutionnaire Nationale pour le Développement (MRND) was formed to mobilize the Rwandan population for development. But the formation of this party was essentially the replacement of one political party by another. Instead of eradicating the roots of conflict, attempts were made, in principle, to reduce conflict by introducing affirmative action quotas based on population ratios of clans and regions in education, employment, and political appointments. In practice, the Northern Rwandans were relatively favoured in the allocation of jobs and in education. The mistakes of Kayibanda were repeated in another form.

Scarce resources were also diverted to the building of clientele-based political support for the party and government. The political leadership recognized that Western ideologies were incompatible with the Rwandan environment, but instead of delving into African culture to propound an ideology compatible with the Rwandan environment, the government decided to find a solution by combining some Western ideologies to propound something called "planned liberalism," which it explained in the following words:

> The national economy must be planned: that is why the MRND opted for planned liberalism. It protects private property and supports private initiative, but gives primacy to the interest of the collectivity. It says no to unrestrained capitalism, no to socialism or extreme collectivism that stifles freedom and individual initiative. The creation of state-owned or mixed ownership enterprises is recommended and co-operatives are encouraged.[10]

The solution made no mention of the incorporation of any aspect of African cultural communalism, such as the adaptation of co-operative labour to development. The technique of co-operative labour has been employed by Africans for thousands of years to enable individuals to cultivate large farms and to construct houses and lanes cheaply. The combination of co-operative labour and modern equipment might enable the construction of a hundred-mile road in Africa to be awarded to ten African contractors instead of one. By pulling their resources together, and under the inspiration of invigorating African songs, the road could be completed in a month instead of, when awarded to one contractor only, a year. The co-operative venture has the added advantage of distributing income among ten contractors and their employees instead of one contractor and his or her few employees. Co-operative labour expresses the fundamental African principle that one should not eat all the cake alone but share it with brothers and sisters. Thus, in Africanism, democracy extends even to the economic and survival spheres. It is not liberal democracy but collective democracy; it is not the survival of the atomized individual, it is the survival of the collectivity as a whole. Habyarimana appeared to have forgotten his own African culture and its value system.

Despite the much publicized collective approach, the government provided credit to individuals and awarded contracts to single enterprises, and in so doing pumped money into the pockets of individuals. Kigali became flooded with foreign goods, including food items and automobiles that increased the demand for gasoline. Beautiful and Western-style luxurious housing sprang up. The government was encouraged in this stance by its windfall profits derived from the enormous amount of coffee smuggled from Congo (Kinshasa) and its position as a communication and supply centre among its economically weak neighbours— Congo (Kinshasa), Tanzania, and Uganda. What resulted was not an egalitarian society, but a society of open inequalities, about which Jean Rumiya commented: "The prototype of the wealthy man is no longer the well-off peasant, respected by his peers, or the government official who returns to his hill, but the city dweller, preferably in Kigali, whose living standard attains an international level in the areas of leisure, transport, or lodging. This paradise has a strong attraction for youth ... but in this type of competition, there are only few winners."[11]

What came out of the planned liberalism was not the authoritative allocation of Rwandan values to Rwandans but the authoritative allocation of Western values to Rwandans by elites who were so completely out of step and tune with Rwanda's cultural values that they were no longer qualified to be called Rwandans. They were Europeans in black African garb. The African egalitarian cultural value of sharing the survival cake with one's brother or sister vanished, replaced by a state of inequality in which the rich lived in luxury while their brothers and sisters lived in abject poverty. This inequality was extended to the rural communities, where absentee landlords comprising civil servants, military officers, and rich civilians living in the urban areas owned the large farms and had easy access to the required inputs.

Rwanda was divided into ten prefectures, each of them divided into a number of communes. In total there were 143 communes. Each commune was further divided into four or five sectors, and each sector divided into ten cells. While this organization might have contributed to an equitable distribution of national resources, partisan political considerations enabled almost 90 per cent of government investments to go to only four prefectures: Kigali in the centre, Cyangugu in the southwest, and Ruhengeri and Gisenyi in the north. The highly populated Gitamara prefecture received only about 0.16 per cent of government investment, and the Kibuye prefecture only 0.84 per cent.[12] It would seem, then, that planned liberalism is about enabling a minority to live luxuriously while the majority of compatriots are marginalized.

The root of the problem rested in the failure to have the ideological symbols of unity transferred from the regional and clan levels to the centre to constitute a strong and united nation that might share the national cake equitably. The Habyarimana government did not learn sufficiently from the lessons of the Kayibanda government—to the effect that a regional concentration of power might lead to political turmoil. Like the Kayibanda regime it replaced, the Habyarimana government concentrated its power in the Northern prefectures of Gisenyi and Ruhengeri, to the degree that by 1990 regional conflict had become stronger than ethnic conflict. The *Journal of Humanitarian Assistance* points out:

> Finally it should be observed that access to power and knowledge came to very few regional groups in the country, notably in the northern prefectures of Gisenyi and Ruhengeri. This concentration took place over a number of years and narrowed down to these two prefectures in the late 1980s. This is seen to happen on all levels, but we shall limit ourselves to three illustrations. In the mid-1980s, the prefecture of Gisenyi alone arrogated to itself one-third of the most important posts in the republic, as well as near-total leadership of the army and security services. According to a survey dating back to early 1990s, 33 public institutions out of a total of 68 were under the directorship of people coming from Gisenyi (19 posts) and Ruhengeri (14 posts). During the period 1979-1986 the "disparity indices" regarding grants to study abroad read 1.83 in favour of Gisenyi and 1.44 for Ruhengeri (the worst off prefecture being Kibungo in the East, with an index of 0.67). By 1990, ethnic conflict had been overtaken or even transcended by regional conflict and—within the dominant region—by small scale antagonisms (for example the prefectures of Gisenyi and Ruhengeri were at loggerheads in the north while Bushiru, Habyarimana's home area, competed with Bugoyi).

The shift of the centre of gravity from ethnic conflict to regional conflict confirms that the political turmoil in Rwanda cannot be interpreted solely in terms of Tutsi versus Hutu, but in terms of other underlying factors, including the centrifugal seeds of partisan politics sown earlier and military rule, both of which are incompatible with Rwanda's culture.

The handling of the refugee problem also left much to be desired. Although planned liberalism was supposed to mobilize all Rwandans, the Habyarimana government put impediments in the way of refugees willing to return. It behaved like the African chameleon that changes its colour at will so that it is difficult to predict what its next colour will be. While it preached a basic principle, it acted to negate that same principle. The regime was unpredictable and unstable. On July 26, 1986, the government declared Rwanda to be too overpopulated to support a mass repatriation of refugees. Instead of providing the necessary support to rehabilitate its returning citizens, the government required the returning refugees to demonstrate that, on their return to Rwanda, they would be able to provide for themselves.

This government stance, in contravention of the provisions of the charters of both the Organization of African Unity and of the United Nations, was rejected at an international conference on refugees held in 1988. Article 12(2) of the African Charter on Human and People's Rights (1986) states, "Every individual shall have the right to ... return to his country. This right may only be subjected to restrictions, provided for by law for the protection of national security, law and order, public health and morality."[13] Article 13 of the Universal Declaration of Human Rights (1948) states, "Everyone has the right to leave any country, including his own, and to return to his country," and article 12(4) of the International Covenant on Civil and Political Rights (1966) states, "No one shall be arbitrarily deprived of the right to enter his own country."[14] The behaviour of the Habyarimana government cannot be explained in terms of compliance with or respect for any of these international provisions, to which Rwanda is a signatory. Meanwhile, as political and economic conditions in Rwanda and the neighbouring states continued to deteriorate, tension between the refugees and the Habyarimana government escalated, though the policy of planned liberalism did not budge.

Planned liberalism also channelled rural development through local government units called communes, which, in theory, were given autonomous status. In practice the heads of the communes, called burgomasters, were appointed directly by the president and were responsible to the Ministry of the Interior. Because, in contravention of African culture, the burgomasters were not elected by the local people, they sought to please the Ministry of the Interior and the president rather than seeking the interests of the local people. At the local councils, instead of listening to concerns expressed by the councillors, the burgomasters tended to dictate. Local input to the decision-making process became ineffective. In addition the burgomasters constituted an integral part of the clientele-based network for government and party. They were responsible for the collection of taxes, dues of all kinds, and the imposition of various fines. Partisan politics was thus transformed into a predatory politics in which both government and party milked the financial resources of the people through the burgomasters. Eventually, as the wise saying goes, the government and the party could fool all the people some of the time, some of the people some of the time, but not all the people all the time. Gradually and finally, the local people came to perceive the role of the burgomasters in their respective areas as serving the interests of the government rather than the interests of the local inhabitants. Moreover, in spite of the many roles expected of the burgomasters, the communes were underfunded by the central government. As a result, rural villagers were compelled to engage in *umuganda* (unpaid labour) against their wishes and to finance the communes by paying various levies, including market and livestock taxes—while they saw contractors and other private enterprises amassing wealth, purchasing luxurious cars, and erecting luxurious houses. In the eyes of rural people, while members of the party and government loosened their belts, they were being called upon to tighten their belts to the bones.

Umuganda should not be confused with the traditional voluntary organizations of African culture. The indigenous voluntary organizations were not based on compulsion. People joined the organizations and offered free services out of their own free will. Because the participants of *umuganda* were compelled against their wishes, they considered it another form of enslavement. In addition to the *umuganda* discontentment, the agricultural extension officers of planned liberalism acted as policemen interested principally in enforcing agricultural regulations. Violations of these regulations carried fines. Indeed, because promotion of an extension officer depended upon the volume of fines he imposed, the extension officers were encouraged to find flimsy excuses for imposing fines. Moreover, they were not trained to teach new techniques or shown how to introduce new seeds to the local population. They also tended to be misogynistic, which, among other things, undermined agricultural productivity. Although women provided about 80 per cent of the labour in the coffee plantations, the government technical information and training concentrated on men, and rural development policies did very little to improve women's productivity.

The international climate also turned against the rural economy. The effects of the oil-pricing and monetary shocks of the 1970s and 1980s were to increase the costs of goods and services purchased by the rural populations. The price of coffee remained fairly stable, while the prices of traded commodities increased, which meant a deterioration in barter terms of trade. As the rural populations became more squeezed, they resorted to selling portions of their anticipated coffee harvests at about 50 per cent below the market price to obtain needed cash. It did not help that the corporate sector in the United States, in search of higher profits and arguing for the fair play of market forces, put pressure on its own government to abrogate the International Coffee Agreement (ICA), which had stabilized coffee prices. Although prices in the international arena are not determined by anything like the free hand of any market, but by oligopolistic pricing within an imperfect market, under U.S. pressure the ICA was abrogated in July 1989. Michael Chossudovsky notes:

> A lethal blow to Rwanda's economy came in June 1989 when the ICA reached a deadlock as a result of political pressures from Washington on behalf of the large US coffee traders. At the conclusion of a historic meeting of producers held in Florida, coffee prices plunged in a matter of months by more than 50%.... With retail prices more than 20 times that paid to the African farmer, a tremendous amount of wealth was being appropriated by the rich countries.[15]

In Rwanda, with what was close to a mono-crop economy, the effect was devastating. Because coffee contributed about 80 per cent of Rwanda's export earnings, the entire economy was thrown into disarray. An onset of famine aggravated matters. This was the time for planned liberalism, if it were an effective ideology, to hold Rwandan society together, but it failed miserably to do so.

Habyarimana tried to hold Rwanda society together, but his efforts were undermined by a constellation of forces: the inequalities that planned liberalism itself introduced, the affluent lifestyles of officials and business persons, and the propaganda activities of the Catholic mission in Rwanda. That the economy was in a crisis as a result of the abrogation of the ICA was undeniable. Moreover, the Catholic bishops were fully aware of the country's inequalities and bloody history, and the resultant necessity for the exercise of restraint to prevent the economic crisis from being translated into a political crisis.

Instead of acting as the ideological apparatus of the Rwandan state, the Catholic mission in Rwanda acted as the ideological apparatus of international political and economic forces, and particularly of the United States, a foreign country. The activities of the propaganda machine of the Catholic mission continuously undermined the genuine efforts of the Rwandan government. Strangely enough, and in an open demonstration of double standards, the Catholic bishops in Rwanda did not condemn the United States for the abrogation of the ICA, which was at the root of the economic crisis. Rather, they diverted attention completely from the United States by blaming it on the affluence of officials of the Habyarimana government. As any sensible government might do under crisis situations, the Habyarimana government downplayed the horrors of the famine in its efforts to keep the peace and maintain order. Its efforts along these lines were rendered ineffective by the Catholic newspaper, which, not long after the abrogation of the ICA, began to publish details about the famine, alleged corruption, relative affluence of government officials, and inequalities in land ownership. Surprisingly, Rwandan intellectuals who should have known better also helped to divert attention away from the abrogation of the ICA and towards official corruption and affluence. This behaviour testified to the inability of the Rwandan elite to build a strong and encompassing coalition capable of absorbing shocks from the international environment. Blinded by partisan politics, they failed to recognize the fundamental issue: that Rwanda is enmeshed in the international economy, where it is only a price-taker subject to unitary price elasticity for its product, where an increase in coffee volume results in little or no increase in revenue. The myopic leaders of planned liberalism could not educate and prepare Rwandans to stand firm against any surprises from the harsh international environment.

The Rwandan political strategists, who combined aspects of Western ideologies to construct the ideology of planned liberalism, failed to take into account that in Western democracies, despite a supposed separation of the two institutions, the church is an apparatus or an instrument of the state. Indeed, as political philosopher Louis Althusser explains, ideology is not an illusion but a social relation or practice. In Western capitalist societies, the church effectively contributes to political socialization. Under planned liberalism in Rwanda, the Catholic Church was not separated effectively and politically from the state, and it was not an apparatus for political socialization on behalf of the state. In difficult times, it acted against the state instead of for the state. As we have seen, in 1959 the circulation of a letter by a Catholic bishop contributed to the massacres that year. In 1989, when the Catholic Church through its newspaper began to attack the Rwandan government, it was acting as the faithful ideological apparatus of external political and economic forces—so much so that the position of the Rwandan government in its negotiations with international organizations became weakened.

In early 1990 the Habyarimana government began negotiations with the IMF and World Bank on stabilization and structural adjustment programs. The IMF's tough conditionalities for African States are well known and have earned it various appellations among African publics. These appellations include International Ministry of Finance, International Mismanager of Finances (to describe how its policies persistently aggravate and deepen the debt and the debt burdens of African countries), and International Monster without Feelings. The World Bank has also earned the name of Worst Bandit because of its disposition to pave the way for foreign business to dominate local economies. Indeed, some Western scholars have appealed for adjustment with a human face. The IMF and the World Bank were fully aware of the delicate political situation in Rwanda, its bloody history, the ongoing famine, and the economic crisis resulting from the abrogation of the ICA. In spite of all that, the IMF and the World Bank, in accordance with their appellations, applied their tough conditionalities on Rwanda to deepen the sufferings of the Rwandan people. According to Chossudovsky:

> After careful economic "simulations" of likely policy outcomes, the World Bank concluded with some grain of optimism that if Rwanda adopted Scenario II, levels of consumption would increase markedly over 1989-1983 alongside a recovery of investment and improved balance of trade. The "simulations" also pointed to added export performance and substantially lower levels of external indebtedness. These outcomes depended on speedy implementation of the usual recipe of trade liberalisation and currency devaluation alongside the lifting of all subsidies to agriculture, the phasing out of the Fonds d'egalisation, the privatisation of State enterprises and the dismissal of civil servants.... A 50% devaluation of the Rwandan Franc was carried out in November 1990, barely six weeks after the incursion from Rwanda of the rebel army of the Rwandan Patriotic Front.

The devaluation was intended to boost coffee exports. It was presented to public opinion as a means of rehabilitating a war-ravaged economy. Not surprisingly, exactly the opposite results were achieved, exacerbating the plight of the civil war. From a situation of relative price stability, the plunge of the Rwandan Franc contributed to triggering inflation and the collapse of real earnings.... The balance of payment situation deteriorated dramatically and the outstanding external debt, which had already doubled since 1985, increased by 35% between 1989 and 1992.[16]

As the economic crisis and the sufferings of Rwandans deepened, in May 1990 the Catholic bishops continued to stir up Christians against the Rwandan government, suggesting more than anything else a pattern of diversionary tactics on behalf of international capital. Jean Newbury writes:

In May, Rwanda's Catholic bishops published a letter to Christians calling for social justice, respect for human rights, freedom of the press, and an end to nepotism, favouritism, and bribes. The letter condemned corruption in the courts, inequities in umuganda (unpaid community labor), land accumulation by the wealthy at the expense of the poor, "diverse forms of theft" and the desire to get rich quickly without any effort.[17]

The letter had the effect of inciting the public to disturb the peace. There were student strikes in the northern city of Ruhengeri and the southern city of Butare, general unrest, and calls for a return to multiparty democratic practice. Both external and internal sources were applying this pressure for a return to multiparty politics, as though multiparty politics were the magic wand for commanding U.S. dollars, productive forces, and peace from the skies, all to enable Rwanda to solve its political and economic problems. To reduce tension, early in July 1990 Habyarimana introduced reforms, including greater freedom for the press, the allocation of government jobs by merit, and changes to the constitution to be implemented within a two-year period. In response to external pressure he also endorsed a return to the same multiparty democracy that, in the 1950s, had divided Rwandan society along clan lines and created a political system in which the Tutsi had little hope. Opposition parties, including a socialist formation, sprang up. The political environment became more complex.

Intensification of the Violent Confrontation

Many of the predominantly Tutsi refugees in Uganda had received military training and experience through serving within the ranks of General Amin's army, and in the guerrilla forces that swept Yoweri Kaguta Museveni to power in Uganda in 1986. These forces included some moderate Hutus, who, because of interregional and intra-Hutu struggles, had turned against the Habyarimana government. With the Habyarimana government placing impediments on their bid to return home, these refugees were waiting for the appropriate conditions to enable them to strike effectively against the Rwandan government. The unrest arising from the economic situation and the activities of the Catholic bishops provided fertile ground for the rebels, who called themselves the Rwandan Patriotic Front (RPF).[18] The programs of reform announced by the Habyarimana government did not please the RPF, whose members had learned from previous experience not to trust or take the promises of the government about refugees seriously. On October 1, 1990, the rebels, with their linkages to the Ugandan Museveni government, attacked from their base in Uganda. By December it appeared that the Rwandan army had the upper hand. However, with its strong linkages to the levers of power in Uganda, the RPF remained determined to press on and win.

The officers of the RPF and the Ugandan army (NRA) had significant connections. The RPF commander, Fred Rwigyema, was the chief of staff of the NRA and deputy minister of defence in the National Revolutionary Council. Paul Kagame, who later became the RPF commander, was deputy chief of intelligence in the NRA, and a large number of the RPF officers had served under Museveni. Evidently, the RPF invasion had the approval and support of the Ugandan government, but Museveni tactically resorted to a double game. He seemingly extended a hand of friendship to the Rwandan government. For example, Museveni denied giving military assistance to the RPF and accused the RPF of having stolen equipment from the Ugandan army. He assured the government of Rwanda that the border had been sealed and that if the RPF retreated back into Uganda its members would be arrested. In practice, Museveni was permitting Rwigyema to build up the RPF within his territory.

After the October invasion and throughout the following war, the RPF commander Kagame travelled several times and openly to Kampala to meet journalists and talk to supporters. He was never arrested by the

Museveni government. The Human Rights Watch report, *Arming Rwanda*, described the support that the RPF received from Museveni's government: "Uganda provided weapons, munitions and other military supplies to the RPF. These included munitions, automatic rifles, mortars, artillery and Soviet-designed Katyushs multiple rocket systems.... Uganda allowed the rebel movement to use its territory as a sanctuary for the planning of attacks, stockpiling of weapons, raising funds and movement of troops."[19]

After the October invasion Habyarimana seized the initiative, trying to apply diplomatic means to resolve the conflict by arranging first a ceasefire and then negotiations with the RPF. Habyarimana projected himself as a lover of peace. He even went to the extent of agreeing to the return of all Rwandan refugees who were interested in doing so and to organize a regional conference on how to solve the refugee problem. Recognizing that the use of identity cards was the most potent instrument for perpetuating divisions along clan lines, Habyarimana abolished the requirement for the specification of clan on the identity card. He appealed for international support to resolve the conflict, and his efforts met with some success, though short-lived. The uncompromising and paternalistic attitude of the IMF and the World Bank, encouraged by the propaganda activities of the Catholic Church, intensified Rwanda's crisis.

The Genocide

The IMF and the World Bank might well be considered the hidden killers—not only in the Rwandan genocide but everywhere in the Third World where the consequences of their policies have caused grave problems. So far, despite the complete failure of their prescriptions to cure economic ailments, those financial institutions have not been held to account. Indeed, because of rules that shield them from any accountability, the IMF and the World Bank officials are encouraged in their irresponsibility towards Third World countries. While others are being brought to justice for the part they played in the Rwandan genocide, the complicity of the IMF and World Bank in those same crimes against humanity has been overlooked. Susan George explains this frustrating immunity of the IMF and the World Bank:

Clearly, the economic policies imposed on debts by the major multilateral agencies—the policies packaged under the general head-ing of "structural adjustment"—have cured nothing at all. They have rather caused untold human suffering and widespread environmental destruction while simultaneously emptying debtor countries of their resources; rendering them each year less able to service their debts, let alone invest in economic and human recovery. The World Bank and the IMF structural adjustors have now had a generous period to impose their plans and cannot complain that their measures have not been given time to work. Had these public debt management officials been corporate executives, with so little to show for themselves, their shareholders would have doubtless sacked them long ago for incompetence. Had they been politicians, they would have been trounced at election time and sent back to where they came from.

Corporate managers and local or national public office-holders can be dismissed for poor performance. No such accountability applies to the international bureaucrats acting on behalf of the creditor governments. The international debt managers need never submit to the judgement of their victims. They answer only to their own equally unaccountable superiors, and, at the top of the bureaucratic tree, to a Board of Governors reflecting the majority voting strength of the richest creditor countries. These lavishly compensated international civil "servants" are consequently still to be found in Washington and throughout the Third World, living exceedingly well.[20]

The IMF and the World Bank were totally insensitive to the sufferings of the Rwandan people or the evident signs of a bloody confrontation developing out of the harsh policies imposed on Rwanda. Whether this insensitivity was racially motivated or not remains debatable, but given the evidence that a similarly harsh and paternalistic stance was not applied to Britain or France during the 1960s, when those countries sought assistance from the IMF, such accusations make sense. With a full knowledge of the belligerent RPF activities, in 1992 the World Bank ordered the privatization of the state-owned enterprise Electrogaz, involving the dismissal of workers and a call to channel the proceeds of privatization into servicing the Rwandan debt. Clearly the World Bank's primary interest was to force Rwanda to pay off its debt, which would in turn enable World Bank officials to continue receiving their fat salaries and would not in any way alleviate the suffering of the Rwandan people. The consequence of privatization was a sharp rise in the price of electricity, which strangled public services. The World Bank, unconcerned with the effects, went on to exert more pressures that served to paralyze the Rwandan economy.

The World Bank recommended the downsizing of some state investment projects and the abandonment of others. Those abandoned included a swamp reclamation program aimed at recovering land for agricultural purposes. Given that Rwanda was a thickly populated country with a severe shortage of land to support its growing population, the reclamation program was a step in the right direction; but it went against the priority of the World Bank, which was debt payments to rich countries. Furthermore, despite the soaring prices arising from the austerity measures imposed on Rwanda, the international financial institutions compelled the Rwandan government to freeze the farm-gate price of coffee at the 1989 level. Meanwhile, following their liberalization imperative, those institutions also deregulated food markets. Evidently, they were playing out a system of double standards. When it came to coffee, the state was to intervene to keep the farm-gate price low for the benefit of international business. When it came to grain and other food commodities, Rwanda was to allow the free operation of the market so that international business might flood the Rwandan marketplace with its goods and suffocate domestic production. The implied agenda of the international policies was to assist transnational business to dominate Rwanda's domestic market while simultaneously impoverishing Rwandan coffee producers to the benefit of Western business. In their frustration, the Rwandan coffee farmers uprooted about three hundred thousand coffee trees so they could grow foodstuffs necessary for their survival—a rational move that had an adverse effect on the Rwandan economy. Meanwhile, the austerity measure aggravated the already volatile political situation.

In Rwanda itself, bitter negotiations with the opposition in 1992 led to Habyarimana giving ten cabinet posts to other parties. Some three months later talks with the RPF opened in Arusha, Tanzania, continuing for thirty-four months. However, those long months of negotiations were disrupted by ceasefire violations and sporadic fighting. The numerous ceasefire problems and the evidence of support for the rebels from militarily stronger Uganda had the effect of encouraging Habyarimana and his supporters to devise sinister contingency plans should the RPF seize power by force. They recruited a large number of extremist Hutus, trained them, and provided them with arms. When the peace talks broke down in 1993, Colonel Theoneste Bagosora of the presidential guard was reported to have said that he was going back to Kigali to prepare for the "apocalypse," meaning the killing of Tutsis and opposition Hutus. Habyarimana reportedly commented, more than once, "If the RPF were to take power, they would find their families dead."[21]

On August 4, 1993, the Arusha Accords were signed, including a power-sharing formula that distributed portfolios in a transitional Council of Ministers. The ruling MRND's portfolios included ministries of defence, planning, and education. The ministries of the interior, youth, rehabilitation, and social integration went to the RPF. The opposition party Mouvement Démocratique Republicain (MDR) had the portfolios of prime minister, ministry of foreign affairs, and the ministry of primary and secondary education. The opposition Liberal Party (PL) had the ministry of justice, the ministry of commerce, and the ministry of labour. The opposition Social Democrats were responsible for the ministries of finance, public works, and agriculture. The signing of the implementation agreement was scheduled for April 1994.

After the agreement was signed, in Dar es Salaam on April 6, 1994, Habyarimana and the president of Burundi, Cyprien Ntaryamira, were returning when the Mystere Falcon plane they were in was hit by a rocket and exploded. The presidential guard accused the RPF of responsibility for the crash. The RPF denied the allegation and, together with the opposition parties, blamed it on the presidential guard, whom they suspected of not being happy with the power-sharing agreement. Immediately after the plane crash, an organized mass murder of Tutsis and opposition or moderate Hutus began. This genocide was encouraged by the political history of Rwanda (including instances in 1959, 1963, and 1973 when thousands of Tutsis were slaughtered) whereby those who committed genocide did so with impunity. Within a period of less than three months, over five hundred thousand opposition Hutus and Tutsis were estimated to have been killed, while the members and staff of an apathetic Divided Nations organization, who enjoy fat salaries and ironically pride themselves in calling that institution a United Nations organization, looked on.[22]

The lukewarm interest of the UN in the Rwandan crisis was nothing new for an African country. However, the scale of killing showed how an institutional apparatus of genocide can carry out its design by capitalizing on a general disinterest towards African problems. It is a classic lesson to Africans, African countries, the OAU, and all people of African descent everywhere not to take the UN, which had long demonstrated a prejudice against people of African descent, seriously in dangers of that nature, but to strive hard to find solutions to the problems of their diaspora. Particularly, in Africa, this demands an operational readiness on the part of African countries to take prompt or pre-emptive collective action to intervene in crisis situations rather than rely on the sweet words or the slow and ineffective processes of a divided United Nations that has little feeling towards or interest in solving problems in Africa.

The massacre was a shameful event, not only for Rwandans but also for the United Nations, which has proved sensitive to crises in Europe, such as the Bosnian conflict, or crises in Asia or the Middle East, such as the Gulf War after Iraq invaded Kuwait. The available evidence seems to suggest that partly because of colour-based prejudice and partly because of the relegation of African countries for centuries to the bottom of the economic vertical mosaic by international political and economic forces, the United Nations is historically insensitive to African problems. In Somalia it acted too late and withdrew too soon. In Liberia it did very little and left ECOWAS (Economic Community of West African States) and its military wing ECOMOG to shoulder the burden. In Sierra Leone, it turned a deaf ear for several months to calls for sanctions and support for military intervention by ECOMOG. In Rwanda it showed a serious interest only after the genocide had taken place, despite considerable information placed at its disposal.

The call for genocide was announced openly on the Rwandan radio, well within the hearing of UN officials in the country. *African Rights* expounds on the actors in the Rwandan genocide:

> The killers include the professional interawhamwe [militias], soldiers, gendarmes, Presidential Guardsmen and local government officials who actually supervised and carried out the killings. Some of these people have been witnessed, with their clothes drenched in blood, at the scene of massacres or at road blocks. And above them, there are the architects of genocide—the men who held the highest offices in the land, who controlled the government, army and radio stations, and who planned and implemented the killings from on high. Few of these people actually wielded machetes or even guns, but it was their policies and works that put guns and machetes in the hands of so many people in Rwanda. Some people travelled the country sowing hatred, or spoke on the radio, others were active behind the scenes encouraging the extremists and lending them logistical, financial, political and diplomatic support.[23]

The evening of the plane crash, and before the killings started, General Romeo Dallaire of the UN forces in Rwanda rushed into a meeting of top Rwandan officers to find out what was happening. In the interest of peace and stability, he suggested to Colonel T. Bagosora of the presidential guard, who was in charge of the meeting, to recognize the prime minister as the head of the state, but Bagosora rejected the idea on grounds that the prime minister was inept and untrustworthy. The next day Prime Minister Agathe Uwilingiyimana and her ten Belgian guards from the UN forces were murdered. In spite of months of awareness of open threats of an impending genocide and its knowledge of the genocidal tendencies in Rwanda since the struggle for independence, the United Nations maintained only a thin military presence in Rwanda. The genocide planners, therefore, had a free hand to achieve their goals. The selective assassination of leading Hutu politicians from the opposition parties followed. The next target group was made up of ordinary Hutus and Tutsis, including civil servants, journalists, and human rights activists identified as being critical of the government. Finally, the mass killing of Tutsis began. Thus, in accordance with a predetermined plan, the killing was started by the Rwandan army before other groups joined. *The Journal of Humanitarian Assistance* wrote about the genocide: "The killings were carried out with extraordinary cruelty. People were burnt alive, thrown dead or alive into pit latrines and often forced to kill their friends or relatives. The survivors were hunted all over the country, even into hospitals and church compounds. Some of the worst massacres were directed against people seeking refuge in churches."[24]

Before the massacre began the UN had received information about the situation in Rwanda and the training of special units for a possible genocidal act. With its knowledge of Rwandan history, the UN could have acted to avert the genocide, but it did not. The UN's immediate focus was on the safety of its own personnel. Instead of taking prompt action to stop the genocide, on April 14 the UN secretariat suggested a threatened withdrawal of the entire UN force unless the RPF and FAR agreed to a ceasefire. The United Nations Secretariat, in a subtle demonstration of its lack of respect for African lives, deliberately covered up information on the genocide. While admitting that tens of thousands had been killed, it avoided using the word "genocide," preferring to call it "widespread violence." No one in the secretariat was fired for gross negligence and irresponsibility.

The Security Council resolution that followed also confirmed how those who wielded power in the United Nations shut their eyes to the genocide and diverted attention in the direction of the civil war between the RPF and the Rwandan army. Clause 4 of the resolution stated, with hypocrisy and irresponsibility, "Obviously, a cease-fire agreement is the first step in establishing a stable and secure environment in the country, thus allowing the organized, co-ordinated and secure delivery of humanitarian assistance and the reactivation of the Arusha peace process." Item 6 contained the words "demands an immediate cessation of hostilities between the forces of the government of Rwanda and the Rwandan Patriotic Front and for an end to mindless violence and carnage that are engulfing Rwanda." Item 7 called for "the active role of the Special Representative of the Secretary-General and of the Force Commander to bring about a cease-fire and to mediate between the parties in order to bring about the earliest resolution of the crisis." Item 8 merely gave the UN representatives in Rwanda the mandate to negotiate a ceasefire.[25]

Even before the April 6 incident, the attitude of the UN mission in Rwanda was questionable, including its response to the Arusha Accord. The Arusha Accord made a request for a force to "guarantee overall security of the country." The UN Reconnaissance Mission report changed that to "establish security zone in and around the capital city of Kigali"—as if that city was in essence the whole country.[26] The UN Security Council resolution 846 of October 1993 watered the Arusha Accord request further by speaking of making a contribution "to the city of Kigali inter alia within a weapons-secure area established by the parties in and around the city." Whereas the Arusha Accord requested a force to "assist in catering for civilians," the report of the UN Reconnaissance Mission narrowed it down: "to monitor the civilian security situation through the verification and control of the Gendarmerie and Communal Police." The UN Security Council resolution narrowed it still further: "to investigate and report on incidents regarding the activities of the gendarmerie and police." Again, on the confiscation of illegal arms the Arusha Accord requested a force to "assist in the tracking of armed caches and neutralization of armed gangs throughout the country" and "assist in the recovery of all weapons distributed to, or illegally acquired by the civilians." The report of the Reconnaissance Mission changed these to "assist in tracking arms and neutralizing armed groups" with armed UN Military Forces and "assist in recovering arms in the hands of civilians"[27] with armed UN military forces and unarmed UN police observers.

The UN Security Council resolution made no provision whatsoever for confiscating arms. In this way, the UN forces were reduced to being mere spectators as the genocide proceeded. In a dispatch by Reuters from Kigali on March 13, 1994, the Belgian UN commander in Kigali, Colonel Luc Marchal, was reported to have complained that within three months of the arrival of the Belgian battalion, they had been able to confiscate only sixteen weapons and one hundred grenades. The same article quoted Marchal as complaining, "It is a problem with the mandate. Stopping and searching people for weapons is forbidden by New York."[28] The Ghanaian battalion in Kigali was frustrated that its numerous calls to the Secretariat were not respected enough to be returned.

The same international political forces that put pressure on Rwanda to return to multiparty politics were unwilling to provide any effective assistance to Rwanda in the crisis arising from that same multi-party politics. After all, it was multiparty politics that led first to power-sharing with the opposition parties within Rwanda, before power-sharing with the RPF, which was essentially another opposition party outside Rwanda.

The disinterest of the UN in Rwanda's plight was confirmed in a statement by the former finance minister from the Social Democrats: "We warned the international community that this was happening, that these people were being trained and armed to kill great numbers of people."[29] The Arusha Accord took such warnings into account; the UN did not. That there was an institutional apparatus for the genocide long before it occurred and of which the UN was made aware was explained by Lemarchand and confirmed by Holly Burkhalter, the Washington director of Human Rights Watch. Lemarchand described the apparatus:

By 1992, the institutional apparatus of genocide was already in place. It involved four distinct levels of activity, or sets of actors: (a) the akazu, "little house," that is the core group, consisting of Habyarimana's immediate entourage, i.e. his wife (Agathe), his three brothers-in-law (Protee Zigiranyirazo, Seraphin Rwabukumba and Elie Sagatwa) and a springing of trusted advisers (most notably Joseph Nzirorera, Laurent Serubuga and Ildephonse Gashumba); (b) the rural organizers, numbering anywhere from two to three hundred, drawn from the communal and prefectural cadres (prefets, sous-prefets, conseillers communaux, etc.); (c) the militias (interahamwe), estimated at 30,000, forming the ground-level operatives in charge of doing the actual killings; and (d) the presidential Guard, recruited almost exclusively among

northerners and trained with a view to providing another slaugh-
terhouse support to civilian death squads.[30]

Burkhalter confirmed that "the army training had gone on for a couple
of years and there were many, many reports that it was organized."[31]
Thus the UN had sufficient time to prevent the genocide, but refused to
do so—again, providing a lesson for all African states as well as for the
OAU, which has been patterned after the UN.

The UN was encouraged in its attitude by the disposition of the
powerful members of the world body, particularly the United States, on
intervention. After the failure of Operation Restore Hope in Somalia, in
which bodies of dead U.S. soldiers were dragged through the streets of
Mogadishu, the attitude of the United States towards humanitarian mis-
sions in Africa changed drastically, back to the lack of concern held
before that special operation. It was not appreciated that the failure of
Operation Restore Hope was due principally to the UN waiting for too
long a period before acting. Thus the UNTAC operation in Cambodia
was costing U.S.$60-70 million per month, and UN peace missions had
increased the U.S. contribution from U.S.$29 million in 1985 to
U.S.$460.4 million in 1993. But when it came to Rwanda, the United
States was most unwilling.[32]

The Clinton administration directed that the United States had to
apply the stringent criteria of national interest before supporting UN
peacekeeping operations, whether or not they involved U.S. troops. The
implication was that the United States would no longer act on humanitarian principles, but would respond based on its own interests and in
particular cases. In addition, the cost of such operations would be
charged against the budget of the Pentagon. Strangely enough, the United States and the North Atlantic Treaty Organization (NATO) would
later find it easy to intervene with armed force in Bosnia. Again, African
states should take note: those who preach and pressure them to adopt
foreign democratic practices could prove reluctant to come to their rescue in a crisis arising from the misfit between that adopted political
practice and the African environment. The future of who should govern
Rwanda was left to be settled on the battlefield.

The Rwandan army proved no match for the RPF, supported by
Ugandan regulars. Kigali fell to the RPF forces on July 6, 1994, and on
July 18 the RPF announced that the war was over. A new government
with two Hutus, Pasteur Bizimungu as president and Faustin Twagira-
mungu as prime minister, was announced. General Kagame of the RPF,

a Tutsi, became the vice-president and minister of defence. The minister of the interior, the minister of foreign affairs, and the minister of justice were also Hutus.

Only after the RPF had won the civil war, over five hundred thousand people had been killed, about two million had fled the country, and about one million were displaced internally did the UN begin to act in a face-saving manner. The mass movements of people created enormous problems, and in relation to those problems the UN wanted at last to be seen as taking action. In that same context the U.S. government, which had been the major obstacle to UN intervention to halt the genocide, began to deliver supplies to Goma to save the lives of the refugees there, and it began to call for the trial of those suspected of genocide.

Meanwhile, the refugees in Zaire included the former Rwandan leadership and the former Rwandan army. They took over the refugee camps and through propaganda and intimidation prevented the refugees from returning to Rwanda. In late December they announced the formation of a government in exile in Zaire, and from the refugee camps there they launched attacks against Rwanda's new government. However, as living conditions in the camps became more difficult and the propaganda of the leaders became less effective, a large number of refugees returned home, leaving about two hundred and fifty thousand still in the camps. The Ugandan-backed rebellion in Eastern Zaire drove these thousands of refugees into hiding, making it difficult for the relief agencies to care for them. The final fall of Zaire to the rebel forces and the exit of Mobutu provided a false hope that the former Rwandan army and the refugees who accompanied it would gain no support from the new Republic of the Congo. That hope did not last long.

The new Rwandan government was also faced with numerous problems, including divisions among its ranks as appointees from each political party pursued their own hidden agendas. On August 8, 1994, Faustin Twagirimungu, the Hutu prime minister appointed at the end of the civil war, resigned and went into exile in Kenya, where he was critical of the behaviour of the Rwandan regime he had helped to establish. On August 30, a new government with Pierre-Celestin Rwigyema as the new prime minister was announced. However, the going was far from easy for the new government. Because both private and public business had ground to a halt during the hostilities and the mass exodus, it proved difficult for the government to raise sufficient revenue to meet expenses. The government came to rely heavily on foreign funding, but response from the international community was not encouraging. In any case, foreign funding with the usual strings attached would imply a compromise on Rwandan sovereignty. The government would have to be selective in its acceptance of funding to protect its sovereignty or to avoid external pressures that could lead the country into more trouble.

The genocide and exodus also meant that a large number of qualified Rwandans were either killed or fled the country. For fear of incrimination and victimization many of these qualified personnel were not willing to return. With the return of hundreds of thousands of both Tutsi and Hutu refugees, the government had the additional burden of accommodating, feeding, and finding them land to live on, or jobs. Although the government recognized the right of property owners, new arrivals who lived outside Rwanda for decades took up land and houses illegally, thus creating difficulties for the Tutsi-Hutu reintegration process. Meanwhile, the identification and prosecution of those involved in the genocide became a sensitive issue that also militated against reintegration. On the one hand, if the government failed to muster the political will to deal with the offenders, the danger existed that there would be no end to the practice of genocide with impunity that had plagued Rwanda since 1959. On the other hand, if the government mustered the political will, its actions could be interpreted by Hutus as a deliberate act of prosecuting innocent Hutus just because some Hutus were accused of genocide. The problem was complicated by the undeniable evidence that a large number of Hutus were killed by fellow Hutus during the genocide. By 1998, although several Hutus accused of complicity in the genocide had been publicly executed, the Hutu rebel attacks had still not been curbed. Contrary to the expectations of the Rwanda-Uganda alliance, Laurent Kabila was not able to keep the Hutu rebels under check. Instead, Kabila, in his attempt to win popular support in the Congo, sacked the Tutsis and limited the activities and privileges of the Banyanmulenge, a Tutsi fraction who are part of the Republic of Congo. The strained relations led to the Uganda-Rwanda alliance to encourage and support a rebellion in the Congo, which drew Angola, Chad, and Zimbabwe (countries that support Kabila) into the conflict.

Rwanda, then, is yet another country in Africa in which the transplantation of foreign democratic practice in the form of partisan politics failed to work in both its single-party and multiparty forms. Military rule also failed to work. The combination of Western ideologies to create a new ideology, planned liberalism, did little to mobilize Rwandans for successful development. Instead, the ideology became the source for an authoritative allocation of Western values to Rwandans, a system in which inequalities abounded. The Rwandan case also teaches that in the absence of a strong and encompassing nationalist coalition forged in accordance with African values, the stresses and strains arising from the international system of oligopolistic pricing can shatter a political system and lead to chaos—and, in this case, genocide.

The Rwandan authorities, by not taking the appropriate action to separate church and state, permitted the Catholic mission to inflame political unrest in 1959 and also between 1989 and 1990, with genocidal consequences. The IMF and the World Bank closed their eyes to the abrogation of the ICA as the cause of the economic crisis and were insensitive to the country's political history. The two international institutions made it clear that humanitarian concerns were less important than their ideology based on the utopian operation of market forces. The debt had to be paid off no matter what. When their prescriptions deepened the sufferings of the Rwandan people and the genocide began, the IMF and World Bank officials and foreign nationals were quickly flown out of the country. It was Rwandans who died.

Also, in the time of crisis, the same international political forces that put pressure on Rwanda to give in to the practice of multiparty politics refused to come to its aid. The UN had ample time to act to avoid genocide, but despite its knowledge of Rwanda's genocidal history and numerous warnings, it refused to do so. It was only after the genocide that the UN and the U.S. government acted in a face-saving manner to mitigate the sufferings of the refugees. The Rwandan experience is a sad, painful lesson to the African states that they must rely first on themselves, and on their own ideologies and not expect that in a time of crisis the UN or other external organization will effectively intervene to save them.

CHAPTER THIRTEEN

CONGO (KINSHASA): "A MOST LETHAL POISON ..."

The 1884-85 Berlin Conference gave undisputed sovereignty of the Congo to the King of Belgium, Leopold II. In accordance with the prevailing colonial logic, Belgium set out to structure the economy of the Congo not to suit the needs of Congolese peoples but the needs of Belgians and the entire Western alliance. The colonial strategy of the Belgian government was to spend very little on the colony while at the same time reaping whatever profits the territory generated. Despite substantial exploitation of the mineral and agricultural wealth of the country, economic development during the colonial era bore little relationship to the needs of the indigenous populations. The production of cash crops was stressed and promoted at the expense of food crops. Profits accrued not to the indigenous populations but to non-Congolese, foreign shareholders of the industrial and agricultural companies of the modern sector, the colonial state that obtained shares in those foreign companies, and the officials of the colonial state apparatuses who enjoyed fat salaries. The colonial state concerned itself very little with basic human needs such as health or education. As a form of dictatorship, it applied coercive strategies to obtain the indigenous labour required for public works and private investment projects. In 1917, for example, a decree was promulgated that required African peasants to set aside sixty days in a year to do agricultural work. Failure to comply with the decree carried severe penal sanctions.[1] The colonial situation simultaneously prevented and discouraged the development of any indigenous entrepreneurial class. Indeed, under colonialism, the Congolese were virtually written out of history by the Belgian masters.

Today the Republic of the Congo is, internationally, a country of both geopolitical and economic importance. It shares borders with several African states, including the Sudan, Tanzania, Rwanda, Uganda, Angola, the Central African Republic, Zambia, Burundi, and Congo (Brazzaville). Its natural resource base makes it a country of economic importance. It is the world's largest producer of cobalt and ranks among the world's top producers of copper, industrial diamonds, zinc, tin manganese, gold, tungsten, tantalum, and niobium. Its Atlantic coast is known to have large reserves of oil. Coal deposits in commercial quantities have also been found. An added advantage is the country's enormous potential in agriculture and hydroelectric energy. It is reputed to have the potential to "feed and power the entire continent."[2] Given its geopolitical importance and economic potential, its successful development might well stimulate the growth of the entire continent.

Despite its enormous natural endowment, the post-independence development experience of the Republic of Congo—which changed its name to Zaire and later to the Democratic Republic of the Congo (Kinshasa)—demonstrates how Western business in conjunction with international political forces and the colonial legacy can act through partisan politics and military interventions to ruin an African country no matter how rich its natural resource base. It shows how a massive transplantation of the political institutions of the West in Africa can weaken an African state, enable external interests to finance particular political parties, and lead to internal divisions. The experience of the Congo serves as a lesson to African states that the pressure from the West on African countries to adopt Western democratic practice may also carry the hidden agenda of making African countries weak enough to be exploited.

Through colonialism, the Congo became an adjunct of the industrial system of the West, in which the wages of the African workers were so low, and the development of indigenous personnel so suppressed, that at the time of independence in 1960 the country had no private indigenous capital and no internal capital market. The largest mining company was Union Minière. Even cash-crop production was controlled by Western businesses, dominated by a subsidiary of the Anglo-Dutch Unilever company, Huileries du Congo Belges, which also dominated palm-oil production. Thus, the Congo was dependent on the West in all factors of production, including entrepreneurship. The consequence of structuring the economy to be so dependent on the West was the economic exploitation of the country, with a negligible real economic development taking place. Furthermore, because the political arena was monopolized by the Belgians, the development of political institutions was stifled. Belgian policy, geared to insulating the Africans from the politics of the country, was continued after the Second World War. However, ethnic associations fostered various ethnic interests.

The postwar years were characterized by political nationalism in Africa, and it became increasingly difficult for the Belgians to keep the Congolese out of the political arena completely. The world economic recession of 1955-56 hit the Congo very hard, with rising unemployment and a fall in investment. Then, in 1957, the world market price of copper fell so low that the profits that Belgian business had derived from copper production were squeezed to the point at which incentive for further investment in copper weakened. Meanwhile, with the prevailing wind of change blowing over Africa, the Catholic Church perceived that an African government in the Congo in the near future was inevitable, and it became increasingly concerned that its support for colonialism in the past might earn it the displeasure of a future African government. Consequently, it changed its policies to support the involvement of Africans in the politics and administration of the country, and it established a Catholic study group, which, in 1956, called for independence in thirty years.

The multi-ethnic structure of the country combined with the effects of the colonial policy of divide and rule, which set the various ethnic groups against one another, plus the low development of the indigenous productive forces, required an encompassing coalition of elites capable of uniting all Congolese ethnic groups to prepare them for the stresses and strains of economic growth. Unfortunately, that is not what happened. To ensure continued exploitation, it was in the interest of the Belgians and their Western allies that the economy of the Congo be neo-colonial. That strategy, in turn, required the existence of a government sensitive and responsive to Western political, ideological, and economic interests. The West rationalized that if the Congo embraced Western culture and Western democratic practices, it would not become a prey to communism, and Western interests would continue to be served. In accordance with this logic, in 1956 the Belgians, supported by the Catholic Church, called for communal elections in the provincial capitals.

How Partisan Politics Created Confusion

Partly because the formation of political parties had been suppressed during the colonial era and partly because political parties were non-existent in the indigenous political culture, most of the new political parties emerged out of the existing ethnic associations and were essentially ethnic parties. One of the most prominent of such ethnic parties was CONAKAT (Confédération des Associations Tribales du Katanga), a party formed by bringing together the ethnic associations of people originating from the tribes of Katanga (now the province of Shaba). It was led by Moise Tshombe, who came from the Lunda tribe of Katanga. Another prominent ethnic party, ABAKO, led by Joseph Kasavubu, sprang from an ethnic association founded in 1950 to promote the culture of the Bakongo. Two other newly prominent parties were again supported largely by certain ethnic groups, though they did not originate from ethnic associations and transcended ethnicity. One of them, the Mouvement National Congolais (MNC), led by Patrice Lumumba, was a nationalist party with a large support among the Bangala speakers who lived around Stanleyville (now Kisangani). The second non-ethnic party was the Parti Solidaire Africain (PSA), a socialist organization led by Antoine Gizenga.

ABAKO and CONAKAT, as ethnic parties, favoured a federalist constitution in which the provinces would enjoy a high degree of autonomy and develop separately. The non-ethnic parties favoured a strong unitary form of government in which ethnicity would be weakened enough to present no threat to political stability. Hence, like Kenya, in addition to competition among the parties, the Congo experienced a rivalry between the federalists and the unitarists. The mining companies, of which the Union Minière was foremost, feared the unitarists and especially Lumumba's nationalist MNC, which they perceived as being not only capable of taxing the mining companies heavily to develop the Congo, but also likely to nationalize them. Because most of the mines were located in Katanga, in their own interests the mining companies decided to back and finance CONAKAT to oppose the unitarist idea. They found in the personality of Moise Tshombe, a failed businessman of the royal house of the Lunda, the combination of selfishness and ethnic-mindedness they required to oppose the unitarist idea. As Lumumba became more popular and succeeded in absorbing smaller ethnic parties into the MNC, the mining companies became more discontented. The fears of foreign business were increased when Lumumba returned from the All-African People's Conference in Accra in 1958 to call for immediate independence—a notable difference from the Catholic study group's call for independence in thirty years.[3] Lumumba's nationalist aspirations led the mining companies to see him as a radical whose policies, ideas, and actions must be checked. They intensified their support and financing of Tshombe.

As Lumumba became more popular, the ethnic-minded Kasavubu,

leader of ABAKO, requested the separation of the Lower Congo from the rest of the country to enable the Bakongo of the Lower Congo to join their ethnic brothers in the French Congo—the Mukongo on the other side of the Congo River—to form one country. Although the Belgian administration appeared to oppose this separation bid, Kasavubu's action encouraged Tshombe to adopt a secessionist stance in Katanga with the support of the mining companies.[4] As the rivalry between the federalists and the unitarists intensified with secessionist feelings, Albert Kalonji was enticed to break away from the MNC branch in Kasai province to join the federalists.

The divisions among the various party leaders worked in the interests of the political and economic forces of neo-colonialism. The Brussels constitutional conference of January 1960 reflected these interests. It provided for a two-chamber legislature for the central government and gave provincial governments and assemblies powers over local affairs. The provincial powers were substantially what the mining companies wanted, because the provinces would have discretionary power to assist foreign business. However, the mining companies wanted something more as well: a situation in which Katanga would be totally aligned with foreign business without any interference whatsoever from a central government. That situation was possible only if Katanga seceded. Under pressure from the mining companies, Tshombe had demanded the right of secession for Katanga from the rest of the Congo—a demand that was rejected.

Elections in May 1960 for positions in the chamber of deputies also served the interests of the neo-colonial forces. Because of electoral victories in various ridings by small parties, no dominant party emerged. Some of these small parties were unitarist and others federalist, but because of a general tendency to shift their allegiances and inclinations, they were relatively unstable. Out of a total of 137 seats, the MNC won 36, the ABAKO 12, and CONAKAT 8. Although CONAKAT fared badly at the national level, it won the largest number of seats in the provincial assembly, where Tshombe became the provincial president. Recognizing that his position at the national level was weak, but enjoying the support of the mining companies, Tshombe stepped up his talk for secession.

Meanwhile, the election results at the national level required the formation of a coalition government. Against the advice of his followers and wanting to break the parliamentary deadlock, Lumumba decided to form a government with Kasavubu. On June 12, 1960, Lumumba became the prime minister, with Kasavubu as president and Gizenga as vice-prime minister.

Entry of International Political and Ideological Forces

Events on the day of independence for the Republic of the Congo in June 1960 included a speech by Lumumba about the new country's colonial legacy, which, contrasting with a paternalistic speech from King Baudouin of the Belgians, helped to turn the Belgian government and its Western allies completely against the African leader. Both Lumumba and Baudouin were less than diplomatic. Baudouin enthused about colonialism, referring to it as a civilizing mission in which King Leopold II of the Belgians had played a courageous role—a position in sharp contrast to the view held by many Africans and people of African descent based on either direct experience or close knowledge of the brutalities, oppression, and greed of centuries of European intervention. Baudouin's speech was provocative, and particularly ill-advised at that time.

Undoubtedly aroused by the Belgian king's speech, Lumumba proceeded to expound on the realities of colonialism as he saw them, including its role as a one-armed bandit whose sole purpose was the exploitation of African material and human resources by force. Lumumba was fully aware of how the Congo was being milked by the mining companies. For example, between 1950 and 1959, the Union Minière alone made a net profit of 39 billion Belgian francs, all of which was repatriated. If this amount or even a good part of it had been invested in the Congo, the country could have made significant gains. After describing colonialism as a humiliating brand of slavery imposed by brutal force—with Leopold II as its chief architect—Lumumba went on to further offend the Belgians present by providing a candid and detailed account of the evils of Belgian rule.

At the same proceedings Kasavubu read a diplomatic speech prepared for him by his Belgian advisers. Although the Belgians had jailed Kasavubu for inciting riots against Belgians in Leopoldville (now Kinshasa) in 1959, they now saw him as an ally and Lumumba as an enemy. From the day of independence the Belgians were bent on seeing the overthrow of Lumumba, and they were encouraged in this by the partisan and federalist-unitarist rivalry between Kasavubu and Lumumba. They were also encouraged by the rivalry between Lumumba and Tshombe, the leader who had the support not only of the mining companies but also of the Western allies, which had been equally offended by Lumumba's open and undiplomatic condemnation of imperialism and colonialism—a condemnation that was, as usual, equated with being in alliance with communism.

Lumumba perhaps made the mistake of thinking that the freedom of speech espoused by the liberal democracies of the West would be fully acceptable to them without giving offence. In this belief he was mistaken, for in the Western democracies freedom of speech has its limits, and if you go beyond those limits you do indeed give offence, followed by lawsuits and energetic, sometimes clandestine activities intended to punish, victimize, or exercise control. The behaviour of the Belgians towards Lumumba after his speech showed that, in a paternalistic manner, the former colonial masters were not prepared to accept any condemnation or statement of any facts about colonialism and imperialism from their former colonies. Indeed, the paternalistic colonial relationship was to be an integral part of the new, latent, or disguised colonialism—neo-colonialism. The Belgians had the added advantage that their officers still controlled the Congo's Force Publique, which had been used in colonial times to repress the legitimate demands of the Congolese people. Because the interests of these Belgian officers were served by their privileged position in the military hierarchy, they were strongly opposed to any Africanization of the Force Publique.

On July 5, 1960, barely six days after independence, the Belgian commander of the Force Publique openly voiced his opposition to Africanization and proceeded to demote an African non-commissioned officer at a time when the ranks of that military institution included not a single African officer. Apparently, although the Congo had become independent, the Belgian officers of the Force Publique had not factored that reality into their way of thinking and behaviour.[5] They continued to see themselves as masters set over inferiors—an air of superiority that was no longer acceptable to the rank and file of the Africans in the Force Publique in an independent Congo. The Africans of the Force Publique mutinied against the Belgian officers. Some Belgian civilians in Leopoldville were also killed. With Lumumba's permission, Belgian troops were flown in to protect the lives and property of Belgian civilians. The Belgians should have been grateful to Lumumba for this protection, but they were not. Seeking to discredit the Lumumba government, the Belgian forces went beyond their mandate, and on July 11, 1960, bombarded the port of Matadi.

The presence of Belgian troops and the bombardment of Matadi encouraged Moise Tshombe to declare the independence of Katanga with the backing of the mining companies, local Belgian administrators, and provincial garrisons. Meanwhile, the bombardment led to African revenge attacks on white people throughout the country. In accordance with a premeditated Belgian response, and without the approval of the Lumumba government, the Belgian army intervened and illegally occupied large areas of the country, including Katanga, where they were allied with Tshombe and the mining companies. Their actions and presence strengthened Tshombe's position, and he proclaimed the independence of Katanga.

At the time there was no united African force capable of driving the Belgians out and ending the illegal occupation of the young country. After ending the mutiny by promising the Force Publique rapid Africanization, and sacking the commander of the Force Publique, Lumumba made a great mistake by appealing to the United Nations for aid—an understandable move given the chaos in the country and the prevalent belief that the UN had overcome the ills of its predecessor, the League of Nations. Lumumba might have been aware that the European-dominated League of Nations had badly disappointed Ethiopia when that country was invaded without provocation by Italy before World War II. But he might have forgotten that the UN was also dominated by the West. That mistake was to cost Lumumba a great deal, including his life.

The UN troops began to arrive on July 15, and by September 4 all Belgian troops were officially supposed to be no longer in the Congo. In reality, Belgian troops were being recruited under cover and arriving in large numbers in Katanga and Kasai provinces, the key areas for the mining companies. Encouraged by the Belgian military presence and economic assistance, in August Albert Kalonji, a former supporter of Lumumba, declared the diamond-rich southern part of Kasai province independent, with himself as king of the Balubas.

The United Nations failed to live up to Lumumba's expectations. The UN could intervene to stop the secession only with the approval of its Security Council, which was dominated by the West. But the West's interests were being served by the secessionists in Katanga and South Kasai, whereas the West saw Lumumba's radical and nationalist stance as a threat to its interests. Added to the mix was the West's erroneous association of African nationalism with communism. Not surprisingly, therefore, an August 9 Security Council resolution on the Congo issue stated: "Reaffirms that the United Nations in the Congo will not be a party to or in any way intervene in or be used to influence the outcome of any internal conflict, constitutional or otherwise."[6] Given that in contravention of the UN Charter Belgium was openly interfering in the internal affairs of the Congo, and that the Lumumba government had called on the UN to end that very interference, which had encouraged secession and rendered the Congo difficult to govern, the resolution itself contradicted the very real justification for the presence of UN troops in that country.

Some may attempt to explain the Security Council's attitude in terms of its policy of non-interference in the internal affairs of member states. However, in this particular case that non-interference principle did not hold. Independent Congo was not an extension of Belgium. Belgium, a signatory to the United Nation Charter, was, in complete contravention of that same Charter, interfering openly in the internal affairs of a member state, and the United Nations had been called on to help bring that interference to a halt. The resolution implied that the UN troops were only in the Congo as spectators to witness the interference of Belgium in the affairs of that country and do nothing about it. What is it, for instance, that would later drive the United Nations to act in the case of Iraq's intervention in Kuwait in the 1990s, but made it so reluctant to act in the case of the Congo that it turned a blind eye to Belgium's intervention there? In his desperation to end the secession, Lumumba solicited the help of the United States, but his appeal was rebuffed by that country—the same country that was, in theory, advocating the right of all peoples of the world to self-determination. He turned to the Soviet Union and received promises of aid, but no immediate help. In an article titled "The Mobutu I Knew," Rajeswar Dayal, the former UN representative in the Congo, wrote about Lumumba's predicament at the time:

Prime Minister Patrice Lumumba was a fervent nationalist, impatient to sever all colonial bonds and unify the country. The most serious problem was the secession of Katanga (now Shaba), which accounted for 75 percent of the country's foreign exchange earnings. It was this problem that brought a head-on clash between Lumumba and the US. Lumumba tried to secure military, financial and political support to end the secession and secure the expulsion of the uninvited Belgian troops. But his attempts to solicit the aid of Washington were rebuffed, compelling him to seek the help of Moscow, which was promised but never delivered. Lumumba's approach to the USSR was enough to dub him a communist. True, he was impetuous and messianic in his zeal to endow his country's nominal independence with substance. But for America, nationalism was equated with communism.[7]

Soviet troops did not directly intervene, but with the assistance of Soviet military equipment and transport vehicles the Force Publique—now renamed the Congolese National Army (ANC)—occupied much of Kasai province. Meanwhile, because of Cold War rivalry and the possible threat to Western interests, the invitation of the Soviets did not please the West. Kasavubu, who had openly identified himself as an ally of the West, was also not pleased with the Soviet connection. With support from the West, Kasavubu announced the dismissal of Lumumba as prime minister and the appointment of Joseph Ileo as the new prime minister. Lumumba responded by announcing the dismissal of Kasavubu as president. Given that under the constitution only Parliament could dismiss the prime minister or the president, both dismissals were unconstitutional. The Western-style democracy emulated blindly and prematurely by the Congolese elite was a total misfit in the cultural environment, leading only to tension and animosity.

The Beginning of Congolese Military Interventions

With tensions mounting, Kasavubu—stimulated by influences from the West, particularly the United States, and wanting to detach the Congolese National Army (ANC) from Lumumba—formed a secret alliance with Mobutu Sese Seko, the Congolese chief of staff of the ANC. Encouraged by this alliance, on September 13 Colonel Mobutu announced that he had seized power and would manage the country's affairs until December 30. Meanwhile, Kasavubu and Ileo continued to be referred to officially as president and prime minister respectively, while Lumumba, who had invited the UN troops to the Congo, was virtually placed under house arrest, having been confined to a house, supposedly under the protection of UN troops.

Mobutu's unconstitutional intervention, which went unchecked, was in itself a reflection of a deep-seated problem. The Congolese elite did not understand Western democratic practice, in which the military does not get involved in politics. Kasavubu and Ileo did not understand that they were teaching Mobutu to use the armed forces for political gain and that they were setting a precedence that could work against them in future. Indeed, by accepting Mobutu's intervention in the political arena, they unknowingly accentuated centrifugal political forces within the Congo itself and set a precedence for coups in Africa as a whole. Later events taught Mobutu more lessons in the art of military intervention and how to eliminate political opponents through assassination. Lumumba, unlike Colonel Mengistu of Ethiopia, was only an African nationalist and not a committed comrade of communism or an agent of Marxism who would enjoy the full support, commitment, and intervention of the Soviet Union. Had Lumumba identified himself as an apostle of Marxism, as Mengistu did, the story might have been quite different. The Soviet response might have been quick, as in Ethiopia, and Mobutu might not have had the audacity to intervene.

In November Lumumba, still in confinement, learned of the death of his infant daughter. In accordance with African culture, it was customary for the father to be present at the burial of his beloved child. On November 27, the combination of Lumumba's desire to escape from his confinement and to attend the funeral of his daughter motivated him to sneak out of the house and head for Stanleyville (now Kisangani). Communication linkages between the UN and the West enabled Kasavubu and Mobutu to learn about his supposedly secret movement. Lumumba was arrested on his way to Stanleyville, severely beaten, and returned to the capital.

The UN could have prevented the arrest of Lumumba or at least rescued him after his arrest, but refused to do so and looked on as the man who had invited them into the country was beaten up, tortured, humiliated, and deprived of the same human dignity that the international organization was supposed to uphold. Lumumba learned too late that the UN, an arena dominated by the West in the Cold War rivalry of the time, was not to be trusted. Meanwhile, Lumumba's deputy prime minister, Antoine Gizenga, announced the move of the seat of government from Leopoldville to Stanleyville and outlined the reconstituted cabinet, which remained, essentially, Lumumba's cabinet.

On January 17, 1961, Lumumba and two of his trusted companions, Maurice Mpolo and Joseph Okito, were transferred to Katanga, where they were assassinated by Belgian officers with the approval of a new alliance of Tshombe, Kasavubu, and Mobutu. Dayal described the conspiratorial involvement of the West in Lumumba's assassination:

I soon began to receive reports that the British Military attache would visit Mobutu every day with bursting bundles wrapped in paper. This coincided with the diminishing demands for financial help from Mobutu and a more defiant attitude toward the UN....

Thereupon, a vicious campaign of vilification was orchestrated by the US and western press against the UN mission and me personally.... On his way to the safety of Stanleyville, [Lumumba] was intercepted by Mobutu's men who overtook him in a helicopter arranged by the American embassy. Lumumba was brutally beaten and since no prison was safe enough to contain him, he was deported in a Belgian plane to Elisabethville (now Lubumbashi) where he was done to death....

The most authentic evidence of the CIA's deep involvement in this conspiracy has been revealed in the report of the Senate enquiry committee under the chairmanship of Senator Frank Church. At one of the innumerable meetings in the White House on the Congo, President Eisenhower exclaimed in exasperation that Lumumba must be got rid of. A CIA scientist, after concocting a most lethal poison, flew to Leopoldville in great secrecy but his attempts to have the poison administered to Lumumba were frustrated by the presence of the UN guard. The CIA, therefore, made other plans to carry out the foul deal.[8]

According to writers Ali Mazrui and Michael Tidy, "No event while Kennedy was alive aroused greater African passions than the assassination of Patrice Lumumba. And Lumumba's death arose out of a sin of omission by the United Nations and, indirectly, by the United States. The UN, which had been called to Zaire by Lumumba, stood by as the man was taken away from Leopoldville and entrusted to the tender mercies of his opponents in Katanga."[9]

Contrary to the expectation of Kasavubu's clique that the elimination of Lumumba was the key to political stability, more confusion and strife followed. Katanga and South Kasai pressed on with their secessionist stance, while the leaders in Stanleyville claimed to be the legitimate government of the Congo. To resolve the confusion, a meeting was held in Leopoldville in which all the rival groups, with the exception of Moise Tshombe, attended. A new government was appointed, with Kasavubu as president, Cyrille Adoula as prime minister, and Gizenga as deputy prime minister.

Cyrille Adoula adopted pro-Western policies that won him the admiration of the West, but at the same time he was strongly against secession, which was being advocated by Western business. The West had to choose between supporting Adoula and thus gaining complete control over and access to all the mineral resources of the Congo or supporting

Tshombe and gaining access to and control over the resources of Katanga. The West decided to choose the first alternative, encouraged by the activities of Gizenga in Stanleyville, which posed a serious challenge to Adoula's government and to Kasavubu, whom the West preferred. That choice may seem to have been in conflict with the desires of Western business, but it was in keeping with the behaviour of the state in capitalist society. As Poulantzas explained in *Political Power and Social Classes* and "The Capitalist State: A Reply to Miliband and Laclau," capitalist states are capable of acting against the short-term interests of capital in order to protect the long-term interests of the capitalist class.[10] This is because the various fractions of the capitalist class may be divided or seek their short-term interests at the expense of their collective long-term interests. The relatively autonomous capitalist state, which is dependent on the capitalist class for its survival, is able to appreciate the long-term interests of the capitalist class because those interests are fused with its own. The Western states therefore acted in the long-term interests of foreign capital in the Congo, although they appeared to be acting against the short-term interests of assisting Tshombe to secede.

The attitude of the Security Council after Lumumba's elimination and the West's switch in support from Tshombe to Adoula showed how the Security Council might be an instrument capable of manipulation to satisfy the interests of imperialism. A new mandate from the Security Council authorized the UN forces to be used to suppress any secession and to expel mercenaries and other foreign agents from the Congo. This was principally the same rationale that Lumumba had used in his invitation of the UN, and that the Security Council had refused to honour on the grounds of wanting not to interfere in the Congo's internal politics. Again, the double standards of the Security Council show that the UN is essentially a Divided Nations organization. This same character would be reflected thirty years later, when the UN became a mere spectator to the ethnic cleansing in Bosnia, and only a joint action by NATO, not the UN, induced some sanity after hundreds of thousands of lives had been lost. With the UN intervention, Katanga's secession came to an end in January 1963, when Tshombe escaped.

The rebellion in Stanleyville was also crushed. With the help of the ANC and the police, the UN looked on as the Adoula government, armed with Western military equipment, proceeded to deal ruthlessly with the supporters of Gizenga and Lumumba in the eastern part of the country, especially in the Stanleyville area. This ruthless operation was to haunt the country in later years. Pierre Mulele, the education minister in Lumumba's government (a witness both to the double standard of the UN and the ruthless attitude of the ANC and the police towards his people in the Eastern Congo), left the country for China, where he received training in guerrilla warfare. Meanwhile, with the help of Western influence Tshombe was allowed to return to the Congo as the prime minister within the context of a new federal constitution. But this very turn of events proved difficult for the Lumumbaists in the Eastern Congo to swallow. Also, as with the continuance of the power struggles with their associated centrifugal forces that tended to break up the country, Mobutu co-operated, watched, and learned a lot.

The military intervention introduced by Kasavubu through Mobutu with the assistance of the West taught the followers of Lumumba and Gizenga that military solutions to political problems were appropriate and desirable. In 1964 a series of military confrontations occurred as Lumumbaists launched offensives against the Kasavubu government from the eastern part of the Congo. Mulele returned from China to Stanleyville with revolutionary ideas, and within a short space of time succeeded in convincing local chiefs and people to rise up against the Leopoldville government. The brutality of the ANC and the police contributed to his success in this regard. In January 1964 the forces organized by Mulele attacked and, although ill-equipped, managed with a combination of local support and determination to rout the ANC and capture a large number of towns. On February 1964 the Mulele forces successfully ambushed and killed the army chief of staff, Colonel Eleya.

Arms and reinforcements poured in from Leopoldville and from the West, but although the Mulele forces lacked modern arms and received no external military help, they were not defeated until April. The Lumumbaists did not lose their morale, and by May they had regrouped, joined by other Lumumbaists who had received guerrilla training and were led politically by Gaston Soumialout, with General Olenga as their military commander. They were well-organized. The political wing of the new rebellion was called Conseil Nationale de Libération (CNL), and the military wing, commanded by General Olenga, was the Armée Populaire de Libération (APL). With popular support, in May they captured many towns, including Stanleyville, and routed the Congolese army. Their successes encouraged Northern Katanga to join them but, at the same time, enabled the West, in July, to convince Kasavubu to accept Tshombe as prime minister. However, the rebellion was so popular that by September the CNL/APL had overrun about half of the Congo and proclaimed a revolutionary government in Stanleyville. With Tshombe as prime minister, however, the government in Leopoldville was able to obtain military assistance easily from the West. The Americans and the British intervened, with massive arms supplies and logistic support, including aircraft. For their part, the Belgians, under the pretext of rescuing European hostages, intervened with paratroopers and military officers, who led military units of the ANC in combat. Mazrui and Tidy wrote about this co-ordinated, massive intervention from the West:

> The most emotionally charged event in Zaire during Johnson's administration was the Stanleyville rescue operation. Lumumba had not been considered worth rescuing, though UN forces were actually there on the scene; but white hostages whose lives were in danger were a different proposition. As Conor Cruise O'Brien pointed out, the humanitarian sensitivity displayed by the West was, at bottom, a case of racial solidarity. No rescue operation of that scale would have been launched by the United States and Belgium if the hostages had not been white.
>
> On the African side there was a further element in the rescue operation which hurt many of them deeply. The Americans had appealed to President Kenyatta, as Chairman of the OAU Conciliation Committee on the Congo, to use his good offices on behalf of the hostages. But it appeared that the Americans appealed to Kenyatta only as a stalling tactic and a diversion, while behind his back they and the Belgians were planning to drop troops on Stanleyville.[11]

Certainly, the CNL/APL could not fight against the combined forces of the West. They were defeated, but not before they had demonstrated to the whole world and to Africa that without intervention from the West, the Congo would have been left in the hands of Lumumba's supporters.

Some Lumumbaists went into exile; others continued the resistance in the countryside until, in 1967, they were defeated with the help of mercenaries from the West and apartheid South Africa. After that defeat the Lumumbaists, including Laurent Kabila, went underground and would later surface to haunt Mobutu. However, Tshombe—who had called for Western military intervention—became so unpopular in both Congolese and African circles that Kasavubu thought it wise to replace him with Evariste Kimba, also from Katanga, as prime minister. Still, Kasavubu could not escape blame. He himself became so unpopular in OAU circles, where he was seen as a puppet of the West, that in conformity with an OAU resolution he proceeded to remove white mercenaries from the ANC to restore his image. The West perceived this corrective action as a shift to the left, deserving of Kasavubu's elimination from the political arena. Mobutu, who had learned his lessons on military intervention in the political arena, was most willing to co-operate with the West in this venture.

Mobutu's Military Kingdom

The West was able to play Kasavubu and Mobutu against Lumumba, and Kasavubu and Mobutu against Tshombe. It was able to intervene to suppress the popular Lumumbaist forces from the eastern part of the country and, finally, to use Mobutu to overthrow Kasavubu. In a coup on October 23, 1965, Mobutu announced the overthrow of Kasavubu in the interests of national unity, and declared himself president. Mobutu, the lion that Kasavubu nourished, had eventually done to Kasavubu what that lion had been taught to do to Lumumba.

Mobutu's rule would go against the grain of the national unity he had advanced to rationalize the coup. The same Mobutu who had supported Kasavubu's federalist stance against Lumumba's unitarist stance abolished federalism and created a strong central government. He proceeded to suppress ethnicism and all forms of regionalism, reduced the number of provinces from twenty-one to eight, and placed all provincial police forces under the ministry of the interior. Continuing with the unitarist process, in 1966 his regime compelled all mining and plantation companies operating in the country to move their headquarters to the capital. When the Union Minière refused to comply, Mobutu seized the assets of the company and gave them to a new state-owned company. In another move, the Congolese government became a partner in other mining companies. Apparently, Mobutu now saw the wisdom in Lumumba's unitarism.

Mobutu was far from being a wise leader. His immediate answer to political opposition was the death of the leaders, often by accusing them of a plot to overthrow the government, and the humiliation of their followers. For example, in 1966, four political opponents accused of plotting to overthrow him were publicly hanged without substantial supporting evidence. In 1967 he introduced a constitution that conferred upon himself the presidency for at least ten years. Also, not long after his assumption of power, Mobutu punitively deprived the region identified as supportive of Lumumba and Gizenga of amenities. This act of deprivation encouraged Laurent Kabila to rise against him in 1967. In 1968 Mobutu granted amnesty to Mulele and then, after Mulele had returned to the country, had him executed. This set a precedent that made any conciliation between Mobutu and his political rivals almost impossible, for they could no longer trust his word. He was so ruthless against political opponents that when presidential elections were called in 1977, nobody dared to oppose him. To cover up his role as a stooge of imperialism, Mobutu compelled all Zaireans to do away with all names that were not African—he changed his own name from Joseph Mobutu to Mobutu Sese Seko. He proceeded to ban the wearing of neckties on the grounds that they were not African. But his own behaviour towards his fellow Congolese was not African at all. In 1978, when the Lumumbaist regions he had deprived of amenities for so long revolted, leading to the death of a single government official, Mobutu ruthlessly retaliated. To teach the rebellious Lumumbaist regions a lesson, Mobutu sent the Congolese army on a three-week rampage that included the burning of villages, looting, rape, and the killing of over two thousand civilians and the brutal murder of Mulele's mother.

Far from scaring people from revolting, the brutal act encouraged refugees in neighbouring countries to take up arms against Mobutu's regime. In a daring act on May 13, 1978, the Front de la Libération National du Congo (FLNC), based in Angola, entered Katanga with only a thousand men led by General Mbumba, captured the mining town of Kolwezi, and routed the nine-thousand-strong units of the ANC in the area. Obviously, those military units were not motivated to fight for Mobutu. In addition, the local people openly demonstrated their support for the invaders. Again, it was only with the intervention of French and Belgian troops and the assistance of foreign mercenaries that the invaders were forced to withdraw. However, before their withdrawal and to discourage foreign interventions in the affairs of their country, the invaders killed eighty European civilians. In retaliation for demonstrating their support for the invaders, the supposedly civilized intervention forces massacred over a thousand innocent civilians.

Having suppressed all opposition, Mobutu proceeded to enrich himself to the detriment of his country. As the economy became weaker, the Congolese were marginalized and shortages of essential commodities became rampant. Mobutu himself amassed a fortune, including ownership of villas in several capitals of Europe and a number of secret bank accounts. Writer Monica Moorehead summarized Mobutu's role:

> Mobutu proved to be a pro-imperialist counterweight to Soviet support for African national-liberation movements. This made Mobutu even more attractive to the imperialists. In fact, President Bush, a former CIA director, referred to Mobutu as "America's oldest and most valued friend on the African continent." Mobutu played a dual role during his tenure. He used the repressive police and military to crush any mass resistance to the brutal super-exploitation of the Congolese people. And he gave carte blanche to monopoly finance capital based in the United States, England, France and Belgium to plunder the extraordinary resources of the Third biggest country in Africa. The imperialists made billions of dollars in profits in the Congo—home to 60 percent of the world's cobalt reserves and rich in many other minerals, including diamonds.[12]

So long as Mobutu satisfied the interests of the West—and no matter how he plundered the coffers of his own country, and no matter how the Congolese were marginalized—he was a good boy in the eyes of Western leaders and interests. Indeed, being touted as America's most valued friend in Africa must have contributed to a dangerously swelled head. Meanwhile the opposition against him went underground, though it would surface later to demonstrate that although Lumumba was dead his political soul, which animated Congolese nationalism, continued to march bravely from the direction of the Eastern Congo to Kinshasa.

With the demise of the Cold War and the emergence of the United States as the only remaining superpower, the West no longer needed Mobutu as a counterweight to Soviet support for African liberation movements. The West was in the Congo not to satisfy the interests of the Congolese, or even of Mobutu, but of its own interests. Furthermore, by amassing assets in the West, Mobutu was creating wealth in the West and not in the Congo. Mobutu himself failed to recognize these crucial facts. His reliance on the West for support had become a liability that the West would no longer accept. In addition, his enormous wealth became a source of embarrassment and criticism. When it became known that Mobutu was suffering from cancer it appeared to be even more obvious that there was no point in the West providing him with effective support, and strategists began to consider ways of ridding themselves of this liability.

Mobutu's Multiparty Games

One strategy considered as a means of loosening Mobutu's hold on the country was to put pressure on him to return to the same multiparty politics that in 1960 had divided the Congo along ethnic lines and raised demands for secession. Given that Mobutu was by then very unpopular with the Congolese masses, it seemed likely that elections would lead to his replacement. But Mobutu proved a clever strategist himself. He resorted to a combination of political appointments and monetary rewards to silence his opponents—spending an estimated U.S.$5 billion in this campaign. Clearly, resources that might have been invested in development projects were diverted to building political support or easing political tensions. Another problem was whether or not Mobutu would allow free and fair elections. Other African dictators, including Rawlings of Ghana and Diouf of Senegal, had legitimized their positions through open, but rigged, elections, and there was no guarantee that Mobutu would not do the same. Indeed, Mobutu had already postponed elections promised for April 1991 to July 1997, with no guarantees that more postponements would not follow over the coming years. He proceeded to violate the provisions of the constitution of the transition for the Republic of Zaire, which he approved.

According to this constitution, Mobutu's term of office would expire at midnight on July 9, 1995, after which the president of the High Council of the Republic would assume the powers of the presidency. But instead of stepping down and making way for Archbishop Mosengwo Pasinya, the president of the High Council, to take over, Mobutu organized his Popular Movement of Revolution (MPR) and an opposition party, the Democratic Union for Social Progress (DUSP), formed and financed by him, but led by his friend and protégé Etienne Tshisekedi, to call jointly for the removal of Mosengwo from his position. Dr. Nzita, the chairman of the People's Progressive Party of Zaire, issued a statement from its international headquarters in Pittsburgh:

> Like Adolph Hitler, Mobutu is a very, very, bright man who has manoeuvred to create illusions of a legitimate political opposition in Zaire by registering over 200 political parties; and secretly conspiring to share limited powers within his syndicate of close friends and family members. Disputes over the spoils is more akin to a Mafioso disagreement, not that of a democratic political opposition. Mobutu's political opponents are all dead, abroad or silent within Church and Chieftaincy Institutions....

It is morally wrong and stupid to believe that Tshisekedi, Kengo, and others appointed by Mobutu are somehow democratically inclined to oppose him. Let it be clear that any disagreement between Tshisekedi, Kengo and Mobutu are nothing more than subordinates complaining of their boss but nevertheless doing what he wants done.

This form of democracy, then, proved both an amazement and an embarrassment to the West, because Mobutu, an African, had fashioned an effective means of meeting the Western pressure for multiparty politics: he had managed to have what was essentially the same party participating in the elections under different names. Whichever party won made no difference.

Fortunately for the West, the Congolese nationalist Laurent Kabila—one of those who had given Mobutu a hard time in 1967, leading to the Stanleyville rescue operation—was also waiting for the convenient time to rescue the Congo from Mobutu's plunder and processes of marginalization. In the last months of 1996, having been convinced that Mobutu no longer enjoyed the support of the West, guerrillas of Kabila's Alliance of Democratic Forces for the Liberation of Zaire-Congo (ADFLC) attacked from northeastern Zaire with nationalist fervour, and amid popular local support routed Mobutu's army and captured Goma, the capital of the eastern province. Perceiving the inevitable fall of Mobutu, Western businessmen, no longer requiring Mobutu's type of assistance, began knocking at Kabila's door for contracts months before Mobutu's government actually fell. On May 17, 1997, the victorious Kabila forces entered Kinshasa, where Kabila declared himself president and renamed the country the Democratic Republic of the Congo.

Despite the enormous amount of arms amassed by Mobutu from the West, the Congolese army put up a limited resistance. As Dayal described the fall of Mobutu:

> While his people suffered, Mobutu waxed richer and richer. From being as poor as a church mouse, Mobutu became one of the richest men in the world while his country, the richest in natural resources in Africa, became the poorest.
>
> With the end of the cold war, Mobutu's utility also came to an end and Washington led the chorus for his resignation. The success of Mr. Kabila's rebellion exposed the brittleness of his regime and the abject cowardice of his tattered army. Western businessmen

began knocking at Mr. Kabila's door, soliciting contracts even before Mobutu's regime collapsed. With the fall of Kinshasa, Mobutu had no option but to flee the scene of his crimes. A fatal illness will do the rest. Truly, "the mills of God grind slow but they grind exceedingly small."[13]

Mobutu, the first Sub-Saharan African to intervene militarily in the political arena of independent Africa, the man who sent thousands of his countrymen into exile or into flight as refugees in various countries, was now on the run, seeking a place of exile. His plane landed in Togo but, faced with popular resentment, President Gnassingbé Eyadéma was not able to let him stay there. Mobutu left for Morocco, presumably as a stepping stone to France, where he had one of his exotic mansions; but there was a great danger that he might be a liability in France as well. Having been abandoned by the West, he died later in Morocco.

Mobutu's Wealth and the Congolese Debt

The Swiss government announced a freeze on the U.S.$2.2 million villa Mobutu had in that country. After initially denying that Switzerland was harbouring some of Mobutu's millions, the Swiss government suspiciously admitted to only U.S.$3.4 million of his estimated U.S.$9 billion held in Swiss banks. Similarly, the initial search for the funds of Ferdinand Marcos of the Philippines had turned up very little, though later the Swiss had admitted to holding U.S.$500 million belonging to Marcos. Meanwhile the majority of the dictator's fellow Filipinos were living in abject poverty. Corrupt politicians such as Marcos and Mobutu rob their own people to make themselves and others rich, and the foreign banks, which lure these dictators with cunning words of safety and security, are understandably pleased with these transactions. Because of the complex nature of Swiss banking, including passwords, secret numbers, and duress provisions, when the dictators die it is the Swiss who inherit the stolen treasure.

Mobutu's wealth was left in the Swiss and other banks of Europe. This wealth is part of the Congo's international debt load. The remaining issue is to determine who is responsible for paying that portion of the Congo's debt, the West or the Congo? Gary Djoli Mokoka, president of the Congolese Committee against Debt, reportedly argued, "We have long campaigned for a write-off of the country's foreign debt. This debt is not the debt of the Zairean people. Loans that France extended to

Zaire stayed in France when Mobutu used it to buy himself chateaux here and there."[14]

The debt problem and its write-off remain the subject of considerable debate. On the one hand the Congo is currently not capable of paying off its debt, and the interest on it continues to grow. On the other hand, the debt itself is a trap by which the West can capture the vast potential wealth of the Congo. The West will, therefore, not be inclined to write off the debt so easily. The Congo may find itself in a dilemma. New loans may be required to rebuild the country. Obtaining new loans may require proving to the IMF and the World bank that it is "a good boy" who will be able to service its foreign debt. Because Western countries will not be called upon to prove that they too are "good boys"—by unlocking their holdings of Mobutu's wealth to defray the debt—the Congo may find itself in a tight corner. The only way, once again, is a practical shift to Africanism: a strong and encompassing nationalist coalition capable of taking consensual decisions in accordance with African cultural democratic practices—a compatible cultural democracy—and capable of consensually withstanding the stresses and strains emanating from the international environment.

CHAPTER FOURTEEN

CONCLUSION: ESTABLISHING AN AFRICAN (JAKU) DEMOCRACY

In accordance with the Western agenda of containment of communism, the political system imposed on African countries as a precondition for the grant of independence represented, in general, a massive transplantation of alien partisan politics. The resulting political regimes were misfits that were weak, politically corrupt, and ineffective. In the Cold War context the West preferred military dictatorships capable of resisting the spread of communism, and the East preferred the same military regimes capable of establishing communism. Coups became rampant as Africa was turned into an immense battleground contested by the giants of the West and the East. As the Cold War heated up, it was the African grass that suffered. Pounded into dust were the encompassing coalitions of the pre-colonial African states that had once drawn support across communal lines and served as forums for bargaining and reconciliation among groups. They were self-reliant states that maintained social and political stability and did not go with caps in hand begging for the crumbs that fell from the tables of any master. In contrast, after decades of blindly emulating the Western ideological and political practices, post-colonial African states were reduced to the role of beggar-states.

Democratic practice existed in Africa long before European contact, and, as we have seen, the indigenous African democratic practice is capable of being modified to suit the present needs of African populations. A modified system built on a non-partisan and consensual democratic practice with a balance between centralization and decentralization would help African society to make decisions by consensus forged at all levels of government. Social choice in that system is more likely to reflect the preferences of individuals comprising society and to be more consistent and coherent.

As the cases studies of various African countries show, before and after the Cold War neither the Western type of partisan democratic practice nor one-party socialism was compatible with African cultures.

Still, that does not mean that democratic practice is not compatible with African culture. The cases substantiate the thesis that what Africa requires is a type of democratic practice that is so compatible with the cultural environment that it enables the elites to forge an encompassing coalition capable of containing the stresses or strains of the development process. It requires some modification of Africa's indigenous democratic practices to satisfy the present-day needs of Africans. This system—one capable of authoritative allocation of African values to Africans by Africans—is what I mean by compatible cultural democracy for Africa, or Africanism. The notion of compatible cultural democracy for Africa makes sense given that the practice of democracy in the countries of the West is not the same. The differences mean essentially that democratic practice has history. It implies that as in the West, compatible cultural democracy in the various countries of Africa might also be similar and African in content, but not necessarily the same. However, when African countries become united under one flag, like the United States or China, then they will have one compatible cultural democracy and one spirit of Africanism.

African countries should not be so naive as to expect that establishing compatible cultural democracy is going to be an easy task. There are problems to be encountered. Internal political and economic forces that continue to gain from the alien system cannot be expected to give up easily. The problem is complicated by the long, bitter history of captive slavery, colonialism, neo-colonialism, and the inherited educational system, all of which has meant that most Africans have come to suffer from a deeply embedded form of mental slavery, a colonization of the mind in which everything African is considered inferior to everything foreign. For five hundred years the African mind was constantly bombarded with the notion of European superiority. For example, despite the inhuman atrocities committed by Europeans against Africans during the era of captive slavery and colonialism, including turning them into commodities and chattels to be sold at the marketplace, the educational and religious institutions presented Jesus, prophets, apostles, saints, and angels to the African mind as white in colour while Satan, demons, and devils were presented as black. Pride in anything African was killed. The consequence was an insatiable preference for European products that inflated the import bills of African countries. Oddly enough, as a result Africans tend to prefer the junk foods of fatty corned beef and sausages to the fresh and more nutritious meat of the African antelope, deer, or gazelle. The African personality has to be restored.

Realization of compatible cultural democracy has to begin from the sphere of the mind to rid the African first of mental slavery. It requires a new education system capable of psychological and ideological transformation of the artificial African created by Europeans—the mentally enslaved African—into the liberated and proud African with an African-centred mind, someone totally committed to his or her country in thought and deed—the new African. This transformation of the African without hope into the new African with hope and dignity yearning for African political, economic, and cultural values has to come through both formal and informal education. Compatible cultural democracy with its advantages over the impoverished liberal democracy in the African environment has to be established first and firmly in the mind of every African, or at least in the minds of the African elites. For this purpose, African studies and Afrocentric values have to be taught in the schools and in the home.

The study of African history, culture, literature, and geography must be emphasized in the home, schools, colleges, and universities of Africa to make the African proud of his or her country and Africa as a whole. The historical linkage between Africans from the continent and Africans in the Americas, the Caribbean, and Europe should be an integral part of the study of African history. The transfer of the ideological symbols of unity to the centre to constitute one nation with a common destiny, the meaning of each symbol, the meaning of the national flag, and the importance of the national anthem should be taught, and these should be proudly recited on independence day celebrations to inject the sense of national feeling so essential in nation-building.

The eradication of mental slavery is not the only challenge. Because of the failure to decolonize Africa, most African countries are indirectly governed from outside by international political and economic forces. Africa is plagued by a one-sided structural adjustment in which the IMF and the World Bank, backed by the Western powers, hypocritically dictate the route of liberal democracy as the only way for Africa to go— hypocritically because pure liberal democracy does not exist anywhere in the West except in its impoverished form of polyarchy in which powerful organized groups usurp power and elected dictators rule the day. International economic and political forces that stand to gain from the political weaknesses arising from the alien political technology cannot be expected to lend their support to the practice of the indigenous democracy with its consensual checks and balances that will frustrate the penetration and domination of outside forces. Despite their economic weakness, African countries must be brave enough to resist and reject the pressure to emulate liberal democracy. While those who genuinely want to help Africa are most welcome, they cannot be accepted as dictators or superiors. However, the ability to stand up against the imposition of liberal democracy from outside requires knowledge about its failures and weaknesses. Teaching and contrasting liberal democracy with indigenous systems, and drawing attention to the impoverishment of Western democracy, will make Africans proud of their indigenous heritage and encourage them to adapt the indigenous systems to suit the requirements for successful development.

The responsibility to expose Western democracy to the African mind as an impoverished form of democracy rests with the African elite as a whole and must be channelled through education. Western democracy was established only after its society had become industrialized enough to meet the people's material demands, and even then the universal franchise was delayed until political stability had been ensured. African society, though, is still pre-capitalist and not industrialized. Liberal democracy in Africa is therefore premature.

The so-called liberal democracy of the West, which has degenerated into polyarchy, promises to protect the interests of the individual as well as the interests of the majority. But even after centuries of practice in Europe and the Americas polyarchy has not been able to solve the problems of crime, racism, and economic inequality. Indeed, these problems have only deepened. Because the practice of *amaniebor* of consensual democracy has never been factored into Western democracy, the election mandate easily becomes a licence to dictate favoured policies for a number of years. For example, there was no referendum to seek the consent of the societies of NATO before the Kosovo war. Similarly, there was no referendum to seek the mandate of the U.S. people before 1999 air strikes against Iraq were ordered by President Clinton at a time when his impeachment was under consideration. The decisions to go to war were purely the dictatorship of the elected.

Furthermore, despite the notion of the existence of a perfect and competitive political market that efficiently allocates political goods to the politicized individuals of society, the actual political market of Western society is oligopolistic, with very few political parties involved. As political oligopolies, they so agree on the status quo that replacing one party with another in government makes very little difference to the individual, for no matter which party wins, the same organized groups—which sometimes cleverly finance the parties—benefit most. The ballot box has been reduced to a smokescreen for satisfying the wishes of the organized few.

Given that the rule of the people cannot be justified in a system in which powerful groups usurp power and the rulers scarcely consult the common people about important decisions, democracy has been redefined in the West as the rule of law, making the notion of government with the consent of the people a misnomer. But the rule of law is not holding, for it has become the rule of technicality in which it is not the truth that prevails but the clever artifice of expensive lawyers. Certainly, the common people cannot afford to hire the services of such lawyers, but the few rich people can. In this way, justice in Western society has become virtually the province and privilege of the rich, and the innocent may as well be a victim of the same rule of law. For example, to take one famous—indeed, infamous—case, whether ex-football star O.J. Simpson committed the offence of murder or not, he might not have been acquitted at his trial had he not been able to hire the most clever and expensive lawyers, because the legal aid accorded the common people in Western society is not sufficient to attract such lawyers. In addition, the rule of law may as well be the rule of brutality. The brutal beating of Rodney King by the supposedly disciplined U.S. police, a videotaped event that drew worldwide attention, is a case in point. But the act of brutality is not limited to the police. Liberalism in the ownership of guns has extended the act to society as a whole, and even to teenagers, making schools no longer safe places for both teachers and students. In the city of New York, a citadel of Western democracy, it is unsafe to walk at night, and the lasting failure to ban the Mafia and the Ku Klux Klan by Western democratic means mocks the very rule of law.

Indeed, in Western society, the rule of law has become a gold mine for lawyers. In the same Western society in which justice delayed is said to be justice denied, a common insurance claim, for instance, can take years to be resolved and, in the final analysis, it is the lawyer who gets the lion's share of the benefit. Civil cases take so long a time that some witnesses may be deprived of the opportunity of providing necessary evidence before their death. All too often justice in liberal democracy seems to favour the criminal at the expense of the victim, and with the abolition of capital punishment criminals such as Canada's Paul Bernardo can rape and kill innocent people with the likelihood that after a stretch in jail they will receive parole and be freed to repeat their crime.

Certainly, in the proposed modernized form of African democracy this poverty of justice will not exist, for justice will aim at the truth and not at technicality; and because lawyers will not be required to defend anybody, members of society will be equal before the law. Justice will not be delayed and thereby denied, for it will be swift. In a matter of days, once sufficient evidence is produced, a social panel of judges, whose responsibility it is to question the accused, will establish whether or not an accused person committed an offence. Insurance claims will no longer pump money into the pockets of greedy lawyers, because lawyers will not be required to establish the truth. The social panel of judges shall order the insurance company to pay once it is established from the evidence available that the claimant deserves compensation.

Convincing Africans to be proud of their own indigenous system is not enough. A common name for that kind of democracy suitable for Africans is required. For example, although there are differences in the practice of democracy in the West, Western democracy has been given the common name of *liberal* democracy, and Western countries tend to be proud of that name, which appears to be ideologically and psychologically satisfying to them. In the same way, despite the minor differences in the practices of indigenous democracy, and to make Africans also proud of their own democracy and accept it as ideologically and psychologically satisfying, the African approach could be referred to as *jaku* democracy. *Jaku* is the Ga word for the common family of Africans, including those inside and outside the continent, as well as an adjective meaning African. *Jaku* democracy would therefore be the type of culturally compatible democracy suitable for Africans. Calling the system *jaku* democracy will send the signal to the African mind that the continent's peoples have their own type of democracy, one they can be proud of, and this knowledge will contribute to an emancipation from mental slavery.

An awareness of the impoverishment of Western democracy is not a sufficient condition for the successful establishment and operation of *jaku* democracy in Africa. All nations require defence and security systems for their survival, and African countries practising *jaku* democracy are no exceptions. However, the organization of defence and security should be African. In conformity with African culture, all able-bodied people should belong to an organized, politicized, and compulsory national militia that would receive basic military training irrespective of the level of education and type of profession, and perform compulsory police and military duties as part of free national service. The discipline and organizing abilities derived from this military training will become useful later in enhancing productivity in the national economy. There would also be a regular core of armed forces and police with special training to handle the more sophisticated weapons, but its size would be small compared to the size of the national militia, of which it would be a part. In this way, there would be a democratization of militancy in which the national militia would provide a check on the regular armed forces and police, and vice versa, to prevent the occurrence of coups.

Just as liberal democracy has found it expedient to establish collective security through NATO, African countries may also require collective defence, for in the past external political and economic forces resorted to organizing coups with the aid of African puppets to overthrow progressive African governments such as the Nkrumah and Lumumba governments. Although the process of re-education to create the new African in combination with the national militia may help reduce this tendency, they might not be foolproof. With Africa still divided into many small and militarily weak countries, the danger of externally directed coups would not be completely eliminated. Re-education must be backed by collective action by African countries through a revised OAU constitution that allows for an African High Command (AHC) with operational readiness to intervene swiftly to foil any coup attempt in any African country. This should not be interpreted to mean that *jaku* democracy is impossible without AHC. It is to emphasize the contribution that the AHC can make towards political stability in Africa. The AHC is essentially the pooling together of military resources and organization for a common African security—as first proposed by Nkrumah and later discussed by the OAU in the 1960s, although the combination of external influences and divisions among the OAU leaders at the time prevented its materialization. Its revival and implementation will discourage coups, because no one African country is capable of fighting against the combined armies of the rest of Africa.

The importance of collective defence should not be underestimated or overlooked. Despite divisions among the political leaders of the Economic Community of West African States (ECOWAS) and problems of commitment, ECOMOG, the military wing of the organization, was able to intervene militarily and successfully to return Liberia to civilian rule and took steps to achieve the same results in Sierra Leone. ECO-MOG is, essentially, an experiment. The mistakes, experience, and lessons drawn from its experience will be valuable to the establishment of the AHC, which in itself could be one of the essential steps towards the realization of the Pan-African Dream—the United States of Africa. Its establishment requires the revival of Pan-Africanism, which animated the struggle for independence after the Second World War but has seemingly long since been shelved. The revival of Pan-Africanism could be achieved through both formal and informal education and buttressed by the establishment of a Pan-African Youth Organization (PAYO), with branches both inside and outside Africa to unite African youth and enable interaction and exchange of views. Pan-Africanism implies the eligibility of African societies both inside and outside Africa for recruitment into the AHC and representation in the OAU. It will open the way for black African soldiers retiring from the U.S. army and elsewhere to join the AHC, bringing with them a much-needed expertise that could serve to discourage fortune-seeking mercenaries from disturbing the peace in Africa. PAYO could serve as the fertile ground for breeding African cadres and preparing them for the difficult tasks of political leadership and economic development.

The AHC's success will depend largely on how its troops are deployed. For example, Nigerian and Ghanaian troops may be tempted or ordered, for whatever reasons, to organize coups in their respective countries. To forestall this possibility, Nigerian and Ghanaian troops could be deployed to serve in Kenya and Tanzania respectively, with Kenyan and Tanzanian troops in turn deployed, perhaps, in Senegal and Sierra Leone while troops from Senegal and Sierra Leone serve elsewhere. Certainly, problems could arise with this shifting around of troops, but those problems would not be insurmountable. For example, logistics problems may require that all troops of the same rank receive the same pay in all African countries. However, the solution of these problems may themselves contribute to unite African countries, because the need to have a common currency, a common defence policy, and a common foreign policy, and to form links through communications and telecommunications will arise and need to be resolved. Considering that Africa, a continent rich in natural resources, has only been made temporarily poor through the ravages of the past five hundred years of history, revitalization of its economy through collective action is possible. The communication and telecommunication facilities would promote intra-African trade and strengthen the economy of Africa as a whole, and because Africa's material resources are vast enough to support its economic reconstruction once the appropriate political conditions are in place, the African common currency would inevitably become as respected as the U.S. dollar.

Still, it should not be forgotten that the self-interests of African leaders contributed immensely to the shelving of Pan-Africanism, undermining of African unity, and stifling of political and economic development. That same selfishness may pose a danger to the establishment of *jaku* democracy. Those self-interests are reflected in their love for power and wealth at the expense of their peoples. Once they gain control over the levers of political power, many African leaders are reluctant to relinquish it. For example, Mobutu Sese Seko was in power for over thirty years, Habib Bourguiba was made a life president of Tunisia, and by 1999 Jerry John Rawlings had been in power for eighteen years in Ghana. African leaders such as these have resorted to various repressive and dubious means to remain in power, including the establishment of one-party states, imprisonment, assassination or detention of political opponents, and the rigging of elections. Such leaders will always see the consensual and selection by merit characteristics of *jaku* democracy, with its checks and balances against corruption and arbitrary use of power, as threats to their personal interests, and even after decades of independence they are unlikely in the extreme to opt for adaptation of that indigenous democracy. It is for the same reason that the Pan-African dream has been shelved for decades, because many leaders prefer to be presidents with considerable power in a fragmented Africa rather than state governors serving under the watchful eyes of the federal government of Africa. Certain leaders will, then, oppose *jaku* democracy in preference to the impoverished liberal democracy of the West. Given this hold on political power, the establishment of *jaku* democracy could well involve a confrontation between the more enlightened and revolutionary PAYO and the entrenched African leaders, also called compradors, in which PAYO would surely win in time and space as the new organization percolates through the administrative machinery of the government of Africa and establishes its effective linkages. The old order will inevitably yield place to the new.

The internal resistance to the establishment of *jaku* democracy should not be taken lightly, for the forces of mental slavery and self-interest placed above all else are potent. Mental slavery is not only a disease of the ordinary African. Many African elites and intellectuals suffer from it. They may resist *jaku* democracy on the grounds that Africans should move abreast with time, as if time should be Eurocentric. As well, the external political, cultural, and economic forces that shape events in Africa are also powerful. That is why they have been able to make Africa politically and economically weak for centuries and continue to do so after decades of independence. It is in their interests that Africa remains a political and economic ancillary, a source of raw materials, cheap goods, and exotic travel.

Unfortunately, the outside interests and the selfish interests of many political leaders and elites of Africa are so fused that they can provide a common front to be buttressed by the mentally enslaved Africans. The establishment of *jaku* democracy for the restoration of the dignity of the African will therefore demand determination and commitment from the new African and particularly from PAYO, the militias, and the AHC to contain both internal and external threats. It is through this commitment that Afrocentricism shall replace Eurocentricism in Africa and *jaku* democracy shall be established not only to achieve the political prerequisites for successful development in African countries but also to realize the African dream of a United States of Africa—a dynamic new domain to which Africans both inside and outside the continent may proudly belong.

NOTES

1. Introduction: Variants of Democratic Practice

1. For detailed information on the formation of nation-states in Western Europe, see Charles Tilly, *The Formation of Nation States in Western Europe* (Princeton, N.J.: Princeton University Press, 1975).
2. Robert Dahl, *A Preface to Democratic Theory* (Chicago: Chicago University Press, 1956), pp.4-60.
3. Emmit B. Evans Jr. and Dianne Long, "Development," in *The Other World: Issues and Politics of the Developing World*, ed. J.N. Weatherby et al. (New York: Longman, 1997), p.50.
4. Claude Ake, *Democracy and Development in Africa* (Washington, D.C.: The Brookings Institute, 1997), pp.1-41.
5. See Arend Lijphart, "Consociational Democracy," *World Politics* 21,1 (1969), pp.207-25. See also Arend Lijphart, "Typologies of Democratic Systems," *Comparative Political Studies* 1,1 (1968), pp.3-44.
6. See Philippe Schmitter, "Still the Century of Corporatism," in *Trends Toward Corporatist Intermediation*, ed. Philippe Schmitter and Gerhard Lehmbruch (London: Sage Publications, 1979), pp.7-52.

2. The Great Transplantation

1. Adu Boahene, *African Perspectives on Colonialism* (Baltimore: The Johns Hopkins University Press, 1987), p.31.
2. The word "imperialist" was a title of honour enjoyed by Europeans returning from the colonies to their home country. An "imperialist" was a European who had amassed wealth from the colonies and held enormous authority and privilege. It was during the independence struggles after World War II that the meaning of the word changed into something more offensive.
3. J.S. Coleman, *Nigeria: Background to Nationalism* (Berkeley: University of California Press, 1958), p.108.
4. T. Walter Wallbank, *Contemporary Africa: Continent in Transition* (Princeton, N.J.: Van Nostrand, 1956), pp.89-90.
5. Kwame Nkrumah, *Towards Colonial Freedom* (London: Heinemann, 1962), p.10.

6. Walter Rodney explains in detail the physical and economic partition of Africa. For more details see Walter Rodney, *How Europe Underdeveloped Africa* (Washington, D.C.: Howard University Press, 1982).

7. The indirect-rule system was found to be so effective in the areas in which chieftaincy was strongly entrenched that, using government-created chiefs, the British extended it to areas where chiefs were weak or non-existent. Although they encountered legitimacy problems, both British and French Africa tended to follow the practice of government-created chiefs.

8. Statement of FRELIMO (Mozambique Liberation Front), Department of Education and Culture, 1968, quoted in Rodney, *How Europe Underdeveloped Africa*, p.205.

9. The famous classical song "O come to Timbuktu, where skies are blue ..." was obtained from England by the Presbyterian Secondary School, Odumasi-Krobo, which I attended. It reflected the greatness of the ancient university of Timbuktu, and provided evidence that Europeans did not bring education per se to Africa, but a European type of education.

10. In his book *Black Skin, White Masks: A Dying Colonialism* (New York: Grove Press, 1967), Frantz Fanon examined how the African elites were transformed into "black skins in white masks" as they became assimilated into European culture and value systems.

11. See, for instance, Roland Oliver and J.D. Fage, *A Short History of Africa* (Harmondsworth, Eng.: Penguin, 1962), p.200; and the section "Extending the System: From Slavery to Forced Labor," in Basil Davidson, *In the Eye of the Storm: Angola's People* (New York: Anchor Books, 1973), pp.107-20.

12. Interviews and discussions with people from East Africa, especially Tanzania and Kenya, confirmed that there is not much difference between the *susu* of West Africa and the *upato* or *kutunzana* of East Africa. Given that the two regions are separated by thousands of miles, the similarity is striking.

3. The Post-Independence Problem

1. J. Lecaillon, C. Morrison et al., *Economic Policies and Agricultural Performance of Low-Income Countries*, OECD Development Centre, Development Studies, 1987, p.39.

2. Evans Jr. and Long, "Development," p.50.

3. The word "Thrasymachian" derives from the character of that name in Plato's *Republic*. Thrasymachus held that it is the natural right of the strong to take more than the equal share of what the world has to offer and that in the arena of justice, "might makes right." The doctrine of Thrasymachus is the basis of social Darwinism and the notion of survival of the fittest.

4. See Albert Hirschman, *Essays in Trespassing: Economics to Politics and Beyond* (New York: Cambridge University Press, 1981).

5. Ibid.

6. See Dieter Senghaas, *The European Experience* (Leamington, N.H.: Berg Publishers, 1985).

7. IBRD, *World Development Report*, 1981, p.25.

8. Degefe Befekadu, "Traditional Adjustment Mechanism, the World Bank, the IMF and the Developing Countries: Survey of Theories and Issues," background paper for the African Alternative Framework to Structural Adjustment Programmes for Socio-economic Transformation, UNECA, Addis Ababa, Ethiopia, 1998. See also J.K. Horsefield, *International Monetary Fund 1945-1965*, vol. 1, *Chronicle*, International Monetary Fund, Washington, D.C., 1969.

9. Evans Jr. and Long, "Development," p.51.

10. F.G. Erb and Valeriana Kallab, eds., *Beyond Dependency: The Developing World Speaks Out*, Overseas Development Council, Washington, D.C., 1976, Annex B-1.

11. See Senghaas, *European Experience*.

12. See "Arusha Programme for Collective Self-Reliance and Framework for Negotiations," adopted at the Fourth Ministerial Meeting of the Group of 77, Arusha, Tanzania, Feb. 12-16, 1969, reprinted in Karl P. Sauvent, *The Group of 77* (New York: Oceania, 1981), Annex 11.

13. Ferrel Heady, *Public Administration: A Comparative Perspective*, 3rd ed. (New York: Marcel Dekker, 1984), p.42.

14. M.P. Todaro, *Economic Development of the Third World*, 3rd ed. (New York: Longman, 1993), p.79.

15. Susan George, "How the Poor Develop the Rich," in *The Post-Development Reader*, ed. Majid Rahnema and Victoria Bawtree (London: Zed Books, 1997), pp.207-13.

16. Samir Amin, *Imperialism and Unequal Development* (New York: Monthly Review Press, 1977); Andre Gunder Frank, "The Development of Underdevelopment," in Frank, *Latin America: Underdevelopment or Revolution* (New York: Monthly Review Press, 1969).

17. L.K. Mytelka, "Unfulfilled Promise of African Industrialisation," *African Studies Review* 32,3 (1989), pp.77-137.

18. John W. Mellor and B. Johnston, "The World Food Equation: Interrelations among Development, Employment, and Food Consumption," *Journal of Economic Literature* 22 (1984).

19. Tekeste Negash, "Contradictions between Western Democracy and African Cultures," in *Democracy in Africa*, ed. M. Melin (1995), pp.61-75.

20. Ake, *Democracy and Development in Africa*, chapter 5.

21. Claude Ake, "The Unique Case of African Democracy," *International Affairs* 69,2 (1993), pp.234-44.

22. V.G. Simiyu, "The Democratic Myth in the African Traditional Societies," in *Democratic Theory and Practice in Africa*, ed. W.O. Oyugi et al. (Portsmouth, N.H.: Heinemann, 1988).

23. Richard Sandbrook, "Liberal Democracy in Africa," *Canadian Journal of African Studies* 22,2 (1988), pp.240-67.

24. Richard Sandbrook, "Transitions without Consolidation: Democratization in Six African Cases," *Third World Quarterly* 17,10 (March 1966), p.69.

4. Typical African Political Systems

1. Meyer Fortes and E.E. Evans-Pritchard, eds., *African Political Systems* (London: Oxford University Press for International African Institute, 1940), pp.5-7.

2. Merran McCulloch, *The Ovimbunda of Angola* (London: London International African Institute, 1952), describes the political system of the Ovimbunda.

3. For more detailed information about the Zulu social formation and political organization, see Fortes and Evans-Pritchard, eds., *African Political Systems*, pp.27-55.

4. Ibid., p.33.

5. Ibid., p.35.

6. Ibid., p.31.

7. See R.S. Rattray, *Ashanti Proverbs* (Oxford: Oxford University Press, 1916), p.41.

8. See Ivor Wilks, *Forests of Gold* (Athens: Ohio University Press, 1993), p.70.

9. Ibid., p.111.

10. Ibid., p.115.

11. Ibid., p.116.

12. *Asafoiatsemei* is the plural form of *asafoiatse*, a war captain. *Asafoianyemei* is the plural form of *asafoianye*, a female war captain.

13. A traditional area is a town and the villages that come under its jurisdiction. A principal chief is the chief of a town.

14. The relationship between agency and structure here is similar to Anthony Giddens's theory of structuration, which explains that structures may be constraining but not determining and that there is a role for agency despite structure. This particular African experience demonstrates that a structure that may later become constraining is itself created through agency. It emphasizes that despite the constraints of the external environment, the African pre-colonial experience shows that Africans can still make their own history.

15. Habermas, a German philosopher and professor at Frankfurt (1964-71), was concerned with identifying and destroying all oppressive and exploitative power-relations to enable human beings to organize their societies for the benefit of all. See his *Knowledge and Human Interests*, 1968; *Legitimation Crisis*, 1973; *Communication and the Evolution of Society*, 1976; *Theory of Communicative Action*, 1982; and *The Philosophical Discourse of Modernity*, 1985.

5. Towards the Modification of African Political Culture

1. *Susu* was not only an indigenous and pre-colonial banking system, but also used to raise funds for the realization of projects. In the same way that only those who have funds in modern banks can have access to credit, only those who belong to a *susu* group can borrow from it. The borrower does not pay any interest rate.

2. During Ghana's independence struggle, the CPP government organized successful mass education programs. I was a voluntary teacher of a group at Teshi, Accra, and was impressed by the speed at which older people learned how to read and write in the local Ga language. Unfortunately, as partisan politics intensified, requiring diversion of scarce resources to the political front, the mass education programs were given less attention and faded away.

3. I do not agree with Hyden's "uncaptured peasantry" theory. I see the economy of affection as a cultural force that in the absence of the welfare benefits of Western society has enabled Africans to survive the stresses and strains of colonial and capitalist exploitation. The problem is not with the economy of affection per se but with enhancing

productivity within it. Capitalism has the character of creating unemployment after depriving peasants of their land and forcing them to sell their labour on a market that is in theory expected to be free but is not so in practice. The weak African economies do not have the capacity to introduce welfare benefits for the unemployed. Increasing productivity within the economy of affection will enable extended families to care for their less fortunate members. This will free the state to divert resources, solving more pressing problems of the economy. The economy of affection is therefore economic power in disguise. See Goran Hyden, *Beyond Ujamaa in Tanzania: Underdevelopment and the Uncaptured Peasantry* (Berkeley: University of California Press, 1980).

4. Kenneth J. Arrow, *Social Choice and Individual Values* (New York: John Wiley and Sons, 1963).

6. Ghana: Tactical Action, Socialism, and the Military

1. See W.E. Ward, *History of Ghana* (London: George Allen and Unwin, 1958), pp.356-58, 398-402.
2. For a more detailed account of the Coussey Committee's impact on Ghana's development, see Daniel Osabu-Kle, "The Economic Crisis of Ghana: Non-Conformity with the Indigenous Political Culture as the Root Cause," Ph.D. dissertation, Carleton University, Ottawa, April 5, 1994, pp.123-38.
3. Bob Fitch and Mary Oppenheimer, *Ghana: The End of an Illusion* (New York: Monthly Review Press, 1968), p.38.
4. Ibid., p.44.
5. Ibid., p.45.
6. Quoted in Dennis Austin, *Politics in Ghana: 1946-1960* (London: Oxford University Press, 1964), p.360.
7. Ibid., p.361.
8. Fitch and Oppenheimer, *Ghana*, p.75.
9. J.H. Mensah, "The Relevance of Marxian Economics to Development Planning in Ghana," presidential address by the chairman of the National Economic Planning Commission to the Economic Society of Ghana, 1962, p.15.
10. *The Economic Bulletin of Ghana* 9,1, p.14.
11. Ibid.
12. "Program of the Convention People's Party for Work and Happiness," cited in David Apter, *Ghana in Transition* (New York: Princeton University Press, 1963), pp.393-421.

13. See, for instance, S.E. Finer, *The Man on Horseback* (London: Pall Mall Publishers, 1962); Morris Janowitz, *The Military in the Political Development of New Nations* (Chicago: Chicago University Press, 1964); and Lucien À. Pye, *Armies in the Process of Political Modernization* (Chicago: Chicago University Press, 1962).

14. Among the vital projects abandoned was a project designed by the Drevici Group to enable Ghana to process cocoa right from the pod to the main desired products, with soap and fertilizer as by-products. The project included the construction of silos for the preservation of cocoa and foodstuffs. This project, which was underway when the CPP was overthrown, could have given Ghana a strong economic backbone through the value-added factor and the opportunity to influence the price of cocoa on the world market. The cost of the failed project to Ghana was over $20 million. This was something I witnessed personally as a member of a team of engineers who inspected the remains of the project in 1983.

    Equipment for expansion of a tire factory arrived in Ghana just before the coup. Due to disunity within the Ghanaian political elite, and the subsequent discontinuity in government, the equipment was allowed to rust at the Air Force Station, Takoradi, where it was in transit to Bonsasu. The cost to Ghana was estimated at several million dollars.

15. Mike Mason, *Development and Disorder: A History of the Third World since 1945* (Toronto: Between the Lines, 1997), pp.217-18.

16. Crawford Young, *The Colonial State in Comparative Perspective* (New Haven, Conn.: Yale University Press, 1994), p.5.

17. For an account of how Ghana's sovereignty was compromised, see Osabu-Kle, "Economic Crisis of Ghana," pp.261-64.

18. Rawlings's mother is a Togolese Ewe who migrated illegally to Ghana. Records show that Rawlings enrolled in Achimota College as a Togolese student. Since Ghanaians do not carry identity cards, Rawlings succeeded in joining the Ghana Air Force by posing as a Ghanaian Ewe. Since then he has claimed Ghanaian citizenship and his mother claims to be a Ghanaian Ewe.

19. *The Ghanaian Chronicle*, Jan. 26, 1998.

7. Nigeria: Oil, Coups, and Ethnic War

1. Robert Melson and Howard Wolpe, eds., *Nigeria* (East Lansing: Michigan State University Press, 1971).

2. For more details, see I. Ukwu, "Federal Financing of Projects for Development and National Integration," paper presented at the National Institute for Policy and Strategic Studies, Kuru, Nigeria. See also Samuel Oyovbaire, *Federalism in Nigeria: A Study of the Development of the Nigerian State* (New York: St. Martin's Press, 1984), p.234.

3. Larry Diamond, "Social Change and Political Conflict in Nigeria's Second Republic," in *Political Economy of Nigeria*, ed. I.W. Zartman (New York: Praeger, 1983), p. 48. See also Adele Jinadu, "Federalism, the Consociational State, and Ethnic Conflict in Nigeria," *Plubius* 15 (Spring 1985), p.89.

4. Diamond, "Social Change and Political Conflict," p.63.

5. Billy Dudley, *Instability and Political Crisis in Nigeria* (Ibadan: Ibadan University Press, 1973); Larry Diamond, "Class, Ehnicity, and Democracy in Nigeria: The Failure of the First Republic," *Journal of Modern African Studies* 17,4 (December 1988); Richard Sklair, "The Nature of Class Domination in Africa," *Journal of Modern African Studies* 17,4 (December 1979), pp.531-52.

6. Government of Nigeria, *Constitution of the Federal Republic of Nigeria* (Lagos: Government Printer, 1978), pp.3-4.

7. Alex Gboyega, "The Federal Character or the Attempt to Create Representative Democracies in Nigeria*International Review of Administrative Sciences*, 50,1 (1984), pp.17-24.

8. Eghosa Osaghae, "The Complexity of the Nigerian Federal Character and the Inadequacies of the Federal Character Principle," *Journal of Ethnic Studies* 16 (Fall 1988), pp.1-25.

9. J.B. Babalakin, *Commission of Inquiry into the Affairs of the Federal Electoral Commission, FEDECO (1979-83)* (Lagos: Government Printer, 1986).

10. See "Awolowo Interviewed," *West Africa*, Nov. 21, 1983, p.2674.

11. B.O. Mwabueze, *Nigeria's Presidential Constitution: The Second Experiment in Constitutional Democracy* (London: Longman, 1985), pp.75-77.

12. Alex Gboyega, "Intergovernmental Relations in Nigeria: Local Government and the 1979 Constitution," *Public Administration and Development* 5,2 (1985), pp.281-90.

13. As the case of the Congo (chapter 13) shows, Mobutu was an expert in organizing the same political party under different names to give an impression of multiparty politics to the outside world.

8. Kenya: Settler Ideology and the Struggle for Majimbo

1. See United Kingdom, *White Paper on Kenya*, London, 1923.
2. Peter Kabisa, a schoolmate of mine at the Presbyterian Secondary School, Odumasi-Krobo, Ghana, in the 1950s, explained to me that the British mistakenly took the Land Freedom Army's "Uma! Uma!" (meaning "Go away! Go away!") as "Mau Mau." According to Kabisa, the words Mau Mau held absolutely no meaning in themselves and made no sense.
3. Mason, *Development and Disorder*, p.225.
4. Oginga Odinga, *Not Yet Uhuru* (London: Heinemann, 1968), p.11.
5. *Majimbo* may be regarded as the local word for a federalism that respects regional autonomy.
6. See *The Political Economy of the Kenyatta State*, ed. Michael Shartzberg (New York: Praeger, 1987), for detailed information on the activities of the Kenyan state; and, in particular, David Troup, "The Construction and Deconstruction of the Kenyatta State," in that collection.
7. Mason, *Development and Disorder*, p.229.

9. Tanzania: Ujamaa, Compulsion, and the Freedom of Association

1. Positive Action was a concept used by Nkrumah at the beginning of the independence struggle in Ghana, and its use in Tanzania is an indication of the close relations between Nyerere and Nkrumah. The concept itself means the use of legitimate and constitutional, but effective, means to bring about political change. It implies the use of non-violent instruments such as newspapers, education, boycotts, and non-cooperation with the government—tactics similar to those advocated by the Indian leader Mahatma Gandhi.
2. Quoted in Immanuel Wallerstein, "Elites in French Speaking West Africa," *Journal of Modern African Studies* 3,1 (May 1965), p.24.
3. Julius K. Nyerere, *Freedom and Socialism: A Selection from Writings and Speeches 1965-67* (Dar es Salaam: Oxford University Press, 1968), p.15.
4. Ibid.
5. Hyden, *Beyond Ujamaa in Tanzania*, p.103.
6. Ray Abrahams, "Sungusungu: Village Vigilante Groups in Tanzania," *African Affairs* 343 (1986), pp.179-96.

10. Somalia: Experiments with Democracy, Military Rule, and Socialism

1. Helen Chapin Metz, ed., *Somalia: A Country Study*, Area Handbook Series, Library of Congress, Washington, D.C., 1993, p.xxii.

2. Quoted in *Somalia: A Divided Nation Seeking Unification* (Mogadishu, Somalia Republic: Public Relations of the Ministry of Information, in co-operation with Somali Embassy, Bonn, 1965), p.28.

3. Ibid., p.29.

4. Ibid.

5. See *Somalia: The Potential for Resource-based Industrial Development in the Least Developed Countries*, no.6, Dec. 16, 1983.

6. Metz, ed., *Somalia*, p.xxi.

7. For more information on clan structure, relations, and conduct of affairs, see S. Touval, *Somali Nationalism* (Cambridge, Mass.: Harvard University Press, 1963); and P.H. Guver, *Somali Culture, History, and Social Institutions: An Introductory Guide to the Somali Democratic Republic* (London: London School of Economics and Political Science, 1981).

8. I.M. Lewis, *A Modern History of Somalia: Nation and State in the Horn of Africa* (Boulder, Col.: Westview Press, 1980).

9. See Metz, ed., *Somalia*, p.xxi.

10. S.M. Makinda, *Security in the Horn of Africa*, Adelphi Paper, no. 269, London, 1992.

11. Between 1506 and 1542, the Somali hero Ahmed Ibin Ibrahim al-Ghazi succeeded in occupying the Ethiopian heartland. Subsequently, Somalis came to occupy parts of Ethiopia including the Ogaden. Somali irredentist claims to areas in Ethiopia where Somalis have occupied or nomadic Somalis had grazed their livestock derive in part from the al-Ghazi era. These claims remain unresolved despite the failure of the Somali state.

12. J. Predergast, "The Forgotten Agenda in Somalia," *Review of African Political Economy* 59 (1994), p.67.

13. This statement was obtained through an interview with a Somali of the Hawiye clan, who, in full, angrily asked: "Are the Generals fighting in Bosnia warlords? Were the Generals fighting in the Gulf War warlords? Is General Colin Powell a warlord? Is President Bush a warlord? What kind of racism is this?"

14. S.M. Makinda, "Somalia: Political and Military Outlook," *The Indian Ocean Newsletter*, July 18, 1992, p.4.

15. Some observers hold the view that because there is no "effective government" in the North, the relationship between the self-proclaimed republic of Somalia in the North and the rest of Somalia is unclear. This view arises from the perception that the only effective government is one organized to the taste and satisfaction of the developed nations and enjoying international legitimacy. But is seems to me that Somalia has learned a lot from the mistakes of the past. The councils of the clans have the potential of developing a federal constitution and a democracy that will be compatible with the Somali culture and will help them to pursue nationalist development aspirations free from irredentism.

16. M.A. Salih and L. Wohlgemuth, eds., *Crisis Management and the Politics of Reconciliation in Somalia* (Uppsala, Sweden: Reprocentralen, 1994), p.93.

11. Senegal: From French Colonialism to the Failure of Partisan Politics

1. See G. Wesley Johnson Jr., *The Emergence of Black Politics in Senegal* (Stanford: Stanford University Press, 1971), p.vi.
2. Ibid., p.66.
3. Ibid., p.102.
4. Quoted in ibid., p.156.
5. Ibid., p.174.
6. The word "almost" is used here in recognition that the ideological symbols of unity were not properly transferred from the Casamance ethnic groups to the centre. That neglect is at the roots of the Casamance secessionist movement, which has become a thorny issue in Senegal's political development.
7. B. Vincent Khapoya, *The African Experience: An Introduction* (Upper Saddle River, N.J.: Prentice Hall, 1998), pp.122-23.
8. W.J. Foltz, *From French West Africa to the Mali Federation* (New Haven, Conn.: Yale University Press, 1965), p.187.
9. Ali Mazrui and Michael Tidy, *Nationalism and the New States in Africa* (Portsmouth, N.H.: Heinemann Educational Books, 1985), p.291.
10. Ibid.

11. For more details see Benoit S. Ngom, *L'arbitrage d'une démocratie en Afrique: La Cour Supreme du Senegal* (Paris: Editions Presence Africaine, 1989), also cited in Crawford Young and Babcar Kante, "Governance, Democracy and the 1988 Elections," in *Governance and Politics in Africa*, ed. Goran Hyden and Michael Bratton (London: Lynne Reinner Publishers, 1992), p.66.
12. Young and Kante, "Governance, Democracy and the 1988 Elections," p.66.
13. Radio Libreville, Africa No.1, March 15, 1993.
14. Ibid.

12. Rwanda: From Success Story to Human Disaster

1. Catharine Newbury, "Rwanda: Recent Debates over Governance and Rural Development," in *Governance and Politics in Africa*, ed. Hyden and Bratton, p.193.
2. See Jean-Pierre Godding, "Foreign Aid as an Obstacle to Development: The case of Rwanda's Development Projects," in *International Perspectives on Rural Development*, ed. Michael Lipton et al. (Lewes, Eng.: University of Sussex Institute of Development Studies, 1984).
3. Richard Nyrop et al., *Rwanda: A Country Study* (Washington, D.C.: Library of Congress/ U.S. Government Printing Office, 1985), p.6.
4. Ibid.
5. As an African from one of the royal houses of Africa, I am aware of how wise elders of Africa humorously answer questions that they believe are unnecessary. In time such humour forms the basis of tales that are told over and over to children to entertain them. These tales develop later into ideological stories for establishing hegemony. Europeans who are not aware of this cultural attitude might make the mistake of accepting such answers as serious historical facts.
6. Quoted in "Colonial Period and Independence," *Journal of Humanitarian Assistance*, June 11, 1997, chapter 3, p.2.
7. Ibid.
8. For detailed information about the "Statement of Views" and resulting developments, see *Rwanda: A Country Study* (Washington, D.C.: Library of Congress, Federal Research Division, 1982).
9. *Journal of Humanitarian Assistance*, June 11, 1997, chapter 3.

10. Christopher Mfizi, *Les Lignes de Faite du Rwanda* (Kigali: Office Rwandais d'Information, 1983), trans. and cited in Catherine Newbury, "Rwanda: Recent Debates over Governance and Rural Development," in *Governance and Politics in Africa*, ed. Hyden and Bratton, p.202.

11. Jean Rumiya, "Ruanda d'hier, Rwanda d'aujourd'hui," *Vivant Univers*, no.357 (May-June 1985), pp.2-8, quoted in Newbury, "Rwanda," p.203.

12. Andre Guichaoua, *Destins paysans et politiques agraire en Afrique centrale*, vol. 1, *L'ordre paysan des hautes terres centrales du Burundi et du Rwanda* (Paris: Editions Harmattan, 1989), p.173, cited in Newbury, "Rwanda," p.203.

13. *Journal of Humanitarian Assistance*, June 1997.

14. Ibid.

15. Michel Chossudovsky, "Third World Network Features," Third World Network 228, Macalister Road, Penang, Jan. 24, 1995. Michel Chossudovsky is a professor of economics in the Faculty of Social Sciences, University of Ottawa.

16. Ibid.

17. Newbury, "Rwanda," p.214.

18. The RPF was not, as commonly thought, entirely Tutsi in its membership. Although it was predominantly Tutsi, there were many Hutus within its ranks.

19. "Arming Rwanda," *Human Rights Watch* (report), 1994, p.10.

20. George, "How the Poor Develop the Rich," p.210.

21. "Death by Design: Planning for the Apocalypse," Associated Press article, May 21, 1994, p.4.

22. Tod Hoffman, " . . . And So It Happens Again," *Queen's Quarterly*, Spring 1999, gives the astounding figure of 800,000 deaths (p.93). Hoffman cites author Gérard Prunier as saying "the daily killing rate was five times that of the Nazi death camps" (also p.93).

23. See *African Rights*, 1994, cited in "The Genocide," *Journal of Humanitarian Assistance*, chapter 5, 1997, p.2.

24. Ibid.

25. See "Genocide."

26. Ibid.

27. Ibid.

28. Ibid.

29. "Death by Design."

30. "Genocide."

31. "Death by Design."

32. *Journal of Humanitarian Assistance*, 1997, Endnotes.

13. Congo (Kinshasa):"A Most Lethal Poison ..."

1. Sandra Meditz and Tim Mevill, eds., *Zaire: A Country Study* (Washington, D.C.: Library of Congress, 1994), p.140.
2. Ibid., Introduction, p.xxxv.
3. Newspapers in Ghana, including the *Daily Graphic, Ghanaian Times,* and *Evening News*, were very vocal on the conference and its aftermath. Lumumba's call for immediate independence was hailed as similar to Nkrumah's call of "self-government now," which culminated in Ghana's independence. Lumumba himself derived inspiration from Nkrumah.
4. The Belgian political strategists appeared to be opposed to Kasavubu's separatist bid. However, given the support that the same strategists accorded to the mining companies, which were aligned with Tshombe and his secessionist stance in Katanga, the credibility of the Belgians in their relations with Kasavubu was doubtful.
5. Quite possibly, the behaviour of the Force Publique commander was calculated to cause confusion in order to make it difficult for Lumumba to govern.
6. Quoted in Mazrui and Tidy, *Nationalism and the New States in Africa*, p.200.
7. Rajeswar Dayal, "The Mobutu I Knew," *The Times of India*, May 28, 1997.
8. Ibid.
9. Mazrui and Tidy, *Nationalism and the New States in Africa*, p.217.
10. Nicos Poulantzas, *Political Power and Social Classes* (London: NLB and Sheed and Ward, 1973); Nicos Poulantzas, "The Capitalist State: A Reply to Miliband and Laclau," *New Left Review* 95 (January-February 1976).
11. Mazrui and Tidy, *Nationalism and the New States in Africa*, p.217.
12. Monica Moorehead, "What's Next after Mobutu?" in *Workers World Newspaper*, May 29, 1997.
13. Dayal, "Mobutu I Knew."
14. Gary Djoli Mokoka, "Congo: Recovering Mobutu's Ill-Gotten Gains," *PeaceNet*, June 4, 1997.

BIBLIOGRAPHY

Abrahams, Ray. "Sungusungu: Village Vigilante Groups in Tanzania." *African Affairs* 343 (1986): 179-96.

Adamolekum, Lapido. "Institutional Perspectives on Africa's Development Crisis." In *African Governance in the 1990s,* working papers, Second Annual Seminar of the African Governance Program, Carter Center, Emory University, Atlanta, 1990.

___, and Bamidele Ayo. "The Evolution of the Nigerian Federal Administrative System." *Plubius* 19 (Winter 1989): 157-76.

"African Charter for Popular Participation in Development and Transformation." International Conference on Popular Participation in the Recovery and Development Process in Africa, Arusha, Tanzania, 1990.

African Governance in the 1990s. Working papers, Second Annual Seminar of the African Governance Program, Carter Center, Emory University, Atlanta, 1990.

Agyeman-Duah, Baffour. "Ghana 1982-86: The Politics of the P.N.D.C." *Journal of Modern African Studies* 25,4 (1987): 613-42.

Ake, Claude. *Democracy and Development in Africa.* Washington, D.C.: The Brookings Institute, 1996.

___. "The Case for Democracy." In *African Governance in the 1990s,* working papers, Second Annual Seminar of the African Governance Program, Carter Center, Emory University, Atlanta, 1990.

___. "The Unique Case of African Democracy." *International Affairs* 69,2 (1993).

Almond, Gabriel A., and Sidney Verba. *The Civil Culture: Political Attitudes and Democracy in Five Nations.* Princeton, N.J.: Princeton University Press, 1963, 1980.

Amonoo, Ben. *Ghana 1957-1966: The Politics of International Dualism.* London: George Allen and Unwin, 1981.

Anyang' Nyong'o, Peter, ed. *Popular Struggles for Democracy in Africa.* London: Zed Books, 1987.

Apter, David. "Program of the Convention People's Party for Work and Happiness." In *Ghana in Transition.* New York: Princeton University Press, 1963.

___. *The Politics of Modernization.* Chicago: University of Chicago Press, 1965.

___. "Things Fell Apart? Yoruba Responses to the 1983 Elections in Ondo State, Nigeria." *Journal of Modern African Studies* 25,3 (1987): 489-503.

"Arming Rwanda." *Human Rights Watch*, report, 1994.

Arrow, Kenneth J. *Social Choice and Individual Values*. New Haven, Conn.: Yale University Press, 1963.

Austin, Dennis. *Politics in Ghana: 1946-1960*. London: Oxford University Press, 1964.

Awiti, Adhu. "Economic Differentiation in Ismani, Iringa Region: A Critical Assessment of Peasants' Response to the Ujamaa Vijijini Programme." *African Review* 3,2 (1973): 209-39.

"Awolowo Interviewed." *West Africa*, Nov. 21, 1983.

Ayoade, J.A. "Ethnic Management in the 1979 Nigerian Constitution." *Plubius* 16 (Spring 1986): 73-90.

Babalakin, J.B. *Commission of Inquiry into the Affairs of the Federal Electoral Commission, FEDECO (1979-1983)*. Lagos: Government Printer, 1986.

Bamishaiye, A. "Ethnic Politics as an Instrument of Unequal Socio-Economic Development in Nigeria's First Republic." In *Ethnic Relations in Nigeria*, ed. A.O. Sanda. Ibadan: Caxton Press, 1976.

Barkan, J.D. "Further Reassessment of 'Conventional Wisdom': Political Knowledge and Voting Behaviour in Rural Kenya." *American Political Science Review* 70,2 (1976): 452-55.

Bekadu, Degefe. "Traditional Adjustment Mechanism, the World Bank, the IMF and the Developing Countries: Survey of Theories and Issues." Background paper, African Alternative Framework to Structural Adjustment Programmes for Socio-Economic Transformation, UNECA, Addis Ababa, Ethiopia, 1998.

Berg-Schlosser, Dirk. "Elements of Consociational Democracy in Kenya." *European Journal of Political Research* 13 (March 1985): 95-109.

Bestemen, Catherine. "Violent Politics and the Politics of Violence: The Dissolution of the Somali Nation-State." *American Ethnologist* 23,3 (1996): 579-96.

Bing, Addo. "Popular Participation Versus People's Power: Notes on Politics and Power Struggles in Ghana." *Review of African Political Economy* 31 (1984): 91-104.

Boahen, Adu. *African Perspectives on Colonialism*. Baltimore: The Johns Hopkins University Press, 1987.

Bollen, Kenneth A. "Issues in the Comparative Measurement of Political Democracy." *American Sociological Review* 45,3 (June 1980): 370-90.

Borrows, John. *Kenya into the Second Decade: A Report of a Mission Sent to Kenya by the World Bank*. Baltimore: The Johns Hopkins University Press, 1975.

Bosen, J. et al. *Ugamaa: Socialism from Above*. Uppsala, Sweden: Scandinavian Institute of African Affairs, 1997.

Boulle, L.J. *South Africa and the Consociational Option: A Constitutional Analysis*. Cape Town: Juta, 1984.

Busia, K.A. *Africa in Search of Democracy*. London: Routledge and Kegan Paul, 1967.

Callaghy, Thomas M. *The State-Society Struggle: Zaire in Comparative Perspective*. New York: Columbia University Press, 1984.

___. "Culture and Politics in Zaire." Department of State, Bureau of Intelligence and Research, Washington, D.C., 1987.

___. "The State as a Lame Leviathan: The Patrimonial Administrative State in Africa." In *The African State in Transition*, ed. Zaki Ergas. London: Macmillan, 1987.

Chabal, Patrick, ed. *Political Domination in Africa*. London: Cambridge University Press, 1986.

Chazan, Naomi, and Donald Rothchild. "Corporatism and Political Transactions: Some Ruminations on the Ghanaian Experience." In *Corporatism in Africa: Comparative Analysis and Practice*, ed. Julius Nyang'oro and Timothy Shaw. Boulder, Col.: Westview Press, 1989.

Chilcote, Ronald H. *Portuguese Africa*. Engelwood Cliffs, N.J.: Prentice Hall, 1967.

Chossudovsky, Michel. "Third World Network Features." Penang: Third World Network 228, Macalister Road, 1995.

Claridge, G. Cyril. *Wild Bush Tribes of Tropical Africa*. New York: Negro Universities Press, 1969.

Collier, Ruth B. *Regimes in Tropical Africa: Changing Forms of Supremacy 1945-75*. Berkeley: University of California Press, 1982.

Coleman, James S. *Nigeria: Background to Nationalism*. Berkeley: University of California Press, 1958.

"Colonial Period and Independence." *Journal of Humanitarian Assistance*, 1997.

Coulon, Christian. "Senegal: The Development and Fragility of Semidemocracy." In *Democracy in Developing Countries*, vol. 2, *Africa*, ed. Larry Diamond, Juan Linz, and S. Martin Lipset. Boulder, Col.: Lynne Rienner Publishers, 1988.

Coulson, Andrew, ed. *African Socialism in Practice: The Tanzanian Experience*. Nottingham, Eng.: Spokesman, 1979.

Daalder, Hans. "On Building Consociational Nations." *International Social Science Journal* 32,2 (1971): 355-70.

Dahl, Robert. *A Preface to Democratic Theory*. Chicago: Chicago University Press, 1956.

___. *Polyarchy: Participation and Opposition*. New Haven, Conn.: Yale University Press, 1971.

Dayal, Rajeswar. "The Mobutu I Knew." *The Times of India*, May 28, 1997.

"Death by Design: Planning for the Apocalypse." Associated Press article, May 21, 1994.

Development Alternatives Inc. (DAI). *The Rwandan Social and Institutional Profile*. Washington, D.C.: Development Alternatives Inc., 1986.

Diamond, Larry. *Democracy in Developing Countries*. Vol. 1. *Persistence, Failure, and Renewal*. Boulder, Col.: Lynne Rienner Publishers, 1988.

___. "Social Change and Political Conflict in Nigeria's Second Republic." In *Political Economy of Nigeria*, ed. I.W. Zartman. New York: Praeger, 1983.

___. "Class, Ethnicity, and Democracy in Nigeria: The Failure of the First Republic." *Journal of Modern African Studies* 17,4 (December 1979).

Dudley, Billy. "Instability and Political Crisis in Nigeria." *Journal of Modern African Studies* 17,4 (December 1979).

Dunn, John. "The Politics of Representation and Good Government in Post-Colonial Africa." In *Political Domination in Africa*, ed. P. Chabal. London: Cambridge University Press, 1986.

The Economic Bulletin of Ghana. Accra: Government Press.

Edwards, Adrian. *The Ovimbundu under Two Sovereignties*. London: Oxford University Press, 1962.

Ekeh, Peter. "Colonialism and the Two Publics in Africa: A Theoretical Statement." *Comparative Studies in History and Society* 17,1 (1975): 1-112.

Elaigwu, J. Isawa. "Federalism and the Politics of Compromise." In *State Versus Ethnic Claims: African Political Dilemmas*, ed. Donald Rothchild and V.A. Olorunsola. Boulder, Col.: Westview Press, 1983.

Erb, F.G. and Valeriana Kallab. *Beyond Dependency: The Developing World Speaks Out*. Washington, D.C.: Overseas Development Council, 1976.

Fallers, Lloyd A. *Bantu Bureaucracy: A Study of Integration and Conflict in the Political Institutions of an East African People*. Cambridge: Cambridge University Press, 1956.

Fanon, Frantz. *Black Skin, White Masks: A Dying Colonialism*. New York: Grove Press, 1967.

___. *The Wretched of the Earth*. New York: Grove Press, 1968.

Fitch, Bob, and Mary Oppenheimer. *Ghana: End of an Illusion*. New York: Monthly Review Press, 1968.

Foltz, W.J. *From French West Africa to the Mali Federation*. New Haven, Conn.: Yale University Press, 1965.

Fortes, Meyer, and E.E. Evans-Pritchard, eds. *African Political Systems*. London: Oxford University Press for International African Institute, 1940; New York: Kegan Paul International, 1987.

Fortmann, Louise. "Peasants, Officials and Participation in Rural Tanzania: Experience with Villagization and Decentralization." Cornell University Center for International Studies, Ithaca, N.Y., 1980.

Foster-Carter, Aidan. "Neo-Marxist Approaches to Development and Underdevelopment." *Journal of Contemporary Asia* 3,1 (1973): 14-15.

Gboyega, Alex. "The Federal Character or the Attempt to Create Representative Democracies in Nigeria." *International Review of Administrative Sciences* 50,1 (1984).

＿＿. "Intergovernmental Relations in Nigeria: Local Government and the 1979 Constitution." *Public Administration and Development* 5,2 (1985).

"The Genocide." *African Rights*, 1994; also in *Journal of Humanitarian Assistance*, chapter 5, 1997.

George, Susan. *Ill Fares the Land: Essays on Food, Hunger, Power*. Washington, D.C.: Institute for Policy Studies, 1984.

＿＿. *The Debt Boomerang: How Third World Debt Harms Us All*. Boulder, Col.: Westview Press, 1992.

＿＿. "How the Poor Develop the Rich." In *The Post Development Reader*, ed. Majid Rahnema with Victoria Bawtree. Dhaka: The University Press, 1977.

Gester, R. "How to Ruin a Country: The Case of Togo." Dossier 71, Institute for Development Alternatives (IFDA), May 1989.

Gitonga, Afrifa, K. "The Meaning and Foundations of Democracy." In *Democratic Theory and Practice*, ed. Walter O. Oyugi et al. Portsmouth, N.H.: Heinemann, 1988.

Godding, Jean-Pierre. "Foreign Aid as an Obstacle to Development: The Case of Rwanda's Development Projects." In *International Perspectives on Rural Development*, ed. Michael Lipton et al. Lewes, Eng.: Institute of Development Studies, University of Sussex.

Guver, P.H. *Somali Culture, History, and Social Institutions: An Introductory Guide to the Somali Democratic Republic*. London: London School of Economics and Political Science, 1981.

Hagen, Everett. *On the Theory of Social Change: How Economic Growth Begins*. Homewood, N.J.: Dorsey Press, 1962.

Hayward, Fred M., ed. *Elections in Independent Africa*. Boulder, Col.: Westview Press, 1987.

Heady, Ferrel. *Public Administration: A Comparative Perspective*. New York: Marcel Dekker, 1984.

Hirschman, Albert. *Essays in Trespassing: Economics to Politics and Beyond*. New York: Cambridge University Press, 1981.

____. "Indigenization: Problems of Transformation in a Neo-colonial Economy." In *Political Economy of Nigeria*, ed. Claude Ake. London: Longman, 1985: 173-200.

____. "Rethinking African Democracy." *Journal of Democracy* 2 (Winter 1991): 32-44.

Hoben, Susan. *School, Work, and Equity: Educational Reform in Rwanda*. African Research Studies, no.16. Boston: Boston University African Studies Center, 1989.

Hodder-Williams, Richard. *An Introduction to the Politics of Tropical Africa*. London: George Allen and Unwin, 1984.

Horowitz, Donald L. *Ethnic Groups in Conflict*. Berkeley: University of California Press, 1985.

Horsefield, J.K. *International Monetary Fund 1945-1965*. Vol. 1. *Chronicle*. Washington D.C.: International Monetary Fund, 1969.

Huntington, Samuel P. *Political Order in Changing Societies*. New Haven, Conn.: Yale University Press, 1968.

Hyden, Goran. *Beyond Ujamaa in Tanzania: Underdevelopment and the Uncaptured Peasantry*. Berkeley: University of California Press, 1980.

____. *No Shortcuts to Progress : African Development Management in Perspective*. Berkeley: University of California Press, 1983.

____, and Michael Bratton, eds. *Governance and Politics in Africa*. London: Lynne Rienner Publishers, 1992.

IBRD, *The World Development Report*. Washington, D.C., 1981.

Jaycox, E. *The Challenges of African Development*. Washington, D.C.: World Bank.

Jinadu, Adele. "Federalism, the Consociational State, and Ethnic Conflict in Nigeria." *Plubius* 15 (Spring 1985).

Johnson, G.W. *The Emergence of Black Politics in Senegal*. Stanford, Cal.: Stanford University Press, 1971.

Kaplan, I. *Angola: A Country Study*. Washington, D.C.: The American University, 1979.

Khapoya, B. Vincent. *The African Experience: An Introduction*. Upper Saddle River, Bergen, N.J.: Prentice Hall, 1998.

Killick, Tony. *Development Economics in Action: A Study of Economic Policies in Ghana*. New York: St. Martin's Press, 1978.

Lancaster, Carol. "Democracy in Africa." *Foreign Policy* 85 (Winter 1991-92): 148-65.

Lecaillon, J., C. Morrison et al. *Economic Policies and Agricultural Performance of Low-Income Countries*, Development Studies, OECD Development Centre, 1987.

Lewis, I.M. *A Modern History of Somalia: Nation and State in the Horn of Africa*. Boulder, Col.: Westview Press, 1980.

___. *Pastoral Democracy: A Study of Pastoralism and Politics among the Northern Somali of the Horn of Africa*. New York: Oxford University Press, 1961.

Library of Congress. *Somalia: A Country Study*. Washington, D.C., 1993.

Lijphart, Arend. "Consociational Democracy." *World Politics* 21,1 (1969).

___. "Typologies of Democratic Systems." *Comparative Political Studies* 1,1 (1968).

Lugard, Frederick J.D. *The Dual Mandate in British Tropical Africa*. London: Cass, 1922.

Makinda, S.M. *Security in the Horn of Africa*. Adelphi Paper no. 269. London, 1992.

___. "Somalia: Political and Military Outlook." *The Indian Ocean Newsletter*, July 18, 1992.

Mason, Mike. *Development and Disorder: A History of the Third World since 1945*. Toronto: Between the Lines, 1997.

Mazrui, Ali, and Michael Tidy. *Nationalism and the New States in Africa*. Portsmouth, N.H.: Heinemann Educational Books, 1985.

McCulloch, Merran. *The Ovimbunda of Angola*. London: London International African Institute, 1952.

Medith, Sandra, and Tim Mevill, eds. *Zaire: A Country Study*. Washington, D.C.: Library of Congress, 1994.

Melson, Robert, and Howard Wolpe, eds. *Nigeria: Modernization and the Politics of Communalism*. East Lansing: Michigan State University Press, 1971.

Mensah, J.H. "The Relevance of Marxian Economics to Development Planning in Ghana." Presidential address by the chairman of the National Economic Planning Commission to the Economic Society of Ghana, 1962.

Mfizi, Chrisopher. *Les lignes de faite du Rwanda Independence*. Kigali: Office Rwandais d'Information, 1983, translated into English; also cited in Hyden and Bratton, eds., *Governance and Politics in Africa*.

Midgal, Joel. *Strong Societies and Weak States: State-Society Relations and State Capabilities in the Third World*. Princeton, N.J.: Princeton University Press, 1988.

Miller, Joseph. *Kings and Kingsmen*. Oxford: Clarendon Press, 1976.

Minter, William. *Imperial Network and External Dependency: The Case of Angola*. Beverly Hills: Sage Publications, 1972.

___. *Portuguese Africa and the West*. New York: Monthly Review Press, 1972.

Moorehead, Monica. "What's Next after Mobutu?" *Workers World Newspaper*, May 29, 1997.

Mwabueze, B.O. *Nigeria's Presidential Constitution: The Second Experiment in Constitutional Democracy*. London: Longman, 1985.

Mytelka, L.K. "Unfulfilled Promise of African Industrialization." *African Studies Review* 32,3 (1989):77-137.

Negash, Tekeste. "Contradictions between Western Democracy and African Cultures." In *Democracy in Africa*, ed. M. Melin (1995).

Ngom, Benoit S. *L'arbitrage d'une democratie en Afrique: la Cour Supreme du Senegal*. Paris: Editions Presence Africaine, 1989; translated into English; also cited in Hyden and Bratton, eds., *Governance and Politics in Africa*.

Nkrumah, Kwame. *Towards Colonial Freedom*. London: Heinemann, 1962.

Nyerere, J.K. *Freedom and Socialism: A Selection from Writings and Speeches 1965-67*. Dar es Salaam: Oxford University Press, 1968.

___. *Freedom and Development*. Dar es Salaam: Oxford University Press, 1973.

Nyrop, Richard et al. *Rwanda: A Country Study*. Washington, D.C.: Library of Congress, 1985.

Oakley, R. et al. "Somalia and Operation-Restore-Hope: Reflections on Peace Keeping and Peace Making." *The Times Literary Supplement* 4839 (Dec. 29, 1995): 11-12.

Odinga, Oginga. *Not Yet Uhuru*. London: Heinemann, 1968.

Oliver, Roland, and J.D. Fage. *A Short History of Africa*. Harmondsworth, Eng.: Penguin Books, 1962.

Organski, A.F.K. *The Stages of Political Development*. New York: Knopf, 1965.

Osabu-Kle, D.T. "Economic Crisis of Ghana: Non-Conformity with the Indigenous Political Culture as the Root Cause." Ph.D. dissertation. Carleton University, Ottawa, 1994.

Osaghae, Eghosa. "The Complexity of the Nigerian Federal Character and the Inadequacies of the Federal Character Principle." *Journal of Ethnic Studies* 16 (Fall 1988).

Oyovbaire, Samuel. *Federalism in Nigeria: A Study of the Development of the Nigerian State*. New York: St. Martin's Press, 1984.

Poulantzas, Nicos. *Political Power and Social Classes*. London: NLB and Sheed and Ward, 1973.

—. "The Capitalist State: A Reply to Miliband and Laclau." *New Left Review* 95 (January-February 1976).

Predergast, J. "The Forgotten Agenda in Somalia." *Review of African Political Economy* 59 (1994).

Rattray, R.S. *Ashanti Proverbs*. Oxford: Oxford University Press, 1916.

Rodney, Walter. *How Europe Underdeveloped Africa*. Washington, D.C.: Howard University Press, 1982.

Salih, M.A., and L. Wohlgemuth, eds. *Crisis Management and the Politics of Reconciliation in Somalia*. Uppsala, Sweden: Reprocentralen, 1994.

Samatar, Abdi I., and Terrence Lyons. *Somalia: State Collapse, Multilateral Intervention, and Strategies for Political Reconstruction*. Washington, D.C.: Brookings Institute, 1995.

Samatar, Ahmed I., ed. *The Somali Challenge: From Catastrophe to Renewal*. Boulder, Col.: Lynne Rienner Publishers, 1994.

___. *Socialist Somalia: Rhetoric and Reality*. London: Zed Books, 1988.

Samatar, Said S. *Somalia: A Nation in Turmoil*. London: Minority Rights Group, 1991.

Sandbrook, Richard. "Liberal Democracy in Africa." *Canadian Journal of African Studies* 22,2 (1988): 240-67.

___. "Transitions without Consolidation: Democratization in Six African Cases." *Third World Quarterly* 17,10 (March 1966).

Sauvent, Karl P. *The Group of 77* (New York: Oceania, 1981).

Schmitter, Philippe. "Still the Century of Corporatism." In *Trends Toward Corporatist Intermediation*, ed. Philippe Schmitter and Gerhard Lehmbruch (London: Sage Publications, 1979): 7-52.

Senghaas, Dieter. *The European Experience*. Leamington, N.H.: Berg Publishers, 1985.

Shartzberg, Michael, ed. *The Political Economy of the Kenyatta State*. New York: Praeger, 1987.

Shils, Edward A. *Political Development in the New States*. The Hague: Mouton, 1962.

Shinnie, Margaret. *Ancient African Kingdoms*. London: Arnold Publishers, 1965.

Simiyu, V.G. "The Democratic Myth in the African Traditional Societies." In *Democratic Theory and Practice in Africa*, ed. W.O Oyugi et al. Portsmouth, N.H.: Heinemann, 1988.

Sklair, Richard. "The Nature of Class Domination in Africa." *Journal of Modern African Studies* 17,4 (December 1979).

Spikes, Daniel. *Angola and the Politics of Intervention*. North Carolina: Mcfarland and Company, 1993.

"Somalia: A Government at War with Its Own People." *Africa Watch*, Africa Watch Committee, 1990.

Somalia. The Potential for Resource-based Industrial Development in the Least Developed Countries, no. 6 (December, 16, 1983).

Somali Republic. *Somalia: A Divided Nation Seeking Unification*. Bonn, 1965.

Sommerville, Keith. *Angola: Politics, Economics and Society*. Boulder, Col.: Lynne Rienner Publishers, 1986.

Tilly, Charles. *The Formation of Nation States in Western Europe*. Princeton, N.J.: Princeton University Press, 1975.

Todaro, M.P. *Economic Development in the Third World*. 3rd ed. New York: Longman, 1993.

Touval, S. *Somali Nationalism*. Cambridge, Mass. Harvard University Press, 1963.

"Uganda/Rwanda: Picking up the Pieces." *Africa Confidential* 31,23 (1990).

Ukwu, I. "Federal Financing of Projects for Development and National Integration." Paper presented at the National Institute for Policy and Strategic Studies, Kuru, Nigeria, 1980.

Wallbank, Walter T. *Contemporary Africa: Continent in Transition*. Princeton, Mass.: D. Van Nostrand Company, 1956.

Wallerstein, Immanuel. "Elites in French Speaking West Africa." *Journal of Modern African Studies* 3,1 (May 1965).

___. "Voluntary Associations." In *Political Parties and National Integration in Tropical Africa*, ed. J.S. Coleman and C.G. Rosberg. Berkeley: University of California Press, 1964.

Watson, Catherine. "Rwanda Relying on Equilibre." *Africa Report* 34,1 (January-February 1989): 55.

Weatherby, J.N. et al. *The Other World: Issues and Politics of the Developing World*. New York: Longman, 1997.

Wilks, Ivor. *Forests of Gold*. Athens: Ohio University Press, 1993.

Winans, Edgar V., and Angelique Haugerud. "Rural Self-Help in Kenya: The Harambee Movement." *Human Organization* 36 (1977): 334-51.

Young, Crawford. *The Colonial State in Comparative Perspective*. New Haven, Conn.: Yale University Press, 1994.

___. *The Rise and Decline of the Zairean State*. Madison: University of Wisconsin Press, 1985.

Zartman, I.W., ed. *The Political Economy of Nigeria*. New York: Praeger, 1983.

INDEX